Bound to be Read

LONDON BROADCASTING LIMITED
COMMUNICATIONS HOUSE
GOUGH SQUARE, EC4P 4LP

from a drawing by Hubert Williams

Bound to be Read

Robert Lusty

JONATHAN CAPE
THIRTY BEDFORD SQUARE LONDON

FIRST PUBLISHED 1975
© 1975 BY ROBERT LUSTY

JONATHAN CAPE LTD, 30 BEDFORD SQUARE, LONDON WCI
ISBN 0224 01171 5

PRINTED IN GREAT BRITAIN BY
BUTLER AND TANNER LTD
FROME AND LONDON

Contents

Acknowledgments

Certain pieces in this book have been adapted from occasional contributions to *The Bookseller*, and I am grateful to its Editor and its Proprietors for giving me permission to do this.

Press Low the Stop-Cock, Plumbers appeared in the *Spectator* during the editorship of Iain Hamilton, and to him as well I am similarly grateful.

The Excuse

THE immediate reaction was one of mild affront. After all, I had not then retired in any final sense. Nor, so I like to believe, have I since, except from involvement with the affairs of the publishing organization to which I devoted twenty-five of my forty-six years in 'the trade'. I had relinquished the reins of alleged command to my chosen successor only a few weeks before. During those weeks I had been more or less around the place, becoming increasingly aware of new faces and new attitudes a little alien to the procedures and attitudes inbred by the working experience of nearly a lifetime.

And then the simple beauty of the phrase, with all the exquisite delicacy of interpretation, became evident.

I had wanted to examine an author's contract of my time. There appeared to be some hectares of office space devoted to an activity hitherto allocated a minimal square footage. The lady who had most efficiently controlled the operation in my day was not at home. She was at a meeting. So was her assistant. Both, of course, were known to me and I to them.

But, as tends to happen in any change of government, there had been a certain proliferation; and new recruits, alight with ardency, were busy around the place. They were young and charming and none would have looked out of place with the Crown of Mecca upon her head. I stated my modest requirement, but it seemed beyond comprehension. 'Never mind,' I said, 'I will come back another time,' and turned to go. With a charming bewilderment and touching delicacy, Miss World gazed upon the old gentleman. 'And who may I say called?' she asked.

She was not to know it, but slowly, gently and inexorably the fall of a curtain had begun.

Dedication

The trouble with you, said a friend, is that you are frightened of women. This, then, is dedicated with respect and affection to:

Joan and Babs (who were good enough to marry me) and Elizabeth, Noreen, Molly, Joan, Juliet, Betty, Patricia, Lena, Anne, Patricia, Amanda, Jenny and Sarah, to all of whom, for one reason or another, I remain for ever in debt.

I

My Literary Background

OVER my years in and around publishing I have been
continuously grateful to Miss Lob. Until this moment
she has, to the best of my knowledge, made but one
appearance and this in the writings of George Bernard Shaw, who
somewhere recorded an encounter with her. She has always sustained my waning confidence when I have listened to the recollections of my more literary, erudite and sophisticated colleagues.
I have heard recounted tales of tea with Kipling, of encounters
in a wood with Hardy, of holidays with Arnold Bennett and
of what Wordsworth really said about the daffodils to somebody's grandmother. It is on such occasions, which are nearly
always delightful, that my mind turns gratefully to Miss
Lob and an afternoon on the platform of Swindon station not
far off sixty years ago. And Swindon then was Swindon, the
headquarters not of Messrs W. H. Smith but of the Great
Western Railway, where they made such mighty engines as
The Great Bear to convey us at holiday-time from Bristol at
sixty miles per hour, scooping water on the way and slowing
down whenever due to pass a friend travelling in the opposite
direction.

My Aunt Helen was involved, and so were William Morris
and his daughter May and my own maternal grandfather and
Kelmscott Manor. The sights and sounds and delectable smells
of farmyards come back on the instant and I begin to feel as
literary as anyone else in publishing and possibly more so than
some of today. I must have been around six or seven years old
and the First World War had been in progress for some two
years: I had paid my penny to the Primrose League to suspend

weighted strings from my ears which, when twanged, were reputed to convey the rumble of distant guns from across the
Channel; and from a little prep school on the front at Teignmouth
I had seen a passing coaster hit a mine and sink within moments.
We played rounders on the sands, while near by soldiers curdled
our blood by their shouts and charged suspended sacks with their
fearsome bayonets.

But Kelmscott was the centre of our lives. My mother's family had farmed in Kelmscott and around for many generations.
R. W. Hobbs & Sons in gilt lettering on the splendid wagons
signified to me the whole glamour and enchantment of the world.
There were the Turners and the Plumbs and the Arkells who
farmed areas not required, so I supposed, by my grandfather.

It was my grandfather who sold Kelmscott Manor to William
Morris, in order, so I imagine, to finance the upbringing of his
eleven children, ten by his first wife — who had died at the age of
thirty-six — and one, my Aunt Helen, by his second, who had
been the family governess.

This immense family had been brought up at the Farm, and it
was to this haven of exciting activity that my sister and I were
taken each summer and each Christmas of our childhood days.
The place was full of uncles and aunts and cousins and it was the
centre of our world. Alas, the last of the family departed from
Kelmscott only a little while ago and a yeoman saga came to its
end. I still go there when I can, for it has scarcely changed
through all the days that I have known it, except that an abomin-
able complexity of television aerials now sprout from the quiet,
grey Cotswold roofs. The tiny school has been closed and its infant population long since transferred to some glass forcing-house
in nearby Langford. In my day Auntie Jackets, as we then called
her, had been in charge of the school, but she later became my
grandfather's third wife and put on airs and became Auntie
Lottie instead. It was recollections of this tiny village school I
had in mind many years later when I wrote to 'Miss Read' following an article from her in the *Observer*, and persuaded her to
write the book which became *Village School* and launched
its author on a writing career of remarkable and enduring
success.

Opposite the school is the tiny church whose graveyard contains William Morris and many of my aunts and uncles in addition to my grandfather and his three wives. It was to this still spot, so tranquil and serene, that many years later I was to take the ashes of my dear first wife, Joan, and scatter them in peace. A sudden gust of wind blew them around me and I could hear her Scottish laughter.

I can never hear the simple ringing of a solitary church bell without the full memory of the place and of all my associations with it come flooding back. 'Are you sure, Bob, that it is safe to be leading that great horse? Does Uncle Henry know?' 'Of course it is, Mummy, I'm five and he's only three.'

But I should get back to Swindon where I had been driven fast over the hump bridges from Lechlade on that summer afternoon by my Aunt Helen in an early 'tin Lizzie' with its klaxon horn, to meet a new land-girl. 'And where', she inquired, 'is our Miss Lob?' We looked around for a likely land-girl and could see none. The platform slowly emptied, leaving only one memorable figure upon it. It was extraordinary even to my innocent eyes: squat, mannish and a little threatening. 'That', said my Aunt Helen, 'cannot surely be Miss Lob?' But indeed it was and with her odd baggage she heaved herself into the back of the car and we drove in silent contemplation back to Kelmscott.

Certainly, as viewed on Swindon station, no emanation derived from Miss Lob which suggested affinity with the pre-Raphaelites of Kelmscott Manor. William Morris had of course been dead for many years and Mrs Morris more recently so. I remember quite vividly being taken by my mother to the manor and meeting her. She seemed somehow to be surrounded by lace, harps, lavender and her daughter May. I think it must have been a single visit and I recall little now of May Morris except that I saw her more often. She was quite a friend of my mother; and again I can remember harps and lavender and blue china, much of it brought from Italy by Rossetti and presented to Mrs Morris. I now indeed possess some, for it was sold after May's death and pieces of it acquired by my Aunt Helen and given my first wife and me on our marriage.

Miss Lob lost no time in becoming a figure of controversy. I do not know where she was put to live, but I do remember that it quickly became imperative for her to work in the fields alone. None of the men would tolerate the foulness of her invective. In due course Blacksmith Adams, known far and wide for the ferocity and ingenuity of his own vocabulary, felt unable to tolerate so formidable a competitor. Complaints were laid before my grandfather. He had another farm at nearby Bampton and he was taking my sister and me to inspect it. From the 'top road', which a little isolates Kelmscott from the infrequent traffic that uses it, we saw Miss Lob with her tractor and plough. She was alone and deserted even by the gulls which so often swooped around more friendly apparitions and foretold rain. My grandfather stopped the car and sounded its klaxon horn. 'You must stay where you are,' he instructed us. 'I have a job of work to do with Miss Lob.' He looked stern as he plodded his way across to his newest land-girl, halted in her tracks by the sound of the klaxon. My grandfather was never a man to mince his words. We adored him and as the twins of, I think, his favourite daughter, we seemed to occupy a special place in his affections. He rode a white horse called Bess. 'What are you going to do when you grow up, Bob?' 'Ride about on a white horse like you and do nothing.'

I do not apologize for these digressions; publishing encourages such things. Very few publishers, when in conversation with 'their' authors, keep to the point of what they want to say. At any rate, I can well remember my grandfather charging down on his white Bess to the village Cross to drive two robed nuns from the scene. They had accepted his hospitality for the previous night and had then sought to stir up trouble among the men. I was to recall them during the Second World War when nuns with hairy wrists were for ever picking up dropped Bibles in railway carriages and then being led away as suspected forerunners of invasion.

My grandfather did not take long in dealing with Miss Lob. He looked relieved on returning to the car. 'I have sacked Lob,' he said and we proceeded on our quiet way to Bampton.

After that, much of the story, and by far its oddest part, is conjecture. But Miss Lob was to remain in Kelmscott for the rest of her strange life until she died there towards the end of the 1950s. I doubt if any know how she first came to meet May

Morris at the Manor. Certainly what strange alchemy of natures brought together this brutish, truculent creature and the delicacy and refinement of May Morris in a partnership of some forty years must remain a psychiatric problem.

From her tractor Miss Lob repaired almost at once to the Manor and May Morris and dominated the scene there for the rest of her life. From time to time she terrorized the village, and she was the subject of endless speculation. She aroused, as I have mentioned, the curiosity of Shaw; and the compassion of Sir Basil Blackwell as well, who leapt to her defence when on some occasion I referred to her as 'foul-mouthed'.

A yard adjoining the Manor housed a number of my grandfather's Shorthorn bulls (for which he was famous), and on Sunday evenings my sister and I, with anyone else around, would accompany him on a traditional after-tea tour of inspection. My sister knew all the bulls and cows by their romantic names — Barrington Duchess, Kelmscott Wonder and suchlike. I devoted my time and attention to the almost equally famous Shire horses, the responsibility of my Uncle Henry and in the care of 'Shire' Brown. It was on such expeditions that we used occasionally to catch sight of the increasingly grotesque figure of Miss Lob, who would gaze upon us with menacing threat. 'Take no notice,' commanded my grandfather, 'stay close to me.' And we did.

When in time May Morris died, it was assumed in the village that Miss Lob 'had summit to do with it'. But I think it more likely that she was broken-hearted. She continued to dominate the Manor for a while, and presently took to her bed with brandy and a loaded pistol which she flourished before those who sought to tend her. When she died, and the strange, sad story came to its close, her body, to the relief of all, was taken away to distant Cornwall, but by whom and to whom seems unknown.

Such is my single contribution to literary history. I am able to go quite often to Kelmscott now, for I live not far away. During my last visit Concorde flew slowly overhead to its landing at nearby Fairford. Outwardly the village has changed very little, but one remembers with astonishing clarity childhood delights untainted by sophistication, and forgets that in human terms so much has withered away. But it remains, from that childhood which I see no reason to 'put away', the most quiet, the most still, the most unchanging spot to have belonged to the whole of my life. 'The still point of the turning world,' as Eliot has written.

2

The End Seemed Nigh

To be an unpaid reporter on the *Kent Messenger* in January 1927 was a traumatic experience for one who had left a co-educational Quaker school in December. In those days, progress towards examinations was leisurely. After seven years at Sidcot School in the Mendip Hills of Somerset it was anticipated that one would pass Senior Cambridge and, a year later, matriculation. Dr Bevan Lean, an admirable if forbidding headmaster, was proud of his school's record in such matters. This he kept unsullied by the simple process of suggesting that any inhibited by doubt or density should leave. My sister, free of either, stayed on to become Head Girl. Ingloriously I left. My only achievement, which brought a certain notoriety, had been the receipt of two guineas from the *Daily News* for an article I had sent them about the great coal strike of those days. They called it *A View Without Smoke*, and attributed it to A Boy At School. The news editor of the day had two children at Sidcot but I easily persuaded myself that this was fortuitous. I was a rather gutless and silly child and learned almost nothing that I can remember. We lived in Kent at that time and my father contrived that Mr Pratt Boorman, who owned the *Kent Messenger*, should enjoy free of charge the benefit of my journalistic skills.

The *Kent Messenger* was then, and remains still, a local paper of the highest distinction. Mr Pratt Boorman owned it then and another Mr Pratt Boorman owns it still, having successfully and triumphantly resisted overtures from every likely direction. Against all financial temptation, which must have been considerable, it has retained its unsullied independence. In the 1920s it advertised itself across the two sides of every railway bridge in

19

the county with the simple message: THE KENT MESSENGER
FOR MAIDS AND MISTRESSES: TWOPENCE A LINE. I once
came across an irreverent lavatory in Scotland that displayed the
poster, which had been smuggled over that Calvinistic border.

The Editor, appropriately enough, was Mr Reader and he
clearly felt obliged to shield me from those aspects of life thought
alien to Quakers and their schools. That I was not a Quaker
seemed irrelevant. He was a most kindly old gentleman, rather
gaunt and anxious, with a moustache that had perished fairly
early in its life. As I recall it 'we' reporters sat in a row on stools
at a writing-desk which occupied the length of a room. There
was a rather fat and jolly girl who seemed nicely impressed by
the extent of the first report of mine accepted for printing by
Mr Reader. It recorded the Induction and Institution of the
Reverend F. W. Linton-Bogle to the Living of Offham. The
hymn 'O Thou Who Makest Souls to Shine' was sung with gusto
on that Thursday afternoon. The good Bishop of Rochester explained that Mr Linton-Bogle had come from Alnmouth and the
parishioners there had wept in the streets on his departure. My
only instructions from Mr Reader had been to mention as many
names as possible and spell them rightly. I had little idea of what
either an Induction or an Institution implied, but the organist
was helpful and after emphasizing the inspired nature of his
contribution, and spelling out that his name was Goddard, explained all that it was necessary to know.

Mr Reader decreed that I should have some cautious experience of 'the courts'. I was to go only in the company of a more
senior and responsible reporter, and I was to be at once dismissed
from the precincts should 'anything nasty' come to light. From
time to time during those three months the administration of
justice in the county town of Maidstone was brought to a halt
until the newest recruit to the *Kent Messenger* had been bustled
from the scene. The nearest to nastiness I was able to report was
the evidence of some old harridan of the town that the accused
had threatened to 'kiss her with his razor'. It made my first
headline. In the grander setting of the Assizes I fell, or so I
thought, within the grave displeasure of Mr Justice Horridge. I
had never seen a judge before. This one appeared to bear a
perpetual and sardonic half-grin. He looked very small and very

wizened and very menacing in the great seat of justice which
accommodated him. I cannot recall the precise nature of the
'nasty' case before him, but it presumably related to some aber-
ration of sex from which Mr Reader thought I should be protected. In any event my accompanying guardian ordered my
departure. I had some way to go and many knees to scramble
by along the narrow passage. Mr Justice Horridge appeared to
fix his beady little eyes upon me and his smile seemed more in
the nature of a snarl. Both followed me in accusing astonishment
until I had gone from the scene. It was not until many years
later, at the Garrick Club, in which many judges are wont to
play, that I could regard them with equanimity.

It was a pity that Mr Reader's local researches had not un-
covered some of the less desirable propensities of the town's
leading clergy. I was summoned socially to the official abode of
one who, with his wife, entertained me to after-dinner coffee. In
a short while she departed early to bed and I was bidden to sit
beside the reverend gentleman on the sofa. He suggested that
we might combine our intellectual resources to solve the children's crossword puzzle in the *Evening News*. I thought it
rather odd that he should want to hold my hand, but nothing
in the little book the good Dr Lean of Sidcot School had loaned
me to read in preparation for the world had mentioned tendencies of this sort. Having solved for the Canon the problem
of a three-letter word for a favourite pet beginning with 'c', I
made an intuitive escape.

The faded yellowed cutting from all those years ago is before
me: BURHAM BABY'S DEATH proclaims the headline. The in-
quest on a small and very young baby was to be held in the
public bar of the village local during closing hours. I was there
to report it, knowing nothing of inquests and less about the
likely causes of infant mortality. I was much embarrassed by
manifestations of parental distress. A weeping mother, a dis-
traught father, a formidable midwife, a kindly doctor: all seemed
involved. The baby, according to my report, had suffered from a
little wind for which brandy had been prescribed by the midwife.
Perhaps a little too much, said the doctor. I recorded the evidence as best I could, making certain of the names. Then, as
now, I did not hear as well as a young reporter should, but so

far as I could make out the unfortunate infant, with a surfeit
of brandy, had been overlaid by its considerable mother, herself
much fatigued after 'two bad nights'. I was not at all sure what
it all meant, but it seemed a pitiable accident and the sad little
drama came to its end. Awaiting the bus back to Maidstone, I
remained in the bar composing my piece for Mr Reader. A
substantial and obviously senior policeman approached me.
'What', he asked, 'are you saying the medical evidence meant?'
'I am saying', I replied with all the authority of the press in
support, 'that the baby died after being pressed too closely to
its mother's breast.' The policeman pondered on this. 'That's
all right,' he said, 'it doesn't really matter so long as we sing in
unison.'

I seem to have reported a long series of People's Lectures illustrated by lantern slides, the manipulator being always recorded
with care. I lived in rooms opposite the house of Mr Reader, and
had to beware of my landlady's dog who disliked lodgers. For
one evening I became the *Kent Messenger*'s operatic critic and
was sent to Boughton Monchelsea to witness the village operatic
society's production of *Les Cloches de Corneville*. I had never
been to an opera before. As befitted the importance of the
occasion, the paper's operatic reporter arrived early, announced
himself and was escorted to his seat. With an audacity he could
not match today, he at once complained and explained that he
was a little hard of hearing. Could he be accommodated rather
nearer the stage? His request was granted and he was escorted
thither by an elderly officer of the society who was to have his
revenge. He looked with some pity upon the lanky, thin stripling
sent to pronounce upon the evening's activities. 'Would you',
he asked, 'care for a glass of lemonade. And perhaps a nice bun
to go with it?' I reported in fact with some enthusiasm, but I
wonder where Miss Amy Sunnucks might be today and whether,
after nearly fifty years, she has forgiven me? 'Miss Amy Sunnucks', I wrote, 'was good to a point, but she did not appear to
have sufficient confidence in herself to go beyond that point.'
The music of the opera, in the considered view of Kent's fore-
most authority, was one of its most attractive features, and in no
way was that feature spoilt at Boughton Monchelsea on that
evening of long ago.

The son of Mr Pratt Boorman, whose own son has now succeeded him, most kindly invited their unpaid reporter to accompany him to the Boat Race of that April in 1927 and following it I was to return to my parents for the weekend. I found myself standing next to Mr Stanley Baldwin, who was smoking his pipe and looking for all the world exactly like Mr Stanley Baldwin smoking his pipe. I returned in a state of some elation to my parents and the next morning accompanied my mother to church. The vicar, who enjoyed very much the sound of his own voice, was proclaiming the Litany in full. I was on my knees and became aware quite suddenly of an odd commotion in the beating of my heart. Furthermore, I could hear it. I diverted my mother from her prayers. 'Listen,' I commanded. 'What is that noise?' she inquired. 'I think it's my heart,' I said. 'We will call on the little doctor after church,' she said and returned to the Litany. The little doctor stored within his bustling frame every attribute of the family doctor. He knew something of my heart already for I had fallen in love with his daughter within five minutes of arriving in the village some years previously. But that was over and something more serious now intervened.

There was perplexity in the world of medicine. No one's heart should announce its presence to all within earshot. Any irregularities should be routed only via stethoscope to trained listeners. The only optimist was our family doctor. He remained confident that life would continue and that all would be well within three years. He was right, but my journalistic days were over. The *Kent Messenger*'s newest and cheapest reporter withdrew from activity and took to his bed.

3
Cracking the First Crib

SEVEN inglorious years of scholastic failure, followed by three months of local journalism and a year of severe illness could not, even in the greater latitude of the late 1920s, be regarded as altogether adequate qualifications for entry into the then dynastic world of book publishing. I had neither passed, nor indeed taken, any examination of any kind with the exception of the entrance examination to Sidcot School. A question within had required the interpretation of SOS. It was long before the days of Switch Off Something and I was proud of the diplomacy of my reply, Sidcot Old Scholar.

Little did I know that not so far away and at roughly the same time, one of the two most distinguished 'communicators' of our time confronted a similar problem. Allen Lane, to become in later years one of my closest friends, had completed his education at Bristol Grammar School. His examination record was as mine and when the time came to compare notes, we decided that probably we were the last two to scrape our way to activity without benefit of scholastic success. No A-levels, no O-levels, no degree in literature, none of those educational attributes without which today a citizen can hardly scramble from his pram. The deprivation, so Allen Lane and I discovered, gave us both an inherent uncertainty we did our best to conceal from others. We shared an anxiety that we might one day find ourselves thrown upon the world and unable to find a way owing to our lack of academic qualification. We thus made a pact to the effect that either, finding himself ingloriously bereft, would employ the other. Alas Allen Lane no longer enlivens the world with his presence. My examination record remains undefiled

24

except that I have passed the Advanced Drivers' test and have a certificate saying so.

But in this respect the 1920s were more lenient. I would never have made a good journalist and it was a merciful providence which removed me from that activity. Contrary to most expectations I had survived the first year of illness, but confronted the next two with instructions to operate with great caution. I must on no account mount to the top deck of any omnibus. My fragility was considerable and obvious and the outlook uncertain, to say the least.

I cannot recollect how it was that publishing entered my head. I hardly knew what it meant. I liked books and the reading of them and upon reflection had enjoyed my short experience on the *Kent Messenger*. I had collected together everything I had written for the Sidcot School Magazine and in response to an advertisement had sent the lot to Messrs Stockwell who operated as publishers in Ilfracombe. They had replied almost by return that they would be glad to publish and proposed their terms. The proposal induced an elation which the terms failed to sustain. But it was enough and I obtained a copy of *The Writers' and Artists' Year Book* and set about the compilation of as persuasive a letter as I could manage. I wrote seven copies in a 'fist' no more legible then than I am informed it is today. I aimed at the top. Stanley Unwin was, of course, a recipient and so was Basil Blackwell. Sir Godfrey Collins was on my list with Sir Frederick Macmillan and Jonathan Cape. Sir John Murray of Albemarle Street had a copy and so too did Sir George Hutchinson who appeared to preside over Messrs Hutchinson & Co. in Paternoster Row. This labour exhausted all my energies.

It did not seem at the time remarkable that each recipient should reply to my importuning. Sir Frederick Macmillan responded with a four-page letter in his own hand-writing which I should certainly have had the sense to keep. I have retained an affection for that firm ever since, which became much fortified many years later when Harold Macmillan, then Prime Minister, appointed me a Governor of the BBC. Others replied with equal, if less personal, kindness. Stanley Unwin invited me to call upon him, and so did some emissary of Jonathan Cape. Stanley Unwin received me with precision and wanted to make quite certain that I had read or would read *The Truth About Publishing*. For my visit to Messrs Cape in Bedford Square I borrowed my father's bowler-hat and was astonished to be interviewed on a Wednesday afternoon by an impressive gentleman in resplendent plus-fours of an exaggerated disposition. It is agreeable to know that sartorial informality has been a continuing tradition. But a little later than the others came a letter from Walter Hutchinson containing a more positive approach to my problem. His father, Sir George, had recently retired and he now, he explained, was in control. He had, he wrote without more ado, the very job for me and would I be so good as to pay a visit to his Mr Wright and Mr Brown. My father seemed prepared to get through another day without his bowler-hat, and thus in it I presented my slender form to destiny and 34 Paternoster Row.

The general climate of the premises seemed even to me to be lacking some of the more civilized ingredients encountered in Mr Cape's Bedford Square and Mr Unwin's Museum Street. There was nothing but a waiting-room on the ground floor and this was almost pitch dark. But the girl behind the switchboard near the window looked glamorous and was kindly. Later in her life she was to become Mrs Macdonald and her future husband, at that time in charge of the contract department upstairs, subsequently founded the imprint which still publishes under his name. She manipulated the ancient entrails of her switchboard and announced that both Mr Wright and Mr Brown would meet me at the top of the stairs. These I clambered with some caution, remembering the advice given me and reflecting that it would be disconcerting to expire at the feet of Messrs Wright and Brown.

They stood together in a passage both dim and dingy. To the wall near them was affixed a contraption which I learned subsequently was a clocking-in machine much disliked by everyone in the building, but useful to a singularly unpleasant gentleman who extracted the card of any who met with his disapproval and submitted it in dreadful betrayal to Mr Walter. All the employees of Messrs Hutchinson & Co. (Publishers) Ltd were obliged to record their 9 a.m. arrival; their 1 p.m. departure for lunch; their 2 p.m. return and their 6 p.m. re-entry into the comparative orthodoxy of their private lives. On every Saturday we worked from 9 a.m. until 1 p.m. Two weeks of holiday was thought adequate; and on Christmas Eve a gift of ten shillings was handed round a few minutes before the usual closing hour. So far as I know, only Mr Walter was free to disregard the regulations of the establishment. Was it not God who made them High and Lowly and Ordered their Estate?

Neither Mr Wright nor Mr Brown fulfilled my admittedly limited expectancy of what publishers should look like. Mr Wright was large, rather portly, somewhat hot and ill-at-ease. Mr Brown was small and dark and had either come from a funeral or was about to go to one. Their interest in me was cursory and who can blame them? I would give much to know the nature of their instructions.

'When', asked Mr Wright 'would you like to start?'

'Start what?' I inquired, not, I thought, unreasonably.

'Working here,' replied Mr Brown. 'You will be with Mr Lunn, but I don't think', he said, glancing at Mr Wright for confirmation, 'that it is necessary for you to see him now.' Mr Wright clearly agreed. He, it transpired, had been acquired by Mr Walter as one of the more important assets of the firm of Messrs John Long. At that time the imprint specialized in the publishing of whodunits and westerns and Mr Wright was in charge of its operations. Mr Brown managed the firm's warehouse and dispatch department at Ireland Yard in the tortuous streets around St Andrew's Hill. They were subsequently to form an alliance and found the publishing imprint of Messrs Wright & Brown.

Such knowledge was not vouchsafed to me at this juncture of our acquaintanceship. 'It is understood', said Mr Wright as an obviously unnecessary afterthought, 'that you will get no pay for two years.' It was not, in point of fact, all that well understood, but as I had previously gathered that some kind of apprenticeship payment or premium was fairly common in the world of publishing, it seemed not unreasonable, and I hoped my father would share this view. Messrs Wright and Brown clearly awaited a reply to their first question. 'I will start', I announced, 'on Monday week.'

Returning home I reunited my father with his hat and broke the news. 'Where are you going to live?' he asked. 'I don't know,' I answered. 'What is it going to cost?' Again I didn't know. 'I don't know anything about publishing,' he said. 'Is it all right? Wouldn't you sooner be a lawyer?' Such a thought had never previously been mentioned. All my life before the point of embarking upon it had seriously arisen, I had wanted to be a farmer – to ride around on a white horse like my grandfather and do nothing. I didn't think that I wanted to be a lawyer.

Walter Hutchinson did not himself work from nine o'clock until one o'clock on Saturdays and it was thus on the Friday before my arrival that he hurled himself, for this seemed to be the normal manner of his transit, into the partitioned cubby-hole which served Erle Lunn as an office. Mr Walter, in the office at any rate, was never in other than a mood of intense irritation. His whole demeanour conveyed such and he announced, so the good Mr Lunn subsequently told me, that 'You have a fully qualified journalist joining you on Monday. He will help a lot.'

My naivety was such that for quite some time I thought Erle Lunn was indeed as his name. He conveyed a suggestion of elegance which I imagined befitting to an Earl. He greeted me on that Monday morning with quite exceptional kindness and I quickly knew that I could not have been entrusted to more considerate or more sympathetic attention. My Earl was a most charming, cultivated but always apprehensive man. He took one look at his 'fully qualified journalist' and concluded that his demise was imminent.

I had found lodgings in Bloomsbury at the Penn Club in Tavistock Square which operated then, and still does but from another address, as a residential centre for Quaker students and transients. I was there allotted a cubicle and provided with breakfast and dinner each weekday with full board at weekends for two guineas a week. This of course had to be paid by my father together with all my other expenses. I cost him then £4 10s. a week and on this I lacked nothing; but it was important to my rather hesitant morale that I should achieve financial independence at the earliest possible moment. Two guineas from the *Daily News* while at school was fine for a while but not a satisfactory basis from which to regard finance as an irrelevance.

I can see her now as I saw her then on that first evening of my

London life. The student residents of the Penn Club were in
various pursuits and studies. There was a nucleus of, I suppose,
some fifteen or twenty residents forming a group which somehow kept remarkably in contact through later years. She was
sitting in the dining-room having a late supper. She was taking
a course at the London Foot Hospital which was as near to
medicine as her widowed mother in Glasgow could afford. Her
face was alert and her eyes sparkled as they always did. She was
lovely to look upon and her Scottish voice was music. It took
eleven years to persuade her that we should marry. But that
is another story.

My route to Paternoster Row from Tavistock Square was by
an 18 bus which I caught near Holy Trinity Church, from
the basement of which Allen Lane was later to launch his
Penguin books. I dismounted, always from the lower deck, at
the Old Bailey and walked down Warwick Lane, passing Messrs
Hodder & Stoughton, to Paternoster Row. Messrs Simpkin
Marshall were across the road, Messrs Longmans opposite,
Messrs Whitaker and *The Bookseller* round the corner and
Stationers' Hall near by. I could hardly have come nearer to the
heart of publishing and the centre of its inheritance. The only
doubt, already simmering in my mind, was whether the heart of
Hutchinson beat in unison.

Mr Lunn was a man who found decision-making normally
difficult, but he came to a rapid one within a few moments
of the arrival of the one 'who will help you a lot'. He decreed
that I was to make the return journey to Tavistock Square not
later than half past four of an afternoon. It seemed to him
essential that I should not be subjected to the buffetings of the
six-o'clock rush-hour. Unpaid, I was given no time-card upon
which would be recorded this early defection from duty.

To add to my perplexity about Lunn and his earldom he
appeared to be in constant touch with 'the Yard' by telephone.
This, I assumed with increasing excitement, must be Scotland
and the publishing involvement with the underworld much deeper
than Stanley Unwin's *Truth About Publishing* revealed. Alas, it
turned out to be Ireland which accommodated our trade counter
and our warehouse. Trade counters have almost disappeared
now and a sad deprivation this entails. Almost every publisher

then maintained his counter, to which would traipse through every day a succession of mostly ancient 'collectors' with burdensome sacks over tired shoulders. Each had his round and would collect for one bookseller or another his daily requirements, thus providing the customers with an extraordinarily quick service. The sales were often considerable; and trade counters were useful and lively centres of trade gossip. But their cost in terms of space and personnel has become prohibitive and one by one publishers have closed them down and customers have to wait with patience for what they want.

The activities of Mr Lunn's department were carried out within two small cubicles. The one telephone was shared with the adjacent advertising department which conducted its hectic life on the other side of the partition. Erle Lunn's cubicle was next to the window from which was observed Mr William Longman at his desk across the road. A Miss Hubbard was housed with Lunn and occupied a table fractionally bigger than the typewriter she administered. I never knew her other name, nor can I recall the usage of any Christian name through all those early years at Hutchinson. A small table was found for me in the second cubicle which was little more than a cupboard whose door had been removed to ensure a right of way. The other occupants of the cupboard were a large desk, a comfortable but dangerously dilapidated leather chair allegedly made redundant upon the retirement of Sir George Hutchinson, and a youngish, prematurely balding man named Dawson-Scott. He was agreeable and pleasant. I never learned how he got there; nor his other name, nor where he lived, nor how he lived, nor even his age. For three months we lived within inches of one another and all I ever gathered was that his mother was Mrs C. A. Dawson-Scott who founded P.E.N., which, a long time later, when David Carver was its secretary, elected me its first publishing member.

A succession of artists, art-agents, blockmakers and others would crowd daily into our tiny office for, under Lunn, Dawson-Scott was responsible for the wrappers of all Hutchinson novels. It was the business of the department, of which I made the fourth member, to produce all wrappers; to compose all blurbs; to prepare all catalogues; to deal with all illustrations for a never-ending succession of 'Large, Handsome Volumes Profusely

Illustrated'; to contrive all promotional material except press advertisements; and to issue a quarterly 'house' journal, *The Booklover*. It was not at all a bad journal either, and I rather regret that in an unaccustomed mood of convivial consideration I returned all my copies to Messrs Hutchinson a year or so ago for their files. We all of us did a lot of 'reading', but were not much involved in the editorial processes of rejection and acceptance of manuscripts. I never succeeded in discovering who was.

I suspect that somehow it was Mr Walter. He did not, however, believe in authors, and certainly not in seeing them. 'You can't run a publishing house and find time for authors,' he would say. Fortunately for me, Erle Lunn's activities brought us more in touch with authors themselves than any others in the building. We appeared very often to be their only point of human contact with their publishers.

Our daily lives however centred around the comings and goings of Mr Walter. When he was in, all activity became mildly hysterical and could be punctured alarmingly by the shrill buzz of some antiquated internal system of communication on which the flashing of a yellow light heralded a summons to the 'front room' and Mr Walter.

I have been reliably told that Walter Hutchinson was kind to animals. His treatment of human beings, dependent upon him for their living, was of a nature so vicious and tyrannical that the only possible defence of those obliged to endure it was to proclaim his insults and humiliations in a sort of riotous spirit of oneupmanship. The more extravagant his excesses, the more unreasonable his attitudes, the more preposterous his requirements, the more outlandish his arrogance and the more bullying his behaviour, the greater became accentuated a sort of lunatic happiness experienced by well-nigh every man and woman involved in the madness of those Paternoster Row years.

Today, getting on for half a century later, there still exists among a dwindling few a certain nostalgia for the goings-on which never ceased while Walter Hutchinson was alive. To the observant his presence even now can somtimes be detected; and whatever may have happened to the firm since his death, and whatever changes the future may contrive, the legend of Mr Walter will survive.

But I had not, as yet, reached this stage of comprehension as I sat at my makeshift table to which a kindly handyman had attached a screen to protect the sweep of my papers to the floor by the breeze of every passing coat-tail intent on the 'mystery and art' of publishing.

As a fully qualified journalist, and with my cuttings to prove it, much of my early ardour was devoted to the preparation of blurbs — those allegedly alluring pieces of descriptive fiction which appear on the flaps of book wrappers and in publishers' seasonal catalogues. They hold untold horrors of composition for those obliged to write them. It was not thought necessary then, nor always so now for that matter, to be more than distantly acquainted with the book involved. Indeed, when required for the catalogue the masterpiece had often enough not been written. It was necessary to obtain a few helpful words from the author and even more necessary to point out that the required appraisal and the words of commendation could safely be left to the publisher.

My first exercise of this kind to gain the immortality of print was for a novel, *An April After* by the one and only Ursula Bloom. With youthful zest I added it to the cuttings from the *Kent Messenger*. Its opening sentence seems to me an archaic gem: 'Anthony Harding, born of a servant girl and a gentleman, was possessed of an artistic temperament and immense ambition.' What continues to astonish me is that it brought from Miss Bloom's husband (now, with Ursula, a friend of many years) the first of two threats I have so far received during my life of a horse-whipping.

The sanitary arrangements provided for the gents of 34 Paternoster Row were repellent in the extreme. Their purpose seemed to be more a receptacle for unwanted galley proofs of unwanted books than the alleviation of human needs. My perambulations around the building in search of those who managed one or another of Walter Hutchinson's innumerable acquisitions had revealed a convenience of exemplary character on the top floor. It contained hot and cold water and an adequate roller towel. Its more advanced privacies, of which there were two, were kept locked. Discreet inquiries elicited the information that they were the private preserves of Mr Walter and Mr John Buchan, whose name appeared on the door of an office housing Messrs Nelson. How he and they contrived to retain possession of themselves in a building dominated by Mr Walter is as great a tribute to John Buchan's fertile ingenuity as any of his splendid novels. A lift of great antiquity, and made for an age of leisure, served this floor from a landing-stage half-way up the staircase to the first. It was controlled by a surly porter who viewed me with suspicion and distaste as I made frequent use of his services, which were not intended for menials. But as our own art department operated on the top floor, my frequent business there was entirely within the law. I kept these very desirable premises under surveillance, and one morning found that Mr Walter had left his key in the lock of his sanctum. Hoping that neither he nor the creator of Richard Hannay would appear, I purloined it and had a copy cut for sixpence during the lunch-hour. Mr Walter's lavatorial luxuries were thus open to me and I did not demean myself with a galley proof during the remainder of my stay.

When I left I bequeathed my key to my good friend Cherry Kearton, who was then in charge of the imprint of Messrs Hurst & Blackett and whom I am inclined to hold responsible for the Second World War. But that too is another story.

4
Goings On

THERE was a curious and unaccountable exhilaration about 34 Paternoster Row if one were young and without the responsibilities of dependants. The country was in the trough of a catastrophic slump and financial anxieties must have been great. Unemployment was dreadful and in most weeks someone or other from Paternoster Row would join its ranks. But at that stage in a career these matters, one has to assume, are looked after by some higher authority. There are jobs to be done, and within the empire devised by Mr Walter neither seniority nor nepotism was of any account. Experience was crammed down one's throat willy-nilly. It was every man for himself so far as pay was concerned, and a strange brand of mutual loyalties enabled one to survive the cut and thrust of war with Mr Walter. Some wild rumour was always in circulation and there was no great confidence that Mr Lovell the cashier, who seldom had cash, would arrive with one's pay packet on Friday afternoons. It is recorded that Mr Walter, from his office, would keep his eye on Mr Longman across the road while Mr Longman would reverse the process in order to decide their tactics in approaching their mutual bank as pay-day problems became acute.

For older men the humours were less apparent. My first few months saw the dismissal, for no reason at all that I can recall, of Mr Dawson-Scott. We were all paid weekly and a week's notice evoked no particular resentment or bitterness. When Friday evening came Mr Dawson-Scott simply shook me by the hand and left. No arrangements of any kind were made to replace him. There was no consultation with Erle Lunn, who ran the department. All that happened was that I abandoned my small table and moved the few inches to Dawson-Scott's desk and that coveted and comfortable leather chair, once the throne of Sir George. No one told me that in future I would be responsible for the wrappers of all Hutchinson fiction in addition to the not inconsiderable burdens of helping Erle Lunn. That this should happen within a short time of entering a publishing office for the first time I took then to be unremarkable, and only later experience seemed to indicate a certain eccentricity of management. The work brought me at once in close touch with a wide circle of commercial artists and their agents; with printers and blockmakers and to an increasing extent with authors who are never averse to consultation about their wrappers.

Mr Walter was at the same time gathering a heterogeneous collection of printers, binders and blockmakers scattered with geographical inconsequence throughout the land. They were all obliged to realize that we were likely to be their best customers. My instructions to them, marked I think by an ingenuity frequently divorced from practicality, drove them to a sort of affectionate frenzy. Once Mr Walter had scrawled his initials or his insults across a proposed design I was free to do much as I liked and in those days typographical experiment was cheap and often not charged for at all. A major deprivation of today is the lack of freedom for inconsequential experiment. The cost of typographical change or correction is now so great that innovation is discouraged and a dull conformity prevails. The Hutchinson printers of those days could understand what I was trying to achieve and would interpret my quick scribbles with sympathy and amused enterprise. A corrected proof today, and even more so an original 'lay-out', has to be prepared with the meticulous detail of an architectural working drawing for examination by a 'visualizer' and submission to a printer from whose union-dominated life all interest in his craft has long since been stilled. Threaten although one day they did to throw me into Tiptree's village pond should I show my face in the place, the printers of Anchor Press established a relationship of amused tolerance seldom found today.

The next and equally abrupt departure from our already truncated centre of operations was Miss Hubbard's. I can summon little recollection of her, except of a rather puffed pale little face disinclined to smile. Her particular friend, whose frequent visits were rather less than welcome, performed secretarial duties for Mr Coffin's production department next door. If Winnie-the-Pooh, as she was known, had a 'best friend', he or she had disclosed nothing.

Again, so far as I know, there was no consultation about the dismissal of Miss Hubbard, and no plans were made for the further use of her ancient typewriter. There seemed only one solution. Lusty would assume her duties with two fingers.

The publication of our house journal *The Booklover* ceased for a while on grounds of economy, but one day Mr Walter — who had stopped it — complained violently of its non-appearance, declared that he had been told nothing about it and ordered its instant rebirth. It must have been, even in those days, a costly affair but it proved invaluable for me. Its circulation was free and its pages covered the whole of the Hutchinson water-front. It carried me, in search of news, to all the many imprints and it was also expected that so experienced a journalist would find little difficulty in writing most of the copy.

It must have been at this time that I wrote a note to Mr Walter indicating, with what diplomacy I could, that I appeared to be working rather harder than was reasonable without pay. It seemed to me unlikely that he would, unaided, recall the understanding that I should give my services for two years. Rather to my surprise, he scrawled across my note, 'You can have two pounds a week.' It was not, for those days, a wage to be sniffed at and I was able to reduce the burden upon my father by that amount.

The imprint of Hutchinson may not have been exactly revered in the book world of that time. 'Too highbrow' was a favoured justification for rejection by Mr Walter. But its output was huge. We produced four packed catalogues a year — winter, spring, summer and autumn, with a sublime disregard (which still continues here and there) of what might be the seasonal climate pertaining in our 'colonial' markets. I do not remember the word 'export' being in use at all. The typography of these catalogues was atrocious and Mr Walter insisted that they should be bound in at the end of every published book. It was a diabolical practice and necessitated the printing of catalogues by the hundred thousand or so. Another perverse whim of Mr Walter's forbade any new book carrying the year of its publication. He remained adamant against any argument and frequent criticism from the trade. 'We can't sell books with dates in them,' would be his cry.

Every now and again there was also a curious procedure, not I think exceptional in those days, of stopping the run of certain titles after every five hundred copies and inserting the phrase 'second impression before publication', and so on progressively. The total run might be modest, but the huge advertisements could proclaim 'Three Impressions Before Publication'. The Largest Publisher in the World—which became of obligatory usage—was greatly in favour of capital letters. But the list was never negligible and Walter's perversities and eccentricities extracted a rather similar brand of loyalty from his authors as from his staff. Philip Gibbs, Gilbert Frankau, Rafael Sabatini, Eden Phillpotts, Geoffrey Moss, Cosmo Hamilton were all continuing stars in a crowded constellation and it was a magical world for a gangling young man to perambulate within.

The general side of the list comprised an extraordinary range of books invariably described as 'One Large Handsome Volume Profusely Illustrated'. I became increasingly responsible for the profusion of illustrations, their selection with the authors, their captioning and their exact positioning in the text. This activity again placed me willy-nilly in contact with many distinguished 'names', who were always polite in concealing their surprise at the youth and apparent fragility of almost their only personal relationship with the great firm. I spent, to my own excitement and the wonderment of my friends, a happy afternoon on the floor of Gladys Cooper's bedroom at The Grove, in Highgate, selecting glamorous pictures with her enthusiastic approval. She hadn't found a title for her book. 'Call it "Gladys Cooper by Gladys Cooper",' I suggested and she did. She gave me a box from which to view her current performance and added for good value a little bow and a smile at the final curtain. More fun, I thought, than 'inductions and institutions'.

At about this time I was closely involved in a sad little drama which has never ceased to perplex me and which still comes frequently to mind. Even today I sometimes stop in my tracks

37

on a crowded pavement and wonder of a passer-by 'can that possibly be Friel?', forgetting that the face I recall is an amused and smiling one of over forty-five years ago.

In the Bloomsbury of that time the Bloomsbury Group did not comprise its sole gyrating circus. There were others and Bloomsbury was almost entirely a residential centre for students and young men and women starting upon careers. There was a flourishing bed-sitting room life and it was in those days possible, and indeed financially necessary, to share such a room with a friend of the same sex without the axiomatic assumption that one was a homosexual or a lesbian. Breakfast was provided, lunch belonged to the day's work, and a wide range of little restaurants provided excellent dinners for one-and-sixpence. Affluence might occasionally justify half a crown and a feast of gargantuan proportions.

I had moved from the Penn Club in Tavistock Square to a bed-sitting room in a house a few doors away. I first shared this with a Penn Club friend, but after a short while he was drafted from London and his chosen successor could not make the move for a month or so. Also at the Penn Club was an agreeable, sensible and amusing young medical student from South Africa. His name was Robert Friel. He was not a particularly close friend, but I knew him well enough to suggest that he might like to fill the gap for a month or two, and it suited his purpose.

There were no problems; we went our own ways and on occasions he would be away for a day or so on some hospital course. At the office I was involved in a Large Handsome Volume about horses and riding by Lady Apsley, to be called *To Whom The Goddess*. Lady Apsley had been thrown from her horse some months past and was now most gallantly tackling new problems of life from a wheel-chair. I was much flattered and not a little awed to be summoned to Badminton for the night to select the illustrations.

I made the journey on a Wednesday and when I returned to Tavistock Square on the Thursday evening I noticed that Friel's shaving equipment and toothbrush had gone. I thought nothing of it, accustomed as I had become to his periodic absences in hospital.

As the rest of the week passed by I began to think that it

would have been civil to warn me of this longer absence, but no anxiety arose. I knew that he had a doctor uncle in Harley Street and that he customarily paid him and his wife a visit on Sundays. On the Monday his aunt telephoned me at the office to inquire if I knew the whereabouts of her nephew. He had failed to turn up on Sunday. Her husband had been in touch with the hospital, but he was not there nor had he been since the Wednesday, when he had attended a lecture in the morning. I was not able to help her and for the first time anxiety arose. Various inquiries were put in train. None of his friends at the Penn Club had seen him; neither had other occupants of our bed-sitter establishment. On that Wednesday morning he had taken no more than the requirements for a single night. He had attended the morning lecture with other medical students, who had noticed nothing amiss. At lunch-time he had gone to his bank and withdrawn five pounds, neither more nor less than was his custom. From that moment Robert Friel, aged about twenty-two, disappeared from the face of this earth.

He had no known anxieties, no involvements. He intensely wanted to be a doctor and he had seemed happy in London. The police, having satisfied themselves that no crime was involved, appeared to disclaim all interest. Messages were sent to every ship en route for Africa; and the BBC, as was then its custom, broadcast an appeal. He had not been admitted to hospital or involved in any recorded accident. There was a total blank and no light of any kind has arisen over the years to illuminate any aspect of the story.

Meanwhile, retrenchment continued to apply to every activity within 34 Paternoster Row except the endless profusion of its book publishing under an ever-growing list of battered imprints. It was not customary for Mr Walter to invest in success. Large Handsome Volumes, endless novels, a great variety of cheap reprints and sixpenny paperbacks of magazine size poured from Ireland Yard every Monday morning. The Largest Publisher in the World was in Full Flood, and marked the occasion by giving Erle Lunn a week's notice. It was brutally done. He was then, I suppose, around fifty; he had no resources so far as I know, but no children and a delightful Danish wife. He was not to get another job until some three or four years later when, on my departure, he returned to manage the imprint of Messrs Selwyn & Blount.

I owe much to Erle Lunn. Without his kindness and patience I might well have foundered before ever putting out to sea. He had been in the navy and how he was ever recruited to Paternoster Row I never learned. Certainly his gentle temperament was not one for the hurly-burly, skulduggery of Paternoster Row. He seemed in a perpetual state of rather mystified perplexity. For all he wrote he used a brilliant green ink, which somehow impressed me; and he was devoted to the writing of Algernon Blackwood. He had a habit of seizing one by the wrist when driving home a point. He was an easy target for Walter. The day before he left he wrote to Mr Walter simply reminding him of his departure on the morrow, and to whom should he hand over? I can see now the scrawl of the reply across the green ink: 'Hand over to Lusty. We shall be slack for a long time.' On leaving, Lunn gave me his cigarette-case which he had carried all his life. It was a battered thing, knocked around by life rather like its owner. It was a moving gesture.

There was not much slackness that I could observe. The responsibilities falling upon the department had increased rather than diminished over the three years which had passed since my timid arrival in it. Now alone, it was appropriate to survey my little kingdom.

The 'little doctor' had proved right and I was still alive, with my heart in apparently good order. This had greatly surprised the London specialist who had examined it during a stage in my illness. I had returned to him fairly recently in some pain and rather anxious. 'Shingles,' he said tersely. But he had done his homework. 'I thought', he said, 'that you might live, but I never expected to see you up and about.'

Periodically I had written short notes to Mr Walter about my pay. It stood now at five pounds a week having got there by injections of half-crowns, crowns and even on occasions of ten shillings. I was no longer in need of my father's subsidy, and indeed could boast a certain affluence. I supplemented my income by reading a prodigious number of manuscripts of all kinds for the 'subsidiary' imprints at five shillings a time. I had acquired a murderous little Fiat car for five pounds which I garaged in

Woburn Square. My first drive was to Colchester to see a Penn Club girl-friend. The car seemed to falter and consumed fourteen gallons of petrol in doing so. I was still in persistent pursuit of my Scottish Joan, but she would not go in it. So I sold it and expended seven pounds ten shillings on a marvellous yellow Swift with a dicky. It was possible to live well and save money on five pounds a week, and I had all of thirty pounds in the bank.

I moved myself into the more private pen vacated by Erle Lunn, but in the outer cubicle retained the ornament of Sir George's chair to which, in its increasing decrepitude, I had formed an attachment. It was perfectly obvious that help must come from somewhere, but quite how Eileen Webb arrived on the scene I cannot recall. But she did and with great charm and efficiency looked after me until my 'escape' in 1935.

A great deal has been written of the irascibility of H. G. Wells in his treatment of the many publishers with whom he quarrelled over the years. After preliminary flirtation he seemed to have little use for any of them. Hutchinson at this time were embarked upon the publication of *The Shape of Things to Come* and I have no doubt that Mr Walter was paying heavily for the privilege. It was of course my responsibility to produce both a blurb and a wrapper and to submit them to the judgment of the great man himself. The Greatest I had so far encountered. No doubt about that. He was then living in Chiltern Court, over Baker Street Station, and thither I repaired in, I remember, a singularly untidy and very grubby macintosh. I cannot have presented a publishing image likely to inspire Mr Wells with much enthusiasm or confidence. But I can remember to this day the exactness of the exquisite courtesy and charm with which he received me. He looked himself quite remarkably spruce and immaculate. He may have been writing rude notes to Walter but to this menial no man could have been kinder or more considerate.

An innovation I had introduced to 'my' office was designed to make at once clear from which department any missive of mine had come. The derivation was probably Lunn's green ink, but I acquired for Eileen Webb and her typewriter a ribbon which presented its lettering in a rather effective double-tone sepia ink. Mr Wells commented upon it with amusement when

I placed my quite appalling blurb before him. 'This book', I had started, 'by the world's greatest thinker ... ' H. G. Wells pondered, his pen in suspense, and then neatly inserted 'one of the'. Other corrections he made with the same meticulous care, pondering each one. 'I think that will do very nicely,' he said. 'I am most grateful to you.'

I then unveiled the artist's proposed design for the wrapper. He looked gravely at it for a few moments. 'Well done,' he said, 'I like it.' We had a few moments of further talk before he took me to the door. 'Is this your coat?' he asked, concealing his distaste. 'Yes,' I answered, 'rather dirty I'm afraid.' He smiled and why I should still remember so vividly how it was done I do not know, but I can never forget the gentleness with which he helped me into it. H. G. Wells might have continued to write abusive letters to publishers for the rest of his life, but I can only record that he never paid a visit to Paternoster Row or later to our Michael Joseph office in Bloomsbury without seeking me out to inquire if all was well.

The outcome of that afternoon is possibly regrettable. Wells in due course signed for me a copy of *The Shape of Things to Come* and I had the sense to fasten within it my typewritten blurb containing his written corrections. Not so long ago the Society of Authors celebrated the centenary of his birth with a reception at Madame Tussauds, almost adjacent to Chiltern Court. A small exhibition was contrived and on hearing of this I offered my little piece of Wellsiana. It was gratefully accepted and I was impressed to find it occupying a small showcase of its own, with a massive security guard standing by. That I had found the relic at all was more luck than judgment; and feeling that were I to be dismissed from life by the legendary bus it would convey little to anyone finding it, I thought it should be offered to the University of Texas which, with apparently limitless funds, appeared to be buying everything it could lay hands upon. My friend George Ashley of the Society of Authors was about to visit them and I entrusted him with the commission which was brought, as is said, to a satisfactory conclusion. With the proceeds we added a new cloakroom to our Hampstead home, to be known as the H. G. Wells Memorial Cloakroom. Alas, its life was short. A few years later we sold this house; its new owners immediately gutted it, and our Wells Memorial is no more. I wish now, of course, that I had retained the item for at least a little longer.

Returning from this digression to Paternoster Row, it was at about this time that 'apprentices' began to appear on the scene in some profusion. How they were selected I do not know, and what scale of fees was thought appropriate by Mr Walter was not revealed. But each, I suspect, according to his notion of their means. Among the first was the amiable Jock Gibb, who seemed to my eyes a very sophisticated and assured young man about town. His social activities almost monopolized our one telephone and he had a very knowing wink with which, so to speak, I kept in touch as, after graduating at Paternoster Row, he moved to Methuen and then to Geoffrey Bles which he ran with distinction until his recent retirement.

There was no consultation or instruction, but it seemed that the tuition of these hapless young men would largely derive from me. Some were scattered like chaff among the imprints, but I had seldom less than three or four assorted. Some were a good deal older than myself and none I think were younger. A number remain my friends today; others have disappeared in the maelstrom of our turbulent years. I suspect it is from these early days that derived a reputation, which I rather feebly refute, of not being the easiest of mortals to work with or for. In moments of honesty I have from time to time declared that, given any choice, I would not care to work with or for myself. The first moment of truth came during this period in the Paternoster Row Staff College when I learned that three of the five apprentices toiling within my control were imbibing prescribed nerve tonics at lunch-time.

With my team of tonic-taking apprentices and the invaluable Eileen Webb, the work of the department got done; and, once under control and with more careful planning, it made some impact both within the firm and to some extent in the wider world of book manufacture and literary agency. There is little doubt that to Mr Walter we were hardly more than serfs, but in time social tendencies become manifest within the most arid climate and it was suggested that a staff magazine would demonstrate our solidarity and our common devotion to the Hutchinson scene. His wealth of journalistic experience, his obvious idleness and, for some obscure reason, his Quaker education uniquely qualified young Lusty to be its first editor.

Goings On seemed to me, with its slight suggestion of mischief, an appropriate title; and Mr Walter accepted it without demur. He also accepted with alacrity the proposal that he should contribute a foreword to the first number. As he had 'no time to do this sort of thing' would I write it for him? The first number also contained an ingenious, and again slightly mischievous, competition to identify present notabilities within the firm from some childhood photograph. Mr Walter obliged again, and an unmistakably arrogant infant presented no problem to anyone. I believe that two issues of *Goings On* appeared before the departure of its editor, following which it sank without trace.

One of Mr Walter's publishing acquisitions had been the imprint of Messrs Selwyn & Blount, derived by some strange alchemy from Messrs Ingpen & Grant. It was not without quality, but Walter had done virtually nothing with it. It added to the Paternoster Row stage the personage of Joe Gaute, who succeeded Macdonald in the management of the contract department. Joe Gaute was and mercifully remains a large man with a curiously sideways gait. He contributed much to the climate of 34 Paternoster Row; and once was knocked flat on his back by a character named Heriot who had emerged from somewhere, was an ardent admirer of Sir Oswald Mosley, and was later blown to pieces in an air-raid. Messrs Selwyn & Blount was being run from the offices of Messrs Geographia in Fleet Street (also an acquisition of Mr Walter) and was under the management of Rex Flateau whose subsidiary empire included Messrs Hurst & Blackett, the unlikely publishers, within a few years, of Hitler's *Mein Kampf*.

I was not, at that time, exactly inactive, but was possessed of a certain boredom. Thus, one lunch-time, I wrote a note to Mr Walter suggesting that I might have a small imprint placed within my charge. Back came the response: 'You can have Selwyn & Blount — but only as a hobby. It must not interfere with your Hutchinson work.' Two brown paper parcels were later deposited in my cubicle. One was marked Selwyn and the other Blount, and they were accompanied by Mr Flateau's compliments. Neither contained anything of significance but there was a copy each of three rather dreary new books due for publication within the next fortnight. Thus I became, according to one John Macadam in the *Sunday Dispatch* of that time, England's Youngest Publisher.

5
Mr Walter

IT was not until many years later that I was able to appreciate the remarkably good fortune which directed my first hesitant steps to 34 Paternoster Row and the benevolent malevolence of Walter Hutchinson. It may at this stage be appropriate to take a look at one of the strangest and, I now believe, one of the saddest enigmas to bestride the publishing scene of his day. Within a diminishing group, and some thirty years after his death, he remains a never-ending subject of discussion and speculation. When he died he was accorded one of the harshest obituaries ever to appear in *The Bookseller*, or any other paper for that matter, and no word arrived from any source to deny its truth. Yet I do not think he was a hated man even by those who had good reason to hate him. If the perspective of time tends, as I think it does, to soften the outline as distant haze a scene, it is possible to conjecture that he was less a monster than the victim of an uncontrollable temperament which gradually, but with dreadful certainty, brought about his own destruction and very nearly the destruction of a crazy, haphazard and jerry-built empire.

That he had achieved anything was due as much to Mrs Webb as to himself; she presided over almost all of his working life and she was certainly the most remarkable woman in it. Neither Mr Walter nor the firm could have survived without her then or later. She was never seen to lose her calm however intolerable the situation and the stress. She maintained the peace; protected the weak; interceded for the innocent; recognized the guilty; interpreted that which was beyond the understanding of others to comprehend and after Walter's death worked miracles to en-

46

sure that his empire would survive against all the odds. And from the tranquillity of retirement until the end of her days she emerged only to refute and chastise the ungodly who dared to suggest that Mr Walter was not wholly the paragon of every virtue.

But he was certainly not a villain, nor even a tycoon in the sense of today. He was not even ruthless in the attainment of his own aims; he hardly knew what these were. He did not exploit, in the modern sense, those who worked for him. He simply bullied, shouted, threatened, raved and ranted to so absurd an extent that it succeeded in rallying a certain obtuse loyalty. He simply did not know about people or understand the realities of any life other than his own. He would have made no headway at all in the world of today and he would not have begun to comprehend it. No staff would tolerate what had to be acceptable, at the end of the '20s and in the early '30s, in the interest of basic survival. Mr Walter could deride and ridicule a request from a senior employee for an additional five or ten shillings a week with a contemptuous 'Don't you know it costs me three pounds a week to feed one of my horses?' The reaction would not be one of contempt or hate but rather 'what a story to go the rounds'; a sort of oneupmanship boost to morale. Some of those treated most abominably never ceased in loyalty and even a certain affection.

I have never heard any accusation of dishonesty or even of sharp practice. He was never, it seemed to me, in any sense an experienced man of business. One of the leading literary agents of that time, who sold innumerable books to Mr Walter for advances that no other publisher would dream of paying, told me that he never doubted the word of Mr Walter and never knew him retract any verbal deal.

One does not much question the success or standing of a firm which first employs you for nothing a week, and if it appears to be publishing every Monday morning a huge output of new books and cheap editions of old ones, and if a sort of hectic excitement is engendered every day from nine o'clock in the morning until six o'clock in the evening, one assumes simply that this is what publishing is all about. Walter Hutchinson's father, Sir George, had gone from the scene before I arrived in that April of 1928. I never set eyes upon him; he was never referred to and it was not long before he died.

47

If Mr Walter had a flair it was for the acquisition of failing businesses. So far as publishing is concerned he was probably the first substantial take-overer and he collected imprints as most people collect stamps. There was no vestige of an editorial plan to the Hutchinson operation. Each imprint was conducted in isolation and the five-shilling staff readers might well encounter the same manuscript a number of times as its author or its agent worked the rounds. There was neither rhyme nor reason in any editorial sense. And if specialization could be detected at the time of takeover it very rapidly disappeared. I can remember in 1928 the imprints of Rider; Skeffington; Hurst & Blackett; John Long; Jarrolds; Stanley Paul; Melrose, and there must have been others. Shortly after the war the *Sunday Times* organized the first of its series of Book Exhibitions. It was held at Grosvenor House and upon the eve of its opening I went along to assure myself that all was well with the Michael Joseph stand. This was in close proximity to that of Hutchinson, which announced itself as Hutchinson and 164 Associated Companies. On the following morning I paid another visit and a man up a ladder was painstakingly at work on the Hutchinson stand. Very carefully he was removing '4' and substituting '5'.

The only subsidiary imprint of any distinction was that of Jarrolds, and this was due entirely to Robert Hale who had been acquired with it. He was housed on the top floor and operated with a greater professionalism than pertained in any other part of the building. He was a remarkable and kindly little man who rather scuttled around in an alpaca jacket kept for the purpose, gathering this and gathering that, but certain always what he was about. I suspect that Mr Walter found him elusive and his most considerable claim to fame, spoken of in awe and wonder, was that he was the only man in the place paid one thousand pounds a year. He was invariably kind to me, and I read a great many manuscripts for him at five shillings a time. He left Paternoster Row just about when I did in 1935 to start his own business. In this he published a prodigious number of books and his heirs and successors still do so. Many wondered how it was done, but Robert Hale knew exactly and his calculations would have been always precise.

There can hardly be a collection of family books accumulating the dust of years which does not contain one or another of the ormolu-bound copies of some Hutchinson Standard Part Work. I have always imagined that at one time these must have achieved considerable success both as they appeared in fortnightly parts and later in elaborately bound form. There was Hutchinson's History of the Nations, of the War, of the Empire — a long string of them. At what stage they became 'edited' by Walter Hutchinson I do not know, nor what this editing amounted to. But Walter Hutchinson, M.A.; Barrister-at-Law; F.R.G.S.; F.Z.S., etc., etc. was proclaimed on every title page. He set great store by any distinction he could anyhow acquire, and the bitterest disappointment of his life was the lack of recognition and particularly his failure to obtain a knighthood. To this end he employed every wile and every approach he could think up or pay for. He succeeded only in making himself rather pathetically ridiculous, and was reduced to instructing his staff that everything submitted to him, however trivial, should be addressed to Walter Hutchinson Esq and that instant dismissal would be the penalty of omission.

There was, too, in those days, quite a string of magazines emanating from Paternoster Row. A brilliant little Frenchwoman, Miss Jerome, edited *Woman* which, with *Hutchinson's Magazine*, conveyed what was regarded as 'class'. Less 'classy' were *Jolly* and *Happy*, *True Stories* and others. From another cubby-hole in a corridor came *The Occult Review*, an off-shoot of Messrs Rider, whose editor, Mr Strutton, looked like a little white walrus. He wore rimless glasses and discussed the projection of astral bodies and other topics of space and time and esoteric religions with Erle Lunn. I frequently joined them for lunch at Hill's restaurant, off Ludgate Circus, but this in time had to be abandoned as Mr Strutton became convinced that a waitress of buxom proportions was taking too much interest in him.

The Writer was also a Hutchinson magazine edited by Kennedy Williamson, who had just succeeded, so I learned, a Mr Michael Joseph, whose *How to Succeed as a Writer* was in the Hutchinson list. Michael Joseph had accepted the invitation of Mr Curtis Brown to manage his growing literary agency in Henrietta Street; it contained among others David Higham, Laurence

Pollinger, Cherry Kearton, Geoffrey Halliday and Nancy Pearn. A Miss Juliet O'Hea was Michael Joseph's secretary.

My first direct encounter with Mr Walter may not have meant very much to him, but it greatly sustained me before I had been an unpaid presence in Paternoster Row for less than a month. Nowadays flashing yellow lights signify hazards of one kind and another. It was appropriate that a similar contrivance in Paternoster Row gave warning of a summons to Mr Walter. On this particular spring day it came to life in Erle Lunn's cubicle and as ever he responded with alacrity and agitation. But Mr Walter, it seemed, was in need not of him but of Lusty. This young man, on the verge of leaving for an easy ride home on his 18 bus, was a great deal more than agitated, but he somehow got himself to the curious and forbidding passage which led to Mr Walter's room. At the entrance to this passage was a bell which one pressed and then waited. Sometimes the miraculous Mrs Webb would come to the door at its far end and hand over some scrawl emanating from Mr Walter, or convey some instruction. On the other hand she might beckon one to face the music. There would sometimes be others present in various stages of moral disintegration. Mr Walter would sit or stand behind a great table littered with the disorder of his daily life and the flotsam and jetsam of 150 (take it or leave it) companies. Mrs Webb would be either in hovering attendance like a fielder in the slips ready to catch what she could that Mr Walter would fling around the floor, or at her desk keeping Mr Longman and Messrs Simpkin Marshall, who also lived opposite, under surveillance. On this occasion I passed Robert Hale coming out, looking slightly flushed.

It was some moments before Mr Walter took any notice of me. His scowling gaze was on a finished wrapper design which I had never seen in my life. It was intended for some romantic novel and a not unpleasing girl of the 1920s gazed at Mr Walter from it. She clearly had no hope of getting far with Mr Walter. 'You are Lusty, aren't you,' he shouted. I admitted it. He looked at the girl's head and slashed a brutal pencil through it. 'This is no good,' he bellowed. 'I am not going to pay for a thing like this. There isn't enough paint on it for one thing. If I have to pay four guineas for a wrapper design I want more paint on it.'

He scowled at me and threw the picture on the floor. 'Nothing', he said slowly, 'has gone right with this firm since you've been here. You are ruining it.' It was not a remark to which there was much of an answer. I retrieved the damaged heroine from the floor and was gently ushered from the room by Mrs Webb. 'Never mind,' she said, as a nurse to a child.

I gave the offending wrapper to Scott. 'Here's your design,' I said, 'Mr Walter doesn't like it. He wants more paint. I am ruining the firm,' I added with some pride and left to catch my bus.

Oddly enough this confrontation with Mr Walter was never repeated with the same ferocity for the duration of my stay with him. He threatened me with the sack often enough and once gave instructions that I was to be charged with the cost of remaking a set of four-colour blocks which contained some aspect unacceptable to him. I received the invoice but threw it away and that was that. But it very much alarmed me none the less, and I put the problem to Dwye Evans, who had just begun his publishing life at Heinemann under his brilliant father Charles Evans. Philip Unwin, at about the same time, had begun his long career with his uncle Stanley, and it was he, with an enthusiasm which has never diminished, who organized a small group which met occasionally for lunch to pontificate about publishing. It was at these lunches that I sensed a confirmation of my doubts about the normalcy of life with Walter in Paternoster Row. 'What', I asked Dwye Evans on this occasion, 'do you do at Heinemann when mistakes are made?' Dwye drew himself to his full height and seemed to become aware of an odour at the end of his nose. 'We do not', he said, 'make mistakes at Heinemann.'

Once I was sacked more seriously at the behest of Commander St John Rich, whose involvement in publishing was fortuitous. He had married Walter Hutchinson's sister and in a moment of frankness revealed to me that he had been made a director of the firm in lieu of a wedding-present but that he knew nothing of publishing or books. This was quickly manifest, but he was given a table in Walter's room and told to manage the firm. He did not last long and Walter soon resorted to a process of humiliation. Among the commander's new responsibilities was the approval of wrappers of which Walter later disapproved. On one occasion with Rich in the room, I told an angry Walter that Rich had passed the design he was now rejecting and what was I supposed to do about it. 'You don't want to listen to Rich,' said Walter pleasantly enough, 'the man's a bloody fool.'

During Rich's stay I was away for a while with a bad bout of flu and on my return found that, at Rich's behest, I had been sacked. 'Just keep out of sight for a little while,' advised Mrs Webb and that was the end of that. Later, when I left altogether, I wrote somewhere of having 'escaped' from Hutchinson. This, thought the gallant sailor, is a libel and advised Mr Walter to sue. But he had more sense.

But publishing and its attractions had entered the nautical blood of the commander and he soon departed to found the imprint of Rich & Cowan. He took with him from Hutchinson one of the apprentices, Peter Stucley, for whom I was later to publish a travel book and a novel. At my suggestion the new firm produced a book on green-toned paper in an attempt to brighten the appearance. Nobody appeared to notice the innovation. In due course the firm and the commander foundered. Walter acquired the imprint for his collection but left the commander out in the cold. Poor Peter Stucley dropped dead in a train long before he should have done, and I read of Rich's death in *The Times* only a little while ago.

Typical of Mr Walter was his sudden acquisition of a real, as distinct from a literary, sausage factory. A new name for the sausages became a matter of urgency and the resources of all editorial know-how within the building were mobilized to deal with the problem. I never heard of the outcome of this crisis; nor when, on another occasion, a cosmetic company appeared on the scene and again some new marketing image was required. There was considerable hilarity, and Winnie-the-Pooh emerged a hot favourite.

Walter Hutchinson was a rogue elephant in the world of orthodox publishing. He would not involve himself in trade affairs; but every president of the Publishers Association during Walter's lifetime found himself abused by Walter during interminable assaults by telephone. Very few publishers ever met Mr Walter, nor did many authors. Yet he was the pivot around which a very large organization somehow revolved. In addition, his racing activities absorbed a large part of his time, and later in his life the formation of his Gallery of Sporting Prints became his creditable obsession. Necessarily disposed of after his death, its value today, together with that of Derby House in Stratford Place which he bought, would be immense. In whatever activity Mr Walter became engaged, and however admirable it might be, ultimate disaster seemed somehow to become inevitable as his uncontrollable temperament superseded rational judgment.

In my few years at Paternoster Row I learned much that would have required long apprenticeship in less lunatic stables. Experience was rammed down one's throat willy-nilly. One sank or swam and this by luck rather than by ability, and the sins of Walter's omissions were as valuable, if recognized, as were the virtues of a competence which somehow drove forward and kept going a machine of massive proportions.

Two lessons in particular I have found in principle of a continuing value beyond their immediate implications. On one memorable occasion Mr Walter bought at an auction a pedigree cow for what was then a record price. WORLD'S LARGEST PUBLISHER BUYS WORLD'S MOST EXPENSIVE COW proclaimed Edmond Segrave in *The Bookseller*. The cause of this costly distinction arose from the dispatch by Mr Walter of two emissaries to the same auction with the same instruction to purchase.

On another occasion it was discovered too late for any change of plan that three different imprints within the group were to publish on the same day three different books by three different authors all covering the same series of test matches. It was very much this recollection that many years later convinced me on my return to Hutchinson that priority should be given to the allocation of specialist editorial areas to the many imprints within the organization. I have, in fact, long since convinced myself that it was only those crazy years of apprenticeship in the '20s and '30s under Mr Walter which made slightly less than lunatic my return to the fold twenty-one years later to reorganize for the modern world its manifold publishing operations. It took long enough and longer than I had hoped, but if anything was achieved it was made possible only by the experience of those apprentice years.

Megalomania was developing apace in the mind of Mr Walter. It was a saddening spectacle. He had convinced himself, but no one else, that he controlled the largest book publishing organization in the world. It was never true and it never mattered, but it became a rule that such was to be proclaimed as frequently as possible and certainly in every press advertisement. Edmond Segrave, for many years the brilliant editor of *The Bookseller* (made by him the best trade paper in the world), had little use for Walter Hutchinson and his arrogance. He refused to accept any advertisement from Hutchinson which made claim to size and would report to me with delight the anger and frustration of Walter Hutchinson. I had in my early days first established contact with Edmond when his office was a few yards away in Warwick Lane. Over the next forty years he was to become one of my closest and dearest friends in publishing, and I do not think we ever differed on any point of principle. His death, within a few years of Sir Allen Lane's, has been a personal deprivation of immense sadness. Edmond never concealed his acid distaste for Mr Walter and his ways. He was too aware of the unhappiness and insecurity he engendered.

It was my rather exceptional good fortune in 1935 to depart from the Hutchinson scene of my own volition. No one else, within my years there, had accomplished this. Michael Joseph undertook to acquaint Mr Walter with the news that I was to join him on the formation of his own company as its Editorial and Production Manager. The capital letters seemed to me very big. Michael told me later that he had done so during a somewhat rampageous weekend. Mr Walter had been rather tight at the time and was crawling around his drawing-room on hands and knees. He did not apparently register the news then nor, so far as I know, later. I simply departed with an enormous Webster's Dictionary and a watch, still in use, most generously subscribed to by my friends in Paternoster Row. It was some years before I was again to hear the voice of Mr Walter.

During the war a British publishing mission comprising Geoffrey Faber, Walter Harrap and Bob Wren Howard, now all alas dead, at personal inconvenience and some risk to life and limb visited Canada and the United States. They had important work to do on behalf of us all. The Americans required to be told that despite the problems of war the British publishing activities continued in all its traditional markets and that Canada remained an important part of them. The Canadians needed to be persuaded against the domination of the American version of the English language in their territory. Out of the blue came Walter Hutchinson on the telephone to me in Bloomsbury Street — then the Michael Joseph office. The almost forgotten terrors of Paternoster Row came flooding back. 'Is that you, Lusty?' The voice was unmistakable. 'How are you, Lusty? Never forget that I brought you up, will you?'

No, I assured him, I would not forget it and how was he? 'I'm all right, Lusty. Too busy, you know. Too busy. All these companies to look after. You know something about this bloody silly Publishers Association, don't you? I've no use for them at all. Useless to me, utterly useless. Now, Lusty, what's all this nonsense about Faber, Harrap and Howard going to America? It's a damned disgrace. They will land us all in trouble. Bloody fools the lot of them. Don't forget, Lusty, that I brought you up. Can't you do something about these things? We shall all be ruined. Damned madhouse that Publishers Association ... ' And so it went on seemingly for hour after hour. It was impossible to interject a word and had I been able to it would only have added fuel to his fire. Finally he came to a halt. 'Never mind, Mr Walter,' I said, 'they are all in mid-Atlantic at this moment and none of them may get to New York.' There was a pause. 'Oh no, Lusty, you mustn't say things like that. You mustn't talk in that way. Good men all of them. Sorry you don't agree with me. Goodbye, Lusty. Nice to talk to you. Never forget I brought you up.'

There was one more call to come after the lapse of further years. The same greeting, the same instruction to remember and then: 'You know Edmond Segrave don't you, Lusty? Friend of yours I'm told. He's a bloody fool you know. He won't listen to me. I've told him over and over again that I'm the biggest publisher in the world. He won't believe me. Won't print my advertisements. Losing thousands of pounds of advertising. Damned fool. I think he may believe you. Will you tell him,

Lusty, that I'm the biggest publisher in the world? You know damn well, Lusty, that I'm the biggest publisher in the world. You tell him so.' There was a certain pathos in his voice, almost a pleading, which I found very sad. I had heard of increasing difficulties. 'I don't think, Mr Walter, that he will believe me either. It isn't true is it? Why does it matter, anyway?'

'Of course it's true, Lusty. You know that damn well. It's that bloody fool Segrave ... losing thousands of pounds ... I'm the biggest advertiser he could have. You must tell him, Lusty, for his own sake.'

'I don't think I can, Mr Walter. But I tell you what I will do. If you write a piece proving it, I'll persuade him to print it.' This, I thought, was a masterpiece of diplomacy. 'You are a bloody fool too, Lusty. 1 brought you up and you know damn well I have no time to write pieces as you call them. No time at all with all my companies to look after. You know that perfectly well, Lusty. Well, never mind. Goodbye, Lusty. Don't forget now. I brought you up.'

Thus Mr Walter passed from my life and within a few months from the lives of all. Chaos was closing in upon him. The alien world would not receive him. It had become an impossible place. There seemed only one way out and he found it.

6
Hobby-horse

I RATHER doubt if a young man today, at the age of twenty-two and after four years in a publishing office, could hope to be given an almost extinct but none the less reputable imprint to play with 'as a hobby'. I doubt in fact whether such could be expected in the early '30s except upon the whim of Mr Walter. There was no sort of consultation, nor an instruction of any kind. It was probably Mrs Webb who arranged the removal of the two brown parcels from Geographia's office in Fleet Street to my cubicle in Paternoster Row. After that it was up to me.

A real room with walls was somehow found to be vacant and into it I was moved with Miss Webb, leaving a flush of apprentices in possession of the cubicles and obliged to imbibe their tonics and their publishing wisdom at a distance they probably found more congenial.

I had become a good deal interested in typography and book production. Across the road were Messrs Simpkin Marshall, the trade's largest wholesalers, and their new book showroom was in charge of an agreeable young man later to achieve fame and fortune as the author of *No Orchids for Miss Blandish* and a long string of succeeding best-sellers. It was here that I was enabled to examine the wares of the day and first became conscious that the general level of Messrs Hutchinson & Co.'s production standards did not bear comparison with the majority of its competitors.

The new books of Messrs Cape and Faber and Heinemann looked to me to carry a distinction only very rarely evident in the Hutchinson imprints. More curious still, it was a difference which appeared to derive more from the area within the control

of the publisher than the responsibility of the printer. The Mayflower Press at Plymouth, a part of the Hutchinson Printing
Trust, seemed as perfectly able to print a book to the standards
of Messrs Faber as to those of Messrs Hutchinson. It was not, I
knew, significantly a matter of cost but a matter of care and discernment. Only very lately has the cost of producing a carefully
designed and thoughtfully produced book become any greater
than the cost of mass-producing a typographical abortion.

It thus seemed to me as I surveyed the future for Messrs
Selwyn & Blount that its quickest route to recognition might
be in the direction of production standards higher than those
normally associated with the outpourings from Paternoster Row.
I was, at the same time, determined to extend the role of Miss
Webb's brown typewriter ribbon and evolve a recognizable style
for all the printed impedimenta of a publishing operation. The
colophon belonging to Messrs Selwyn & Blount was hardly an
inspired one, but it served its useful purpose and appeared on
our brown-tinted notepaper, review slips, compliment slips and
the like.

I have believed ever since in the image-making value of a
good colophon and have twice encountered the daunting problem of finding one for all seasons and all moods. The supreme
colophon of my time has been that suggested by Edward Young
and adopted by Allen Lane for Penguin Books. It conveys
exactly that 'dignified flippancy' which, as his life was moving
to its close, Allen Lane declared to have been the image he had
always sought for Penguin. Add to the phrase 'supreme courage',
and it describes with perfect brevity Allen's own approach to
the inevitable end of his final illness.

Editorially, I had extreme good fortune in those early days
with Selwyn & Blount. A few weeks before the bestowal of this
mantle of management by Mr Walter, a Penn Club friend of
mine from the Lake District handed me the script of a first
novel entrusted to him by its author. It had been read as an act
of friendship by Hugh Walpole who was reputed to think highly
of it. Dutifully I had handed it over to the editorial processes of
Messrs Hutchinson and it was being read by Mr Skeffington,
a congenial old boy who had been recently acquired along with
the mainly religious imprint bearing his name. His family, so I

understood, made carpets in Kidderminster a good deal more profitably than he made books in London. I heard rumour that he was much impressed and was about to deliver a cracking good report. It was at once necessary to contrive that this would never reach its destination, but should, in current terms, be hijacked and diverted along the passage to the new office of Messrs Selwyn & Blount. This was satisfactorily achieved. The first novel was *George Ashbury* by O. S. Macdonnell, whose cousin A. G. was enjoying an enormous success with *England, Their England*. *George Ashbury* was a splendidly adventurous story of a fugitive on the run in the Lake District and so well has it survived the passage of time that it is currently in process of reissue.

I devised its publishing with great care and found a gloriously panoramic view of the countryside to serve both as a wrapper and as endpapers to the book. It was, I think, and at any rate at Hutchinson, the first novel to carry an all-round design on its wrapper. It was produced to a rather larger size than was then common to novels, and printed on a cream-toned antique laid paper which some ditherers called yellow and still persist in doing so. An informed observer might suspect that it emanated from the meticulous house of Jonathan Cape in Bedford Square and bore the mark of Wren Howard. It would have been a good guess, for in fact I followed their admirable style as closely as prudence allowed me; and I continued to do this over the next forty years with an occasional variation pinched from Messrs Faber.

In those days the publishing of new books conformed to a much more rigid timetable than it does today, and August was regarded as a month to avoid at all costs. For exactly this reason I was anxious to launch *George Ashbury* into the holiday world of that month and I put the case for doing so to Mr Walter. 'You will fail,' he scrawled, 'but go ahead.' A gesture to remember. Fortunately for me it did not fail and within a week or so of its publication had sold more copies than any other first novel published by any of the Hutchinson imprints up to that time. The reviews were prominent, widespread and enthusiastic, for the reviewers had precious little else to write about. Conditions have changed a great deal, but I still prefer to launch a book of exceptional promise during the last fortnight of August, before the overwhelming floods of autumn.

It is difficult to check figures since so many of Hutchinson's records were destroyed in the war when Hitler wrecked the centre of the book trade. But I seem to remember that the sales of *George Ashbury* reached the ten thousand mark at a time when first novels might sell as few as a couple of hundred and there were no book societies or book clubs or indeed much bally-hoo other than great spaces of press advertisements. But it was all very agreeable to Messrs Selwyn & Blount.

An even greater stroke of good fortune, which again reveals an unfamiliar aspect of Walter Hutchinson, derived from my friend-ship with a brilliant young commercial artist named Arthur Wragg. He had done a number of book wrappers, and when he became aware of my new hobby said that he had a proposition to put before me. The evils of that time were very great: poverty, unemployment, avarice, ignorance, war, lethargy, and all were disregarded to an extent utterly unknown today. However de-spairing mankind may seem to be in the '70s, its conscience has been awakened to an awareness remarkably different to its apathy of forty years ago. Arthur Wragg was a serious young man and he thought it important to do something about the world which troubled him so much. He had it in mind, he said, to illustrate the Psalms of David with a series of contemporary cartoons. Would I be interested?

He brought to the office a sample cartoon. It was in the strongest terms of black and white and the impact was immediate. It was utterly devoid of compromise. It revealed a young, un-employed man crouched against the cold; by his side was a battered dustbin. 'I cried unto thee, O Lord:' ran the caption, 'I said, Thou art my refuge and my portion in the land of the living.' It was perhaps too obvious for the sophistication of today, but it was intensely moving then and the idea seemed a splendid one.

How should I present it to Mr Walter? He had probably heard of the Psalms, but he knew nothing of Arthur Wragg. There were additional problems. He, rightly, did not like his publications to be printed outside his own Printing Trust. The printing of the Bible or any parts of it was then as now quite disgracefully restricted to the printers of the reigning Monarch, and if ever the Restrictive Practice Courts lack a topic here is one they should look at. The King's printers would occasionally allow the use of an alien outsider, but I doubted if their indulgence would be extended to the Hutchinson Printing Trust. There was another aspect which might well deter Mr Walter. At that time the Holy Bible was very much of the Establishment, and Arthur Wragg's presentation of the Psalms was unlikely to appeal to it. It invoked dangerously Leftist reflections. And Messrs Hutchinson & Co. (Publishers) Ltd were in no sense dangerously Leftist publishers. I composed a careful note to Mr Walter and submitted that one cartoon with its caption. Back it came. 'Go ahead,' he had scrawled, and he never referred to the book again.

Ahead we proceeded to go. Walter Lewis, M.A., at the University Press of Cambridge, a King's printer, agreed to print the book but clearly had his doubts. He could not, in any event, allow the work to be done by the Hutchinson Printing Trust. Arthur Wragg and I were delighted. We were assured a good printing job and the book had the benediction, for what it was worth, of a King's printer. Arthur Wragg worked on the completion of his drawings. They were marvellous and the impact of each one with its caption was extraordinarily moving.

Today the book seems somehow strangely dated. Not so very long ago the BBC invited a number of publishers to talk about their publishing of some book which had given them the greatest satisfaction, or unusual pleasure. It made a brief series in the morning radio programme *Ten to Eight*, once called *Lift Up Your Hearts* which change of title was long discussed by the Board of Governors. It is a dangerous occupation for a publisher of many books to single out a favourite, for authors are touchy on occasions. However, I thought no bones would be broken if I talked about Arthur Wragg's *Psalms for Modern Life*. The point I tried to make was that its diminished impact today derives from the fulfilment, at least to a heartening extent, of its purposes of forty years ago. Our compassion is now wider; our society is more conscious of its obligations; the wrongs of the world are more personal to ourselves; and Arthur Wragg's book has played its small part in bringing this about. I had lost touch with Wragg over the years, but within ten minutes of that talk he was on the telephone, much touched and almost in tears, and we were able to meet and talk again of that time which meant so much to each of us.

We thought it would prove helpful if some notability would write an introduction and the obvious choice was the Rev. H. R. L. Sheppard, then at the height of his influence and fame at St Martin's-in-the-Fields.

> When I was first invited to write this introduction [he explained] I asked to be excused. I am old fashioned about the Bible and I feared either a series of arty and painfully clever pictures, or else a number of goody-goody, sentimental drawings ... When the portfolio was opened that I might see the pictures, I gasped, because some of them seemed to pierce the soul like bullets.

It was a wonderful piece and gave the book exactly the impetus it needed. I have before me as I write the copy which both he and Arthur Wragg signed for me. The only concession to Hutchinson tradition I was obliged to make was the omission of the year of its publication.

It gained instant and almost sensational reviews. Hannen Swaffer acclaimed it without reserve in the *Daily Express*; and it was reprinted and reprinted and reprinted many times. Of more importance to myself was that various helpful people began to inquire what was going on at Selwyn & Blount. As a matter of fact, Lusty very nearly went out. For some reason Wragg decided that I should abandon publishing and dedicate myself to working for H. R. L. Sheppard. It sounded a high-minded thing to do; but I was not all that high-minded, and resisted.

It was at about this time that I became first involved in the politics of publishing from which the Hutchinson organization was almost totally divorced. An old schoolfriend of mine, Felix Greene, was now in the talks department of the BBC. Under his charge was a series, *Youth Looks Ahead*, to which a contributor one evening was a young curate from St John's in Smith Square, Westminster, named Joseph McCulloch. His talk was, I thought, magnificent and I managed at once to track down Felix Greene. 'Come with me,' he said, 'I am just going to see him.' I joined him and that evening met Joseph and Betty McCulloch to whom

I have been devoted ever since. I wanted, of course, a book from Joseph on the lines of his talk. 'I am afraid I can't do it for you,' he said. 'Under the terms of my contract with the BBC it is first committed to Messrs Allen & Unwin.'

This, thought England's Youngest Publisher, is quite outrageous. Stanley Unwin might have written *The Truth About Publishing*, but there was nothing about this in its pages. I took a look at McCulloch's contract and there it was in small print. Next morning I trotted round the corner to the office of Edmond Segrave and apprised him of my discovery. 'But this is monstrous,' he said, and we agreed we should have some fun — an exercise we were to repeat at intervals over the next forty years.

Stanley Unwin at that time was president of the Publishers Association and Geoffrey Faber, next in line of succession, its treasurer. We carefully prepared our little piece and it appeared in the next issue of *The Bookseller*. It was a courageous decision of Edmond's for he was fairly new to the scene and had not then transformed his trade paper with the genius of his editorship. He was, in a sense, on probation and the wrath of so powerful a trade dignitary was not to be lightly entertained. As was to be expected there was immediate and great displeasure in Museum Street, but in quarters expected and unexpected there was a good deal of hilarity among those who rather enjoyed the spectacle of Stanley Unwin being caught with his trousers down.

In those days the presidency of the Publishers Association was not the almost total involvement it has since become, and the reigning incumbent had time left over to devote to his own business. But to be critical of the president during his term of office was not thought commendable and Geoffrey Faber was dispatched to the office of Edmond Segrave to acquaint him with the facts of life. 'Segrave,' he said sternly, 'you are of course absolutely right, but I have come to tell you that you were absolutely wrong to do it.' Thus began a very warm friendship between Edmond Segrave and Geoffrey Faber, who was later to be so kind to me and whom Edmond and I always regarded as probably the most distinguished and attractive publisher of our days.

Stanley Unwin's exclusive arrangement with the BBC came to an abrupt close and for the rest of his life there was, to put it mildly, a coolness between him and Segrave. His name was enough to light the glint of battle in Edmond's eye; and at Edmond's name Unwin would rather sadly shake his little head. Shortly before his death, however, Stanley Unwin was returning from an international conference of publishers, and in the plane Segrave found himself sitting next to Lady Unwin. She was a delight and a lady of great spirit and humour and at once captivated Edmond, from whom she accepted, to his astonishment, a glass of white wine. After that Edmond, an Irishman if ever there was one, could never again be quite so critical of Sir Stanley.

He, Unwin, learned soon enough of my involvement in the affair, but it was never mentioned and he was never other than kind, helpful and generous over any problem, and they were many, I put to him over the years. But he refers to the episode in his autobiography where I am cast in the role of a 'jealous competitor'.

Another early and lucky success for Selwyn & Blount was Katharine Trevelyan's *Unharboured Heaths*, which attracted a good deal of attention. Her mother was one of the first women to become an M.P.; her father was at one time Minister for Education and her grandfather was the great historian. More immediately important for me was that she had been head girl during my time at Sidcot. She had trekked across Canada, and this was a much more venturesome undertaking then than it would be today. *Unharboured Heaths* told her story brilliantly, and looking through an old catalogue I discover that Eric Gillet went to town about it in the *Sunday Express*; Cecil Roberts reviewed it with enthusiasm in *The Sphere*; *The Times* found it of 'haunting beauty'; and the *Morning Post*, 'exhilarating'. There were no instant exposures on television in those days, neither do I recall the unending absurdity of 'launching' parties, the invention of a later age. No such event, however, would have been sanctioned for the publications of Messrs Selwyn & Blount; Katharine Trevelyan's book did very well without, and it was reprinted a number of times.

By what process I found myself at the bottom of George Lansbury's garden being photographed with him I cannot recall except that it was somehow through the contrivance of his son-in-law Raymond Postgate, for whom later we at Michael Joseph were to publish a number of books. 'England's oldest statesman with England's youngest publisher' ran the awful caption when in due course Selwyn & Blount published George Lansbury's *My England*. How there emerged a Leftist tendency I do not know, for party politics neither then nor since have ever aroused in me a flicker of interest. Within a short while, however, we had books by Ellen Wilkinson in our list; and in 1935 an anthology, *Young Oxford and War*, edited by Michael Foot, who has probably forgotten it as completely as I had until finding it announced in a fading catalogue of 1935.

I seemed in those days to have a certain capacity for ingenuity. My parents were then living in Shrewsbury and were friendly with a young Shrewsbury master and his family from whom I commissioned an anthology of verse and prose 'from those still at school'. His name was R. W. Moore, and he was later to become headmaster of Harrow and to die tragically young. There was as well *The Guinea Pig's Tail*, a thriller commissioned from one Fielding Hope with instructions to besprinkle it with intentional mistakes. A prize was offered to its most successful reader and in due course a munificent five pounds was sent to one. A further ingenuity attracted a useful constellation of crime novelists—Dorothy Sayers, Margery Allingham, Ronald Knox, Anthony Berkeley, Russell Thorndike and Wills Croft, Each was invited, in a short story, to commit the 'perfect' murder. Each did so and the scripts were submitted to Ex-Superintendent Cornish, late of the C.I.D., with instructions to solve the problems. My recollection is that he did so in every case.

Ageing publishers should not be encouraged to roam the pastures of their publications of long ago. There is too little of substance and much has withered. But each one has had its birth and brings back a flood of memory. So must it be to a midwife thumbing through the deliveries of a lifetime. The prenatal period; the approach to birth; the anxieties of the birth day; the expectancy of success; the wailing author; and all too often the long life of oblivion, but occasionally the prospect of genius, the flowering of talent, the arrival of some Churchill on the scene.

What Mr Walter made of these activities I do not know, but at some stage he must have approved each, since nothing could be done without the authority of his scrawl. My Hutchinson responsibilities still required the major part of every day, but my horizon was being helpfully widened as I visited the literary agents to sell the story of Selwyn & Blount and to display my wares in proof that its image must not be confused with the lack of one in the rest of the Hutchinson stable. Avail yourselves, I would declaim with enthusiasm, of the advantages of the great machine coupled with the personal touch and enthusiasm and experience which six years had accomplished. 'And if ever', I would conclude a little lamely, 'you should hear of an opening somewhere else perhaps you would be so kind as to let me know.' Mr Michael Joseph at Curtis Brown made a note. 'It is just possible', he said, 'that I may hear of something.'

It is curious now to reflect that my Selwyn & Blount existence from its beginning to its end extended over no more than three years. While in many ways the climate was more agreeable and lacked the urgency and bustle and hysteria of today, the actual pace of production and publication was infinitely quicker. What requires a month today was then easily accomplished in a week or less. I do not think that the Selwyn & Blount development could now be done at all within a comparable time and certainly not as a 'hobby'. There was nothing extraordinary about it then.

Alight with zeal, it seemed to me that we should contrive a series of 'topical' books. Quite how he came to me as the prospective editor I do not know, but one evening a wild-eyed, emaciated, limping Indian presented himself before my rather startled eyes. His name was Krishna Menon. He lived in a garret in Gray's Inn Road, and was secretary of the India League. He was already in the process of selling his talents to a Mr Allen Lane of The Bodley Head, who was thinking up a scheme to publish good books at sixpence a time. Did I know him? No, I didn't; but as Menon talked and his wild eyes flashed, I thought he might well be the man to edit Selwyn & Blount's new series. In due course he produced an impressive list of titles and authors, of which the first dealt with the possibilities of a new piece of gadgetry called television. A Mr Gerald Cocks of the BBC had already agreed to write an introduction.

Krishna Menon was an extraordinary man and led an even more extraordinary life. As secretary of the India League he led great marches of protest and agitation through London, operating from his garret, from which every now and again he announced his imminent death. Agitator, editor, lawyer, politician, diplomat, statesman — the range of his life was phenomenal. I owe to him my first meeting with Allen Lane who, I think, with Reith, should be regarded as the greatest educative communicator of our time, and whose contribution to the printed word has never been surpassed. Krishna Menon had come on a late visit to the Hutchinson office to discuss some project on which he was working. 'I am going on to Vigo Street,' he said. 'I have to see Allen Lane. Would you like to come along?'

Sixpenny paperbacks were no innovation to me. Hutchinson published scores, produced in magazine format with covers regarded as lurid in their time, by a whole range of popular authors.

Allen Lane was still in the Vigo Street office of The Bodley Head and at least a year away from the publication of the first batch of his Penguin titles. I do not recall very much of that first meeting, or of any particular interest in his project. He had devised a new format for paper-bound books but there was no magic in this nor, for those days, was sixpence much of an appeal. For ninepence there was a wide range of cloth-bound titles available. He did not look like a revolutionary prophet nor did he talk like one. There was nothing of the missionary about him. He was alert, quick, emphatic. I liked him that evening, but would hardly have remembered the occasion had I not been led to it by the eccentricity of Krishna Menon. How was I to know then that long before his end I, and most of my fellow publishers, would have given a right arm to accomplish in our chosen vocation what this man was to achieve? In the beginning was Vigo Street and, oddly enough, so nearly was the end.

At some stage during his gallant, uncomplaining battle against the hopeless odds of his cancer, Allen laid on a small party in the old Vigo Street office of which, on literally the spur of a passing moment, he had again taken possession. It was an odd party. His family were there in force, including elderly aunts and a grandchild in its pram, a sprinkling of Penguin faithfuls, a doctor from Canada who shook his head when I asked how Allen was, and Bertram Rota, the antiquarian bookseller, who learned that evening that he did not after all possess the complete manuscript of Richard Llewellyn's *How Green Was My Valley*. It was gay as all Allen's parties were. I asked Allen if his signature was still on the window-pane, and we went across the room to look at it. I reminded him that we had first met in that room. He had shown it me then, and here we were looking at it again—Allen Lane, roughly scratched with a diamond. I hope it is somewhere cared for. It should perhaps find its home in that Library of Bristol University to which Allen bequeathed his great signed collection of Penguin titles.

It was not long after that first evening in Vigo Street that Krishna Menon telephoned from his room in Gray's Inn Road and asked me very faintly if I would be kind enough to drop in and bid him farewell. He was, he explained, about to die. Shortly before this he had taken me to the Bloomsbury flat of Ellen Wilkinson to meet Mr Nehru, who was on a secret visit to London, and I had felt conspiratorially involved in great affairs. I was not then at all experienced with death; nor, to be frank, did I feel so close to Krishna Menon as to become involved in so personal a matter. However, it was not an invitation to be declined and I thus betook myself to Gray's Inn Road and clambered to the top floor of a squalid block. I knocked a little hesitantly at a door which proclaimed the office of Mr Krishna Menon and the India League. A vaguely familiar face came to it. 'My name is Carroll,' he said, 'and I am Krishna's doctor.' He took me into a room which seemed completely bare but for the emaciated form of Krishna Menon stretched on what I took to be a bed of nails. A fleshless arm protruded and I took its hand in mine, fearful that it should break. 'I am dying, Lusty,' he said, 'and I want to see you and to say goodbye.' There did not seem much to reply, but I muttered some embarrassed good wishes for the journey and Dr Carroll showed me to the door. 'Is he going to die?' I asked. 'Yes, he is,' replied Carroll, 'unless I can snap him out of it. That's what I've come to do.' He didn't appear to be at all disturbed as I left him to get on with the job. 'Carroll,' I muttered to myself as I descended the decaying stairs, 'Carroll. That name rings a bell.'

One of the most remarkable characters of those Paternoster Row days, in whose debt I am for ever, was Hutchinson's

London traveller—the legendary 'Farmer' Roberts. He was larger than life and not unlike Jimmy Edwards. He was invariably dressed to kill, with a constant button-hole larger and more colourful than a button-hole had any right to be. He wore tweeds of an exaggerated disposition and a gold chain stretched taut against his ample frontage. His eyebrows were large and white and his eyes very blue. A splendid moustache was constantly aquiver. In one hand he flourished a large cane with a golden top and with the other he doffed his hat with a theatrical sweep. He knew every detail of the London book trade and of the men who ran it. He lived at Brixton and in his early days travelled by horse-drawn tram to the West End. He was shrewd for all his garrulous ebullience and he knew about books, caring for them as well. Around lunch-time he would appear in the office on a daily perambulation which very soon included Selwyn & Blount, in which he had detected a change. I became a privileged exhibit and he would now and again take me on his rounds. It was through him that I met the stalwarts of that time: Freddie Richardson of Boots, whose Wednesday repeats could make or mar a title; dear J. G. Wilson of Bumpus; Willy Foyle in the Charing Cross Road, and Christina, whom I lived and laughed with then and love and laugh with still. It was a marvellous experience for a young man new to publishing to be taken around by so welcome and popular a character. I became, because of it, an identifiable parishioner of the book trade.

In the early autumn of 1935 I was invited to the Savage Club to lunch with Michael Joseph. It was for both of us an auspicious occasion; for me especially so. Michael Joseph was a man of the utmost charm, and few could be more persuasive. At his best he had an equal sincerity; at less than his best he hadn't. He was a brilliant agent and had accomplished great things for Curtis Brown. While at that time without much publishing experience, he was a shrewd observer of the publishing scene. His circle of friends and acquaintances was a very large one. He was ten years my senior, but we seemed, without actually formulating how, to share the same approach to publishing. He had watched with interest the goings-on at Selwyn & Blount. He had it in mind, he explained, to set up shop for himself. He didn't know much about the intricacies of publishing, but he was finding agency to some extent frustrating. He had no money to speak of, but he had confided in Victor Gollancz, who was willing to put up most of what would be needed to start in a modest way. Gollancz also had vacant rooms above his office in Henrietta Street and he would make his own administrative services available. He had had a good look round the trade and had decided he would like me to join him from the start. He envied me, he said, my background, which was a remark I couldn't understand then nor do I now. The staff would be virtually non-existent. I was to be his editorial and production manager; there would be a couple of girls and he had already got an office boy in mind — the son of Curtis Brown's office manager — a Peter Hebdon who was many years later to become managing director and to die far too young. It was all very confidential and nothing was finally settled. Was I interested in the proposal? He proposed of course to devote himself mainly to editorial matters, but I was to be closely involved in them too. He would leave production entirely to me. He proposed a commencing salary of five hundred pounds a year. If all went well the new company was to be formed on November 1st; and he would like me to join him on December 1st.

Was I interested? Was I indeed? Not only was I going to be interested, I was going to be rich. Five hundred pounds a year in the publishing of 1935 was almost plutocratic. There would, too, be all the excitement of a new firm bearing the name of a man well established in the whole wide world of books. Light of heart and head I returned to Paternoster Row and it was not many days before the letter came, typed by Juliet O'Hea, confirming that I was to be editorial and production manager of Michael Joseph Ltd and he hoped our association would be long, happy and successful.

7
Nursery Days of a Mermaid

Book publishing is not an operation susceptible to survey, analysis or market research. Nor can slogan advertising, however ingenious or elaborate, induce an appetite for reading. During each generation of book traders the opposite is at least once loudly proclaimed, and those opposed are dismissed as faded reactionaries. To learn that the old-age pensioners of Shropshire read *per capita* more crime fiction than their equivalent in Cornwall costs a great deal to ascertain and has no practical relevance. Recently a firm devoted mainly to the publication of romantic fiction, whose respected products are reputed to be purchased by the yard, conducted an elaborate and costly investigation into the reasons for their great and continuing and expanding success. An elaborate report was produced which contained much of interest, but nothing of relevance that a reasonably equipped publisher would not know by intuition and experience. These are not commodities in much demand today and the purse strings of publishing are held in the main by those who seek guidance from computer analysts. It is just as well that the Michael Joseph mermaid took to the water before the invasion of such infections. There is probably no successful publishing firm in existence which conducted a trade investigation 'in depth' before setting up in business.

There has never been a time 'ripe' for a new publisher to enter the arena. There seemed nothing particularly right or wrong about the year 1936, but hindsight could hardly choose a less propitious moment. Trade was bad and getting worse, the international outlook was gloomy and getting gloomier; and the one certainty within the book trade was that far too many books were being published anyway.

In the previous year Allen Lane had launched his first Penguins and was already wondering if he might be wise to call it a day. There was no particular welcome for the new firm of Michael Joseph Limited. Indeed, its first announcement aroused considerable hostility. This unfortunately welcomed to the new list rather more authors than had entered into a final commitment to come to it, and others who had not informed their current publishers of such intentions. A number of publishers held the view that it was quite improper for a literary agent to set up a publishing shop and a move was made to ensure that this particular upstart should not succeed in becoming a member of the Publishers Association. It failed.

I have never fully understood the motives which persuaded Victor Gollancz to finance and house the new imprint. At no time did there appear to be any particular friendship between him and Joseph. They were totally different in outlook and character, and indeed a more contrasting pair could hardly be imagined. Victor was fiery, impetuous, dogmatic, arrogant and excitable; Michael was cool, persuasive, charming and rather cautious. They shared only a considerable vanity. There seemed little to explain the association and much to justify doubts of its endurance.

The new firm was set up with a nominal capital of £10,000 of which in fact no more than £6,000 was ever utilized. We occupied uninspiring rooms above those Victor Gollancz maintained in a state of deliberate squalor. His administrative services covered our requirements and we used his trade counter and warehouse and also his travellers. Norman Collins, then a directorial colleague of Gollancz's, was on the Michael Joseph board. It is stated in Ian Norrie's up-dated Mumby's history of the book trade that the Gollancz involvement was 'secret'. This is balderdash. It might have seemed mysterious, but secret it most certainly was not.

No theatrical set could equal the minutiae of discomfort and decrepitude of the Gollancz premises. A similar apparent parsimony was the hallmark of their productions. The Gollancz image for many years was that of the vivid yellow wrapper shouting its message with typographical fervour and ingenuity of emphasis. His huge advertisements in the 'Sundays' conveyed the same forceful image. For his wares he used cheap paper and unattractive bindings. There was no nonsense about 'the book beautiful' and shoddiness seemed the desired result. It was a brilliant conception and it worked.

Michael Joseph had installed himself a few weeks previously with Peter Hebdon and a secretary; I was to find my own on arrival. It was originally planned that Juliet O'Hea would be with us, but a last-minute hitch came about and the ranks of publishing lost the services of a woman who could not have failed to become as distinguished a publisher as she has been an agent. I was due to join the firm on the first Monday of December 1935. On that fateful day, however, a small cargo boat with a load of oranges from Spain was hove-to in the Bay of Biscay during a storm of monumental ferocity. I was one of its three passengers, who had paid fourteen pounds each for a month's round trip to the major ports of Spain.

Naturally I anticipated my advent in Henrietta Street with curiosity and excitement. No more cubicles; no more Mr Walter; no more clocking-in and, no doubt, a well-equipped office would be awaiting its tenant. This I was to learn was not Michael Joseph's way of doing things at all. Late but eager, I reached 14 Henrietta Street. Michael Joseph was not at home but Peter Hebdon was, and had instructions to bid me welcome and conduct me to my room. I had seen it only empty and not furbished for the reception of an editorial and production manager. Its aspect had not changed. It contained no vestige of furniture or equipment of any kind. A pile of five uninviting manuscripts were dumped in one corner. The only machinery which I had brought with me from Paternoster Row was a nine-inch ruler I had owned since I was ten. I have it still in retirement with me. In preliminary discussions we had already planned that our first titles would appear on Monday, April 24th. It was the manuscripts of these which awaited me now.

Enter Michael from the wings, very affable and very charming, with that smile it was not always wise to interpret at its face value. 'How good to see you,' he said. 'Now we can get down to things. I thought', he went on, as if he had been thinking of little else for some time, 'that you would much prefer to choose your own furniture and so forth. Let's have a talk as soon as you are

73

fully settled in. And I don't think we want to spend too much on furniture, do we?'

Office furniture of a sub-standard sufficiently acceptable to 14 Henrietta Street was not hard to come by in the dingier areas of the Euston Road and my needs, conditioned by the eccentricities of Paternoster Row, kept cost the acceptable side of extravagance.

The Hutchinson Printing Trust was to do well by my departure. I had brought with me the operating timetable of the Hutchinson production process, which was rapid even for those days, and I drew up an elaborate recording sheet which I believe, after forty years, is still used in the Joseph office. Among the components of the Trust was the Mayflower Press of Plymouth, a first-rate firm, for years owned by the Brendon family and only lately acquired by Mr Walter. They were to print every Michael Joseph title until the night of their destruction by the German bombs of 1940. Both their prices and their service were excellent; and Messrs Dickinson had agreed to maintain adequate stocks of paper in Plymouth in a variety of weights and sizes, to be charged for only as used. All our binding was to be in the hands of Messrs James Burn of Esher's Royal Mills and under the supervision of Lionel Darley who, whether he likes it or not, comes under scrutiny at a later stage. The contrived timetable was tight, but not unreasonably so and was more often than not exactly adhered to. To arrange the publication in April of those five manuscripts occupying an empty room in December presented no great problem.

The magic of a private retrieval system brings back that winter of 1935 and Victor Gollancz's positive expectations of what we should accomplish with his money. Whether he had done the sums himself or whether some other had done them for him cannot be known, but he bade us achieve a turnover of at least £40,000 annually if solvency was the desired outcome. Neither Michael nor I was quite certain what he meant. But Michael thought he knew, which was more than I did. 'I think, Bob,' he said, 'turnover is everything that comes in.' 'And', I added with the air of one alighting on truth, 'more has to come in than go out.' 'Exactly,' agreed Michael.

Financial inexperience is nothing to be condoned, but the

accountant had not then reached dictatorial power in publishing. Had he done so there would be no firm of Michael Joseph today; indeed, I cannot think of any significant imprint now operating in the field of general book publishing whose sole aim from its beginning has been the making of money. Solvency was no less important in the '30s than it is in the '70s; in fact it was probably more so, since the sophistication of finance was less widely shared. It amazes me today how often it is that a firm with apparently no money in its till can find the wherewithal to outbid a well-heeled competitor in the purchase of some dangerously speculative and unwritten story.

At any rate, on the first floor of 14 Henrietta Street Michael was for ever doing sums and £40,000 seemed an awful lot of money. My more immediate task was to ensure the highest possible standards of production (of which Victor Gollancz disapproved) with the minimum of expenditure. I was unhappy unless I could balance my own salary against credit notes and furnish review copies without cost from our 'overs', of which no one today seems ever to have heard. Peter Hebdon's office tea was filthy, but he was already a tower of strength. Our finances were under the wing of a nameless character in whose ingenuity we had complete confidence. He had long been known to Michael, and looked after the affairs of many authors. It was ultimately and urgently necessary, some years after the war, to evict him from his responsibilities and expunge him so far as possible from our memories. He had, it transpired, led us quite a long way up the garden path; and the way down it again was delicate and protracted. A personal aggravation was the limitation imposed on my own holding in the company for reasons which Michael Joseph and I accepted but which in fact was counter to Joseph's wish that I should acquire as much as I could contrive to afford. Had we not been misled and ill advised, the subsequent story of events could well have proved remarkably different.

I had not at this time actually met the alarming Victor Gollancz, although the bellow of his voice, more melodic than that of Mr Walter's, would sometimes reach me from below. There was a memorable afternoon when his anguish seemed so great and was so loudly proclaimed that the stage doorkeeper of the Vaudeville Theatre left his post and crossed Maiden Lane to offer his assistance. I contrived to keep out of his way for he had concluded, according to Michael, that I was not the type likely to prove very helpful. What I did not know was that I disturbed his afternoon siesta.

His customary pull-up for lunch was the Savoy Hotel, hardly more than a stone's throw from the slum of his own office. Returning from his snack, he liked to enjoy a sleep upon his couch. I was unaware that my uncarpeted room was immediately above, and that my perambulating footsteps made adequate repose impossible. Fortunately for me, Michael was neither then nor later to fall in with Victor's whims.

For some time before we opened shop the problem of an acceptable colophon bothered us. With the very recent example of Allen Lane's penguin in mind we felt it to be something of extreme importance. Whether it was the penguin which took us towards the sea, I do not know, nor exactly can I remember the first appearance before us of our mermaid. But she came and she conquered and, with changes to her profile, her figure and her pose, she has survived the years.

Our first list, with a design looking almost contemporary today, covered the spring of 1936; it announced twenty new books and occupied thirty-two pages. An innovation in such productions was 'Irrelevant (and sometimes Irreverent) Decorations by Audrey Wynne'. These carried such captions as 'A Literary Event'; 'Author Taking his Place in the Front Rank'; 'A Good Review at Last'; and so forth. Nothing quite to set the Thames afire, but it had not been done before, nor, perhaps more significantly, has it been done since.

A popular novelist of that time, whose sales may well continue today, was Dorothy Whipple. I think she was published by John Murray who was much put out, and not to be blamed for being so, that she had given Michael Joseph her first non-fiction work. It was an enchanting autobiographical record of her childhood called *The Other Day*. It was to receive the accolade as our first publication, and a specially bound presentation edition of one hundred copies was reserved for 'our friends'. 'This copy', proclaims the one before me now, 'is for Joan C. Brownlie' — but it still did not do the trick. A further three years were to pass before the wedding. It had a most beautiful wrapper by John

Morton-Sale and in its ordinary edition cost eight shillings and sixpence.

Another book for that first day was C. S. Forester's novel *The General*. Forester had previously been published by The Bodley Head and by Heinemann and he had some superb stories to his credit—*The Gun, Death to the French, Brown on Resolution* and others. For some reason they had made little impression and his agent A. D. Peters decided that the new firm should have a shot. It was a splendid piece of good fortune. *The General* made an immediate impression. It was the *Evening Standard* Book of the Month, which was a useful bonus in those days; and a Recommendation of the Book Society, which was also something to crow about. It sold well and soon outstripped the sale of any previous Forester novel in an original edition. More important, it began an association with the firm which was to last until Forester's death and gave to the imprint a continuing series of best-sellers.

Cecil Forester was a curious man, difficult to know but every now and again surprisingly warm in his friendship. It was in the following year that we published *The Happy Return*, the story of the adventures of one Captain Hornblower. There was no suggestion that it was other than another novel in the Forester tradition of story-telling. Forester wrote entirely from research and ingenuity. He had no sea-going experience and no particular interest in history. But he found he enjoyed thinking up problems for Hornblower and then solving them by his own ingenuity. He had come across, in Portsmouth naval cemetery, a tombstone with the name of Hornblower upon it and this had appealed to him. Thus a casual afternoon brought to English fiction one of its greatest characters, whose adventures will continue to be read so long as the English language survives.

Forester once told me that most of Hornblower's conundrums and their solutions came to him unbidden as he shaved. A psychoanalyst had heard this with much interest and was anxious to bustle Forester on to a couch and ascertain the reason. Forester, who would in fact have been rather fascinated by this project, mercifully concluded that the operation might well jeopardize Hornblower's future. I muttered a thankful prayer to God. Our future would have been in the balance as well.

The first Hornblower novels ranged in haphazard fashion over his life. It was only later they became listed in chronological order. Winston Churchill was a great follower of Hornblower and I used to send him a proof copy of each as soon as it appeared. He was always grateful. After the war, and during the period he was out of office, I thought he might enjoy a meeting with Forester and I let him know that Forester was on a short visit to London from his American home. To Forester's delight the immediate response was an invitation to lunch. The old man, it appeared, was in splendid form and Forester was greatly touched by his deference to a distinguished and professional author. 'My man Sawyer', announced Mr Churchill at one point, 'is as great an admirer of yours as I am. I want him to meet you,' and he rang the bell in summons. 'Sawyer,' said Winston when he appeared, 'this is Mr Forester who writes those wonderful stories about Hornblower we both so much enjoy.'

There was nearly another meeting. Forester was to be in London for the première of the only Hornblower film, in which Gregory Peck played the lead. It was not a good film, and it is curious that no other attempt has been made to translate the Hornblower saga into cinema. There is yet hope that the BBC may one day make the attempt. But it occurred to me that Mr Churchill might care to attend the première with Forester and that afterwards we might all dine together. To everyone's surprise and excitement it was on. My wife and I were to pick up the Foresters at the Savoy; with police outriders we would make our way in triumph to Leicester Square; there we would unite with Winston Churchill to view the film. It all went beautifully according to plan, but alas no Mr Churchill. Late in the afternoon a message had come to me in Bloomsbury Street — Mr Churchill was very sorry, but he was suffering from a pile and could not come. There was no beating about the bush.

One of the most splendid novels of the war was Forester's *The Ship*. At that time he was living in America and beginning to suffer from the muscular atrophy which greatly restricted his mobility and was finally to kill him. A light cruiser, H.M.S. *Penelope*, was in New York undergoing repairs, and Forester spent some time aboard her. He then returned home and wrote the story of H.M.S. *Artemis*. *The Ship* is dedicated 'with the deepest respect to the Officers and Ship's Company of H.M.S.

Penelope'; and of it Ralph Straus wrote in the *Sunday Times*, 'this must be one of the most vivid accounts of a modern battle at sea ever written'. At that time it was necessary to submit such books for clearance on security lines, and *The Ship* went off to the Admiralty who, I thought, might help to acquire an extra allocation of paper for it. In due course I was bidden there to meet a most engaging personality, Captain Grahame Johnstone, who was the first R.N.V.R. Fleet Air Arm pilot to reach his rank. He very much approved of *The Ship* and it was through him that we brought out a special Forces edition as a simultaneous paperback. His 'readers', however, had pointed out a technical error. At one stage in the battle H.M.S. *Artemis* was turned to starboard whereas, according to the Admiralty, she should have turned to port. It seemed to me very unlikely that C. S. Forester would have made such a slip, and returning to the office I went into a huddle with Peter Hebdon; with papers and pencils we decided that the Admiralty was wrong. And so, somewhat shamefacedly, Captain Johnstone finally agreed.

I kept in desultory touch with Captain Johnstone, and when he had command of H.M.S. *Vulture*, a Fleet Air Arm station in Cornwall, he invited me down for a weekend. I met there John Moore, one of the most attractive and successful authors of our day, and a young officer, George Griggs, later to be published by Hamish Hamilton. It turned out to be VE weekend and it was extraordinarily moving to be, so far as I could ascertain, the only civilian at the service of Thanksgiving on the Sunday. On the Saturday I had been taken for a picnic by amphibious Duck and I still hold the certificate issued me by Grahame Johnstone that 'he has satisfied me as to his ability to drive a Duck'. Alas, all three men, having survived the war, were to die long before they should have done. Grahame Johnstone contracted a fatal fever of some kind while in Africa on a business trip; John Moore became a victim of cancer; and George Griggs found himself unable to cope with life.

That first spring list for 1936, although hardly sensational and not likely to attain Victor Gollancz's £40,000, was thought not too bad. It is as tedious for readers to accompany a publisher roaming around his lists as it is for a publisher to listen to an author outlining his next six plots, but by the advent of war we appear to have published around a hundred authors. These included Walter Allen (who was to become a tower of editorial strength as our chief reader); Lilian Ashby; Lady Cynthia Asquith; Ursula Bloom; Caryl Brahms; Joyce Cary; Clemence Dane; Monica Dickens; John van Druten; Jacob Epstein; Paul Gallico; Eleanor Farjeon; Philip Gibbs; A. S. M. Hutchinson; Gerald Kersh; Herbert Hodge; Louis MacNeice; Joseph McCulloch; Eden Phillpotts; Lennox Robinson; Vita Sackville-West; H. G. Wells; and a great many others.

Victor Gollancz was not uncritical. He thought we should be less conscious of our production and get some impact into our advertising. He designed a huge double column for us which was fine, except that it was stamped all over as having come from the house of Gollancz rather than the house of Joseph.

There was much liveliness around our domestic scene in those early days. Adolf Hitler did not appear to be friendly, but to redress the balance we published Bertrand Russell's *The Way to Peace* (to the great annoyance of Stanley Unwin, who claimed Russell as his own) and Philip Gibbs's *Across the Frontiers*, which very much upset Messrs Heinemann.

If in this book Philip Gibbs had refrained from a passing criticism of the Russian leaders, the imprint of Michael Joseph would certainly have disappeared on the outbreak of war, if not at an earlier date. Victor Gollancz somehow got hold of a proof copy and his eyes alighted on the relevant sentence. It was intolerable; it was indefensible; it was nonsense. He, Victor, could not even from a distance, be associated in any way with a book containing so wicked a criticism. The offending sentence must come out. He could not allow it.

Gollancz was becoming increasingly impatient with our publishing and possibly apprehensive for the safety of his money. But this editorial interference was something quite new and quite contrary to the whole basis of our understanding with Victor. It was completely unacceptable, and Michael Joseph said so. We would at once buy Gollancz out and go our own way.

This act of calculated bravado required us to find some six thousand pounds with urgency. It was a lot of money, but Michael managed to find it from a variety of sources and within a very short while we had achieved, on friendly enough terms, our severance from Victor Gollancz. We continued in an un-satisfactory way to make some further use of the Gollancz services, but we removed ourselves one door down the street to offices on the top floor of Messrs Mash & Murrell, the wholesale fruiterers. Apart from finance, their banana skins were a major hazard; and we were still reliant on Peter Hebdon's repulsive tea.

Victor certainly cooled towards Michael, and I was not to know him at all well until shortly before his death. But he and his wife Ruth extended great kindness to me, especially after the death of my wife. I encountered him at some party soon after John Le Carré had taken himself to Messrs Heinemann. Gollancz had published *The Spy Who Came in from the Cold*, and had made a triumphant success of it. He expected that he would continue to be Le Carré's publisher and was, not unnaturally, greatly incensed when told that this was not to be. He felt much affronted and was deeply upset. He insisted that he would like me, for various reasons, to hear the whole story and would I lunch with him. I did so, and once or twice again before he died.

Without Gollancz's original contribution the firm of Michael Joseph would have had great difficulty in getting off the ground and would have required a good deal more money to finance those operations entrusted to Gollancz. He made two more contributions of even greater significance to our future. The one was an author and the second a salesman.

Victor Gollancz had published a novel or so by an author with whom he said he could make no headway and whose books were unsuccessful. He was about to reject him from his list but just wondered if we might be interested. He had the manuscript of his new novel and its title was *Charley is My Darling*. The author was Joyce Cary. Thus we recruited to our young list a novelist destined to be recognized as one of the most brilliant and significant of our time. No author could have presented fewer problems of temperament. He was an unforgettable character; a man who lived and wrote with great intensity and power and compassion for his characters. He was not, in current terms, anything like a best-seller, and only after his death was recognition and success accorded him in America. He wrote his novels in quick sequences which he numbered and then fitted together to bring order and unity. He was a delightful man, too, with his rather puzzled look and alert, quick glance. He spoke rather as he wrote, his thoughts moving faster than he could either talk or write. Only his wife could decipher his rapid scrawl, and her death a few years before his own was a sad deprivation.

I visited Joyce Cary in Oxford very shortly before his death, which he awaited with the greatest composure. He had never given the impression of being other than mildly careless about his appearance. He seemed to ignore such irrelevancies. But on this occasion he was immaculate, with almost the look of a dandy. He lay on his couch in the neatest of jumpers, and carefully pressed linen trousers rather deeper in colour; his socks were gay and his shoes neat and highly polished. A monocle dangled from a chain; his face, a little pale, achieved nobility and his eyes had lost nothing of their brilliance. He seemed more relaxed than I had ever seen him. He gave the impression of having done with the worries of the world. We talked of this and that for a while and I made my departure. Within a very little time he died.

Victor Gollancz had recently installed in his basement the young protégé of one of his directors, to whom the youngster had confided his determination to do something with books. As an act of kindness Gollancz had agreed to take him, and he was employed to address envelopes. His heart, however, was not in his work and he nourished the conviction that he could sell books. Whether he wanted to read them as well is another and irrelevant matter. The name of this young man was Charles Pick, and he is now the able managing director of Messrs William Heinemann. Like others since, Victor Gollancz succumbed to his persistence and said that if he would like to sell the publications of the firm to bookshops in the suburbs of London, he could have a shot. But, insisted Mr Gollancz, you must on no account call on any customer within the territory of the London traveller. Thank you, Mr Gollancz, said Charles Pick, touching his brow.

Charles Pick's next call was to the Civil Service Stores in the Strand, where he bought with his own money a cheap suitcase. This he filled with the publications of Gollancz; and he proceeded to perambulate the suburbs and call on any shop in them which seemed remotely likely to sell a book. The outer suburbs is not a trade territory which even yet uplifts the hearts of those who since then have become representatives.

The results from the application of Charles Pick's vernacular of enthusiasm on suburbia were little short of sensational. He had almost to purchase another bag to contain his orders, and the small warehousing staff in the basement of 14 Henrietta Street was put nearly in chaos by Charles's insistence that all these new customers should be given priority in dispatch. It was therefore Charles Pick whom Gollancz plucked from his basement when it was felt that Michael Joseph's books required a traveller of their own in London.

It was necessary to clarify two points. The first was that in no circumstances did we ever want any Michael Joseph book to be 'oversold', and the second that Charles Pick and Peter Hebdon should be regarded as a team of two equal in standing. In due course the titles of sales manager and trade manager were thought up. No one quite knew the difference, but Charles Pick and Peter Hebdon made a complementary team of outstanding talents which proved of immense value to the Michael Joseph imprint from almost its start to the time of its acquisition by the Thomson organization. Together, and later separately, their impact upon the publishing story of our times has been, and in Charles Pick's case continues to be, considerable.

Shortly after Charles had 'taken on' London he suggested that he might perhaps represent us on the continent of Europe as well. Thereafter, twice a year, he would depart from the office to take the Continent by storm. He very wisely, at the same time, seized the opportunity to extend his calls to European publishers, and in this way established contacts of the greatest value to him in his later activities.

At about this time began the saga of what proved to be our first substantial success, achieving for us a recognition for which we might have had to wait many years. As with so much that happens in publishing, it was mainly a matter of luck. Michael Joseph had been persuaded to have his portrait taken by Howard Coster, then at the peak of his fame as the 'photographer of men'. Unwillingly Michael complied and went off for a sitting. During this ordeal Coster remarked that he had a young friend who was wanting to write a novel and had completed a few pages. He would be very grateful if Mr Joseph would kindly look at them and perhaps have a talk with the young man. It was, explained Coster, to be a novel with a Welsh setting and its author was a Welshman. The resultant portrait of Michael was on the gloomy side, for few prospects could be less inviting. Of course he agreed, but would much prefer to read what was available before committing himself to a visitation from the author. Howard Coster was most grateful and handed over a few pages of script which had not even been typed.

Thus it was that the first incomplete chapter of *How Green Was My Valley* appeared in our office. Michael read it and passed it to me. Wisely, he would seldom reveal his own thoughts on such occasions. The pages were very flimsy, the writing small, neat and legible. Forty years later I can remember the first sentence almost exactly. 'I am going to pack my two shirts with my other socks and my best suit in the little blue cloth my mother used to tie round her hair when she did the house, and I am going from the Valley.'

Years later Michael extracted my scribbled report on the early pages. We had both agreed. The novel would turn out either to be quite unpublishable or it would be a natural best-seller. We should, in any event, take the exceptional step of commissioning a first novel on the strength of a few hand-written pages. Michael had his meeting with the author, who had been delightful and delighted and in return for the signed contract had gone away with an advance payment of £150. We were not to hear from him for nearly three years.

Michael Joseph did not like change. It upset his notions of security. He had an extraordinary and rather appealing affinity with the Siamese cats he so greatly adored and about which he wrote so well. He purred when stroked but was often difficult to approach. He was a very fastidious man. At first he saw no reason why we should not continue in our Gollancz office, but he could see that it might be difficult and consented to move a door or so away to the rooms over Messrs Mash & Murrell. These were never intended to be more than a stopgap, but again Michael, once tidily installed, was reluctant to consider anything more suitable. Meanwhile most of the staff and many of our authors were obliged to accept the hazards of soft fruit.

Somehow or other Peter Hebdon and I came across 26 Blooms-bury Street which, sandwiched between two small hotels, was 'to let'. It was rather larger than we required for our immediate needs, but we thought it proper to provide for what is nowadays called 'growth', and thus covers malignant as well as benign. The house had been occupied by a clearly irascible dentist, for the small garden at the back, which sported an aged mulberry tree, was littered with broken picks hurled from an upper window. Bloomsbury was a mainly residential area, but a good many pub-lishers were moving in and Bedford Square, a few yards north, already contained some of the classier ones. The British Museum was behind us and the street itself was rather quieter than it is today. The basement could more than adequately house our ware-house and trade counter. If the tiny lavatory with its minuscule wash-basin was in the garden, what of it? There was another in the attic. Michael was unenthusiastic. He was quite comfortable where he was. In any event the rent was prohibitive and he couldn't get his sums right. What was the world coming to with rents amounting to £350 a year. We didn't have that sort of money to fling around.

Undefeated, we suggested that we might let the upper floors for the time being and we would accommodate ourselves in the basement and on the first and second. Our newest salesman then entered the picture. If he could sell books he could sell space. Of course he could, and from the heart of the Continent extracted a publisher only too ready to operate from Bloomsbury Street.

We had no reason ever to regret that decision. Michael became happy in the smallish back room, undisturbed by the turbulence of traffic and overlooking the garden. I was deputed the larger room in the front since 'with your deaf ear, Bob, you won't be disturbed by noise from the street'. We both had large open fires in the charge of Mr Raper, who was also packing books in the basement.

From the trade department of a publisher in the act of expiring we recruited Harry Thompson. He knew his way around, did Harry. When the war came he found us bicycles and scrounged packing paper in abundance. There were few problems he could not solve, and he and Jack Raper gave to our customers a delivery service beyond the skills of all modern sophistications.

The incomparable Miss Bird had moved with us from the Gollancz establishment. She never, I hope, regretted the change; and in her way she was as indispensable as Harry, and far more so than the rest of us. She kept the books with delicate precision and in a flowing script of such artistry that any cheque from Michael Joseph Limited made its encashment an act almost of sacrilege. Her heart and her hair were golden and her instincts maternal.

During the First World War Miss Bird established a pen friendship with an Australian soldier named Bert. This continued without interruption until destiny called a halt in the early 1950s. Bert then signified his intention of coming to London to wed our 'Dickie'. To describe the office excitement that followed as a flutter does less than justice to the drama. It is supposed that photographs had been exchanged at some stage during the forty years of distant courtship, but neither had set eyes on the other. The day of Bert's arrival at King's Cross (somehow the first and last stop from Australia) saw Miss Bird irresistible in her finery. She was accompanied to King's Cross by our Miss Morris, who concealed about her person a small bottle of brandy should its restorative powers be called for. At the station Miss Morris kept Miss Bird under surveillance, as policemen say. The train drew in and Bert, identified by some alchemy of magic, stepped out. Miss Morris observed, and returned to the office with the brandy untouched. They have lived happily ever after.

We did not publish romantic novels from Bloomsbury Street, we lived them.

Another romance flowered within the nest, but at a time less propitious. The war was in progress and imminent invasion seemed likely. We were bidden to watch the skies for parachutists and ensure that our attics were cleared of rubbish. By this time our European tenants had departed and we occupied the entire house. In a small top-floor room, where the dentist used to confine his servants, Miss Greenfield kept miraculously accurate royalty records which no one was ever known to query. The attic was above her and reached by a ladder on the landing outside. Up it clambered Peter Hebdon intent on his war-time duties. Unfortunately his foot slipped from a beam and, attached to his leg, dropped through the ceiling bringing plaster and dust upon Miss Greenfield and all her royalties. 'Parachutists,' she shouted at the top of her voice and took wise and immediate shelter in a cupboard. But it was, of course, only Peter Hebdon and they married and lived happily; alas not for ever, but until Peter's untimely death just a few years ago.

Indeed, looking back from today it is saddening to reflect how many who shared in these early days are no longer living and were taken from life far too young. I seem to be the sole survivor. Michael Joseph's first wife had been Hermione Gingold, but this marriage had come to an end and his second wife Edna — one of the sweetest and most gentle of women — was to die shortly after the war. Michael Joseph himself is dead, followed soon afterwards by my wife Joan.

8
Portrait of a Bookbinder

I HAVE already declared that whether he likes it or not Lionel
Darley is to have a chapter to himself. He has been retired for
a number of years now and is a quiet man who has never
sought to proclaim his skills or troubled to consider his own
contribution to book-readers of the twentieth century.

There existed at one time a Lionel Darley fan club whose
headquarters were the commodious office of Messrs Faber &
Faber, then in Russell Square, Bloomsbury, and now elsewhere.
A plaque somewhere on that spot should record that Lionel
Darley, Bookbinder, passed by.

As one through the years acquires friends and acquaintances,
a certain small number become an integral part of one's life and
remain, whatever happens, as landlord's fixtures in a house. It
has to be presumed that there was the occasion of a first meeting.
It has passed completely from memory. Someone must once have
asked, do you know Lionel Darley?, and the old rogue would
have grinned and hands were probably shaken.

It should possibly be explained that Lionel Darley is a lover
of books as well as a bookbinder, and for all his working years was
a hired hand (although latterly a director as well) of the great
bookbinding firm of Messrs James Burn whose Royal Mills at
Esher are to be observed by all who make use of the railway
between Esher and Walton-on-Thames. A few years ago Lionel
Darley wrote the history of his firm and Messrs Faber published
it. Its title was (and still is, for that matter) *Bookbinding Then and
Now*; and it is a classic of its kind to be read by any man, woman
or child who cherishes not only what books contain but how
they appear as well.

I believe that I first met Lionel Darley in 1935 when we concluded between us an arrangement that his firm should bind all the books for the new imprint of Michael Joseph Ltd, and from that moment until I left the firm twenty-one years later, it was never necessary to refer to any document again or to have any serious argument. Indeed, there may well have been no document to refer to had the need arisen. From the first I knew, in a moment of rare percipience, that with me was a man of gold, transparently good. And so it was and, mercifully, so still it is.

The book which Messrs Faber published chronicled the first 178 years of Messrs James Burn. I always suspected that the first intention was to cover 150 years, which would be more to the point; but Lionel, I concluded, is a scrupulous and meticulous fellow and, as an author, not to be hurried in any way. Any reading of the book makes clear that its author has tooled every word with the same loving respect and precision that he has tooled for his friends the exquisite hand bindings which from time to time emanate from his workshop at home. For 50 of the 178 years Lionel Darley played a leading part in the development of the James Burn business, but the book gives no hint of this at all. It is a typical omission.

By the grace of God and the insistence no doubt of the Lionel Darley fan club, Messrs Faber, when producing the book, threw all thoughts of economy into Russell Square. It attains a standard of craftsmanship for which we lesser mortals have to fight like devils possessed, but which an artist of Lionel Darley's calibre can keep fresh and stimulating by a look in the eye and a smile. In his writing as well he possesses a wicked charm. 'If at any moment', he writes in his foreword, 'the narrative achieves lucidity, the hand of Mrs Ella Hatt might be suspected. She read the manuscript twice and although she failed to move it towards sublimity at least she earned my gratitude by nudging it a pace or two away from the ridiculous.'

And listen again, for it is music, to Lionel Darley on the subject of Miss Moffat:

Miss Moffat, the last of the gold layers-on, retired in 1936 before ribbon gold could rob her of her indispensability. For more than fifty years she had worked with gold leaf; her

hair, even when grey, had a faint golden tinge as if the
gilder's habit of greasing the gold pad by lightly touching
the hair had left something there of the precious metal.
Rather like a lady at the tea-table Miss Moffat would sit
among her pots of glaire, sponge between two fingers and
thumb, as she deftly washed case after case without leaving
mark or smear. Gentle in her ways, as befitted one who
handled material as flighty as gold-leaf, she was also gentle of
speech, speaking with her lips slightly pursed as though she
found her mouth a little larger than she needed. If Miss
Moffat had an affinity with the characters in any one book
among the untold millions she had handled in her time,
undoubtedly it was with the ladies of Cranford. An enduring
embarrassment to her was the bookbinder's practice of
keeping glaire in utensils having such a strong likeness to
the common chamber-pot.

Here again is Lionel Darley, bookbinder extraordinary, writing
of the men and women crafts-people in language of which any of
the great authors of the past and present, whose books he has
bound, would be proud:

And what characters were about in those days before the
First World War. Lil Jennings with the rude cockney
laugh and the generous heart of a cockney; Peterkin, once a
lighthouse-keeper, now in charge of the warehouse, blue eyes
puckered against salt spray and a voice to outride the storm;
and old Warner (not to be confused with young Warner,
who was nothing), a walking epitome of all bookbinding
wisdom and a great player of chess, wearing a cutaway coat
over his white apron, as was the binder's habit, and never
seen in the street without bowler-hat and slightly corpulent
umbrella; and Mr Cremer at Esher, on intimate terms with
the stars, insisting on the need of a horoscope before any boy
was engaged to help in his warehouse; and Tom Simmonds
who sang *Asleep in the Deep*, and who once belonged to
Christy Minstrels; and, of course, Wag Ward, comedian of
all Esher pantomimes, who could record the genesis of the
Royal Mills, when among other adventures he had gone into
the fields to persuade farm workers to become bookbinders.

The book trade is littered with grateful people whose lives have been enriched by Lionel. Lionel with his dog, a vicious-tempered little beast actually quite abominably trained and spoiled by his doting owner; Lionel as a Home Guardsman, losing his rifle but retaining his sandwiches during an exercise; Lionel, after five years of war, realizing that he had forgotten to insure his house in the firing line of Woking; Lionel, well over seventy, announcing his imminent departure to climb, on feet doubtful and uncertain, a mountain in Switzerland. And he got to the top, very frightened, he reported.

I remember a visit from Lionel during the early days of the war. He was agog, having received a letter from his secretary Ella (probably the same lady to whom he bows so gracefully in his foreword) who had somehow vanished into the maelstrom of that time. 'Let me read it to you,' said Lionel, pink with pleasure. He did so, and came to the passage, 'I expect Mr Lusty is proving as great a nuisance as ever'. At this point I burst into laughter, but only for a moment was Lionel disconcerted. 'She is a nice girl,' he said, 'she would want me to skip that bit.'

He once took from a friend of mine a tattered little Catholic prayer-book which he was to rebind in his workroom. My friend was with us and we talked over a drink of the war, alighting in due course on the Pope. Lionel had no use whatever for the current holder of that office. 'The Pope,' he exploded, 'the Pope — that wicked man!' and betook himself off to his train. On the way home he examined the little book he was to rebind and the truth dawned. 'What have I done?' he asked as soon as he could reach a telephone, 'how dreadful of me.' Distressed as he was, he could only giggle and so of course did everyone else.

The possibility of Lionel Darley giving offence at any time or in any circumstances is not one to be entertained at all. Not that he lacks discrimination or the good fire of temper, but he is as gentle of susceptibilities as Miss Moffat with her gold. 'I may grow to like him,' he said to me of one particularly nasty customer, 'but not this year.'

The financial rewards of publishing books are limited and often illusory, but to attain friendship with one of the calibre of Lionel Darley goes to the credit of an account which is kept somewhere other than in a bank and which can never be overdrawn.

9
Survival Kit

IT is difficult now to recapture the domestic spirit of those early days in Bloomsbury Street, but the limitations of our survival kit were manifold. We had successfully extricated ourselves from Henrietta Street and Victor Gollancz and this was a cause for rejoicing. We had the stimulus, if not the wherewithal, of independence. Our organization, such as it was, now embraced the whole operation of publishing. We were masters in our own house, answerable to no one, and thus we were to remain until the completion of our sale to Sir John Ellerman and his Illustrated Newspaper group in 1954. Ahead of us, but unknown, lay some fifteen years, nearly all of them in the surroundings of war and its aftermath. At that time it seemed much more probable that our demise would be witnessed rather than that our mermaid should attain any flowering maturity. It seemed most unlikely that an Austrian house-painter would take our fragility into account when preparing his programme of aggrandizement. We were still some way from achieving the £40,000 of annual turnover regarded as necessary by Victor Gollancz before we could call our soul our own. We had now to sustain and finance the mechanics of publishing administration which had hitherto been undertaken by Gollancz on a commission basis. Our resources of capital were slight and today would hardly sustain the publication of one major title.

But there was a gaiety of spirit, a certain excitement in the air around us which is always necessary, but seldom nowadays in evidence, if editorial initiative and urgency is to flourish in any abundance. We were a happy ship, with Michael Joseph a little remote from the rest of us on the bridge and I operating as his chief officer. The burden of every day was shouldered by Peter Hebdon, Charles Pick and myself. This was as I liked it; and Michael Joseph, satisfying himself that over all it worked, left us wonderfully free to get on with things.

My relationship with Michael at that time was, in a strange way, rather distant. But underneath the hesitations and reserves was a shared conviction of what publishing was about and what sort of part we wanted to play in it. Michael never bothered himself with the mechanics of publishing or indeed with the politics of the trade. He extended his instinctive and brilliant role as an agent into the activities of publishing; it was his response to what must be the frustrations of agency. In what was to prove a long and towards the end a difficult association with Michael Joseph, I can recall only one serious disagreement about what we should publish or how we should publish it. During all the years of his inactivity he never questioned, as he had every right to do, any title which I added to the list. He sometimes had doubts and expressed them. He thought I paid too big an advance for *Fair Stood the Wind for France*, which was to be the first of our books by H. E. Bates, and he could not understand our enthusiasm for *Doctor in the House* by Richard Gordon. Nor was he pleased when I commissioned *The Smallest Room* by John Pudney. But such instances were not significant and this mutual understanding was somehow communicated to those around us and, more than any other factor, sustained, I think, whatever success the imprint achieved.

I can perhaps illustrate this by recalling the arrival in the office one morning of Charles Pick aglow with a salesman's excitement. He had secured from the young man in charge of Messrs Simpkin Marshall's showroom in Warwick Lane the manuscript of his first novel. He had chosen the pseudonym of James Hadley Chase and the title of his novel was *No Orchids for Miss Blandish*. It would, proclaimed Charles Pick, prove an undoubted bestseller. There was equally no doubt that we were in need of such. Nothing would be more agreeable. We entertained high hopes of that other first novel, *How Green Was My Valley*, but this was still pie in a doubtful sky.

Michael read *No Orchids for Miss Blandish* and then gave it to me. We shared Pick's certainty that it would be a big seller; he

93

had done a good day's work in securing it for us. But neither of us entertained any doubt whatever: it was not a novel we had any inclination to publish. We had to request Pick to restore Miss Blandish to her begetter. The Charles Pick of that day shook his head in sorrow. It was beyond comprehension.

Our list seemed to be developing well. We had greatly extended the popularity of C. S. Forester, and were doing better for Joyce Cary than Gollancz was ever able to do. We had a first novel, *A Bullet in the Ballet*, by a lunatic couple called Caryl Brahms and S. J. Simon, who were to enliven our office and their readers until Simon's untimely death brought the collaboration to an end.

With *The Green Fool* Patrick Kavanagh involved us, for the first time, in libel proceedings. It was a delightfully Irish autobiography and it recorded at one point its author's progression down Grafton Street in Dublin. On the way he espied Oliver St John Gogarty's front door with its brass label. With temerity he rang the bell of Ireland's leading poet. It was answered by a lady whom he assumed to be Gogarty's mistress 'since all poets have mistresses'. The short answer was that she wasn't and they don't, and damages of £250 were awarded in due course. It was this occasion, I seem to remember, which brought us first in contact with that splendid practitioner of forensic debate, Maurice Healy, K.C. We published first his *Stay Me With Flagons*, which introduced us to the pleasures and profits of a modest speciality in books about wine and their consumption. Later came his *Old Munster Circuit*, which if it is not still in print must surely again be so in time. André Simon, Raymond Postgate and Augustus Muir were all to write wine books for us.

At that time Bloomsbury Street was not the one-way road it is today and it was the main route taken by Royalty and newspaper vans to Euston and King's Cross. My window looked upon the road and a sudden proliferation of policemen gave advance notice that Royalty was passing by. Much more alarming were the newspaper vans with their shrieking posters of ever more sensational developments. We were moving towards war with a chilling certainty and none of us knew what would happen to the publishing of books. We certainly had no plans in mind for the survival of our frail craft as it struggled from publication date to publication date every other Monday morning.

We somehow came across a London taxi-driver who, as Herbert Hodge, achieved fame as the author first of *It's Draughty in Front* and, later, of *Cab, Sir?*. He became something of a celebrity as a wartime broadcaster. We published, too, a not particularly distinguished thriller by an American sports writer called Paul Gallico.

For a new publisher working with small capital reserves and from hand to mouth, a best-seller can prove an almost greater financial hazard than no sellers at all. It can swamp his capital and distort the whole basis of his financial calculations. It is a more agreeable anxiety than many and from every other aspect joy can be unconfined. We had heard nothing but occasional rumours about Richard Llewellyn and most of these were contradictory. We were in time to learn that almost everything about Llewellyn was contradictory, and what we thought we knew about him one day was found to be in doubt the next. The cottages in Wales purporting to have been lived in by the author of *How Green Was My Valley* while in the travail of his labours must exceed by hundreds the alleged resting-places of Queen Elizabeth. But there came a day when, out of the blue, the completed manuscript was placed in our charge. Every expectation and very much more was fulfilled. The magic of its first few pages, read some three years before, was in all its six hundred.

Comparatively early in our publishing existence had arrived the moment which every publisher prays for but which many never experience. There is about it an undefinable excitement which sets the mind aglow with plans. We entertained no doubt whatever that a supremely good best-seller was in our keeping, and, moreover, one of which each of us involved could remain proud for the rest of his life. In those days one did not rush down to the Thames and set it alight. The scene was a quieter one. The thought, for instance, of what the paperback rights might be worth did not much enter any calculations; nowadays, excitable and lunatic bidding would be engineered within minutes. We sent no cable to America, nor even a letter; today there would be a successsion of telephone calls. Instead, Michael Joseph caught the *Mauretania* on its maiden voyage and took, with other propositions, a copy of the manuscript which we had decided to entrust to Harold Latham, then of the Macmillan company in New York.

In London the routine of production got under way and we ordered an additional supply of bound proof copies with which to beguile the trade. We held no office meetings of the kind which now proliferate over every trumpery decision. In fact I cannot recall in all the first twenty-one years of Michael Joseph that we ever had a formal meeting about anything at all. We proceeded instead by some alchemy of consensus which left no one in doubt that the new firm of Michael Joseph Ltd had something cooking in its oven. A. E. Barlow, the best lettering artist I have ever encountered, designed a superb wrapper; and we contrived a mammoth book for display purposes thought then to be highly original. It was a long book and its price was 8s. 6d.; we were a little fearful of this sharp increase from the customary 7s. 6d.

No author could have proved more gaily amenable to every whim or more captivatingly infuriating on occasions. He raised not the slightest query about anything at all. Every effort which might be made on his behalf was rewarded with an excess of generous gratitude. Chocolates, flowers and compliments descended on all and sundry. Always dapper, perfectly groomed and with an engaging flamboyance, Llewellyn would exercise his magic on every soul aboard. The exacting passage of time seemed the only phenomenon beyond his comprehension. Thursday was as good as Tuesday for a date, and four o'clock in the afternoon was as good as eleven o'clock in the morning. One would sit for hours in a restaurant awaiting his non-arrival and return fuming and hungry to one's desk. Irate contact somehow established, a surrender to charm would be instant. Of course tomorrow would do as well. Affluence was as yet round his corner, but the assumption and enjoyment of it were not. I have never seen Richard Llewellyn at a loss for cheer. The prospect of war seemed not to bother him at all. It certainly bothered us and our date for the publication of the most important gamble in our short career was scheduled for September 4th, 1939.

Our first printing was to be an edition of 25,000 copies at a time when a first novel was regarded as more than usually successful if it sold as many as one thousand copies in its first six months. After that it was dead. *How Green Was My Valley* had been nominated by Alan Bott's Book Society as its September choice. This in those days was of great value and a vivid band around the book conveyed the message. There was one tiny snag. Alan Bott was a man of percipient caution and into his letter of confirmation he had slipped a condition new to any of us. In the event of war, it ran, the choice would be cancelled.

The point of no return for a publication was then little more than two weeks prior to the final date. Now the technology of computers requires a much longer notice. But at that point, whenever it may be, review copies are distributed and the considerable operation of dispatch to the retailers gets under way. Thus, towards the end of August a decision required to be made. War seemed probable and it was assumed that Hitler's bombers would at once attack London and life as we knew it would come to its end. In the general reckoning, the fate of a first novel by a new writer to be published by a fledgling publisher could not be accorded a high priority. Michael Joseph, who had lied about his age to fight in the First World War, was making preparations to fight in the Second. It was unlikely that either Peter Hebdon or myself would be involved. Peter Hebdon suffered from epilepsy, and in addition to a dicey record with my heart I was stone deaf in one ear, with occasional threats of becoming equally so in my other. Charles Pick was likely in due course to be called up, and it looked very much as though Hebdon and myself would be expected to scrabble through the 'troubles' as best we could.

My own personal life had taken a remarkable turn for the better. My courtship of Joan through three reigns had finally triumphed, and for some reason we never subsequently were able to fathom, we had arranged to get married in the June of 1940. There was, however, another small-print reservation. If war should intervene we would get married at once.

From my vantage point in Bloomsbury Street it was difficult to take other than a grim view of the news as the placards were driven ever faster to Euston. A little way down Bloomsbury Street from the office was the Holborn Registry Office and on August 28th I thought it prudent to pay a call. To my astonishment, the lady in charge was Miss Haldane, who ran a small private hotel next door to No. 26. 'What', she inquired 'can I do for you?' 'I may want to get married rather quickly,' I said, 'and

I don't know how to do it.' 'Nothing easier,' she replied. 'The necessary form will cost you one shilling. I will fill it up for you if you would be so very kind as to go and buy me twenty cigarettes, and we shall be all square.' I have always remembered with ease that cigarettes were then twenty a shilling. 'And what', inquired my wife-to-be later in the day, 'were you doing in Bloomsbury Street this morning? I saw you from a taxi and you had a guilty look.'

Meanwhile, in consultation with Alan Bott, the publication of *How Green Was My Valley* had been deferred until the first Monday in October. On the morning of September 1st I was to visit A. D. Peters in his office off the Strand. As a literary agent he had probably the strongest list of authors in London. He was acting for Vita Sackville-West who had recently joined us; she was to remain with us for the rest of her life and we were to publish some of her best writing. Outside the Tivoli cinema, then reputed to be stacked with coffins for the burial of air-raid victims, the *Evening Standard* poster was brief. WARSAW BOMBED it said. I found the nearest telephone. 'They have bombed Warsaw,' I said. 'I think we should get married today.' 'Wait until lunchtime,' she replied with Scottish caution. On the way back to my office I dropped in upon the friendly Registrar. 'I can marry you at half past four,' she said. 'Don't be late. There will be a rush.'

Lunch-time brought no indication that the war had ended and I telephoned again. 'We can get married at half past four,' I announced. 'You have my car with you. Bring Mr Hanby [Joan's partner] with you, stop off in Piccadilly and buy a ring and I'll be at the Registry Office at half past four.'

I sent a telegram to my parents and gave thought to a best man on the spur of a moment. I telephoned my friend Geoffrey Edgar, late of the Penn Club and a one-time sharer of a bedsitter. 'Joan and I are getting married at half past four,' I told him. 'Can you be my best man?' 'Do you know what the date is?' he asked. 'Of course I do, you bloody fool. Why?' 'You were my best man six years ago today.'

Shortly before zero hour I set forth from a virtually deserted 26 Bloomsbury Street and found Richard Llewellyn in its hall, full of cheer. 'I want to talk,' he said. 'I can't,' I explained, 'I am just off to get married.' 'Who to?' he asked. 'To Joan, of course. Who do you think?' 'God be with you,' he cried, and his was the only mention of God upon that day.

Joan was at the Registry Office with my car, her partner and a ring. The best man just made it in time. Miss Haldane came from her room. 'A slight delay, I'm afraid. We have to telephone the police about the couple ahead of you. A German girl is marrying a Fiji Islander and it's a little tricky.'

We had not many minutes to wait and our marriage was duly solemnized. 'We'd all better have some tea,' I suggested, and we went along to Tommy Layton's Book Restaurant in Great Russell Street and ate the chocolate cake for which he was much renowned.

Joan had a sister in Aldershot to whom she felt we should report our marriage in person. It was a nightmarish drive. We were told to wrap newspapers around the sidelights; and the roads were crowded with mysterious vehicles of all kinds, moving, it seemed, in every direction. Aldershot was a seething mass of mobilization, for which a thunderstorm obligingly provided an appropriate orchestra. My new sister-in-law wept and found some tinned spaghetti on which we feasted. Next morning we returned to London. Joan was a V.A.D. and I a special constable at Bow Street, until they found I couldn't hear, or stand upright with confidence in the dark, and turned me out. My war career was brief and inglorious, but I retained a truncheon.

On the Sunday morning war was declared. We waited for the holocaust. An extraordinary silence settled over central London and its almost deserted streets. The air-raid sirens wailed almost at once, followed in a very few moments by the all-clear. I went home to lunch and met a policeman on the way. 'I hear there is fighting in Seven Dials,' he said, 'but I am going in the opposite direction.' 'My lunch is in the opposite direction too,' I said, but there was never any fighting in Seven Dials.

I do not think that I have consciously determined upon anything in my life. What has happened in it appears to have come about almost entirely by chance. Except once. On almost my first day in London I met Joan at the Penn Club and resolved that in due course we should marry. 'You look ravishing,' I said on that first evening in 1928 when, late, she was eating her cold supper in the Penn Club dining-room. She laughed and I blushed. 'I'm sorry,' I said, 'I meant ravenous.'

There were many little restaurants in the Bloomsbury of those days which catered for the students in bed-sitters who comprised much of the resident population. One whose opening we had witnessed was The Golden Tortoise in Marchmont Street. It was run by a dauntless lady who also accommodated students in her house in Brunswick Square. She was assisted by a more than attractive daughter, who walked with exquisite grace and oper- ated with charm and a beautiful composure. Their treacle tart was unusually superb and cost, I think, twopence a slice. We went often, Joan and I, to the Golden Bug, as we called both the restaurant and the daughter. Joan detected the possibility of release from relentless pressures and for a while diverted me towards the Golden Bug. But not for long. There appeared to be a doctor on the scene. I was always suspicious of him and rightly so, for he married the Golden Bug.

Many years later, after the war when we lived at Cobham in Surrey, I was reading the *Observer* in a desultory way. My eye alighted upon a piece which announced that an international convention of criminologists was to be held in London under the presidency of Dr Denis Carroll. 'Blow me,' I remarked to Joan, 'didn't the Golden Bug marry a chap called Carroll? She was a nice girl; I've often wondered how she has got on.' She had in fact got on very well. She had two sons and her husband had become one of the leading psychiatrists of the day, with a flourish- ing practice in Weymouth Street. I was very glad to re-establish contact — for somehow or other I have managed to keep more of less in touch with the majority of my romantic associates from the age of fourteen onwards.

Alas, in a very short while Denis Carroll died and for seven years his widow had to face alone the education and upbringing of her two schoolboy sons. Joan and I were married for twenty- three years; then, in the June of 1962, a few days after her birth- day she died from leukaemia. It was not a time on which I can dwell, except to record that eighteen months later the Golden Bug and I were married by Joseph McCulloch in the crypt of his re- stored St Mary-le-Bow, to the ringing of Bow Bells. Thus it can be said that I married almost the first two girls I met in the London of the '20s. All who knew and know them marvel at my good fortune. And right they are to do so.

And now back to the farm. Immediately before the war we made useful progress. H. G. Wells, perambulating as he unfortunately did around the publishing world, came to us with *The Holy Terror*. We did well with *On the Night of the Fire* by F. L. Green, who made a considerable name for himself during and after the war as a teller of thunderingly good stories. His slim, rather frail figure and a severe limp were in strange contrast to the power of his writing.

What Charles Pick was doing at a firemen's ball on a Saturday night has never been satisfactorily explained, but it was a merciful providence which guided his steps into partnership with a young and attractive nurse called Monica Dickens. He prudently told her that she should emulate the example of her great-grandfather Charles and write a book. She did and thus appeared *One Pair of Hands* and an author who was to be one of the brightest and nicest stars in the Joseph constellation for the next twenty or so years.

I behaved badly, and it has troubled my conscience ever since, to an author whose first book we published just before the war. I had come across Peter Opie and he was considered to be rather bright. Indeed he was, and, I thought, on the precocious side. But I liked him and encouraged him to write, at the age of twenty-one, an autobiography. He did not, in point of fact, need much persuasion; and *I Want to Be a Success* was the title. Opie had been to Eton and I thought up the notion of reproducing his Old Etonian tie in full colour across the wrapper. This, it seemed to me, would with the title convey the message. Opie was indignant as he had every right to be. I was adamant and should not have been.

At that time I think Peter Opie's notions of success were very different from the triumph which he and his wife have now achieved. The scholarship of their studies into the fascinating labyrinth of the folklore of children is unique in the world. Their anthologies and surveys are known everywhere and they must be among the most widely selling authors ever published by the fortunate Oxford University Press. Every now and again I encounter the quiet and scholarly and gentle Peter Opie and have long since apologized for my arrogance towards him.

In the context of likely war it was difficult for any firm, let alone a new one engaged in publishing, to plan far ahead or to make provision for what was generally assumed would be the breakdown of life and certainly of letters in London. Michael Joseph was for ever doing little sums on scraps of paper. None of them would make sense and he had grave doubts about whether any of us could expect to be paid for very long. It was all deeply sombre as he went off to the wars with his cat Charles. He was not in fact to return to the office, other than on occasional visits, until a short while before the ultimate sale of the company to Illustrated Newspapers in 1954. His military exertions, which he chronicled in *The Sword in the Scabbard*, exacerbated the gastric ulcer which plagued his life in varying degrees of vindictiveness until finally it killed him in the late '50s.

During the week which followed the outbreak of war it was incredibly borne upon us that life was continuing. On the Monday morning our office and everyone in it looked very much as they had on the Friday. The post had been delivered and Miss Haldane's cat was sitting in its accustomed place. An unfamiliar world intruded with the blackout which was hateful. A total deafness in one ear disturbs one's balance in the dark. We had embarked, although we did not know it, upon the 'phoney war'. It soon became difficult to recall any previous existence.

On the first Monday of October, *How Green Was My Valley* was able to enjoy a triumphant publication. The Book Society had restored its accolade and the reviews were immediate, massive and splendid. That we with the rest of Europe were in fact gripped by all the ugliness of war somehow sharpened and simplified a delight in what could be regarded as civilized and decent. It was already clear that, far from falling into decay and disrepute, books were on the ascendancy to a new life of considerable elan. They were 'in' at so great a speed that any traveller on commission — and in those days many of them were — found himself in possession of an income undreamt of by the principal of any publishing company. In due course he was able, if so minded, to sit at home and ration supplies to his favourites.

Paper rationing was known to be drastic and inevitable and our allocation, based on a formative year, was likely to be minuscule. Despite an impassioned plea by Harold Macmillan at an emergency meeting of publishers to discuss participation in a voluntary war risk insurance scheme, London publishers took a gloomy view of the safety of their stocks. Harold Macmillan sat immediately behind me in Stationers' Hall and declared our apprehensions to be quite groundless. There was no chance that any German bomber could get through to London.

The imperative requirement for us was to conserve our paper allocation in every way possible. To keep even *How Green Was My Valley* in the generosity of its first edition would have been prohibitive. We had at once to re-set its original 650-odd pages into the format of what became 'wartime economy production'. The books produced within these limitations, which applied until paper rationing came to an end, were in the main unattractive; but they enabled at least two books to be produced for every one designed in more agreeable times.

Our particular position was an extremely difficult one. A publisher's paper allocation in weight was a percentage of what he consumed during a previous period of twelve months. It was fair enough, but of course there was an element of pure luck. A publisher who happened to have during that year a sequence of successes did very much better than a comparable publisher with an uneventful year. Our previous years had all been formative, although we had enjoyed our successes and used a paper rather heavier than most. We at once reduced our output, which had exceeded a hundred titles in our third year, to a total that more by accident than design never exceeded thirty-two and this we maintained throughout the whole of the war and for a few years after it. We had quite exceptionally good fortune. Our office in Bloomsbury Street remained intact apart from a few broken windows; and a chance introduction brought about a remarkable transformation to our paper problems.

A providential concession, which remained undisturbed, permitted a publisher unable to make use of his full quota to transfer the balance to another publisher. All our paper, from the beginning, had been supplied by the great firm of Dickinson and our account was handled by an always helpful Mr Bradshaw. He one day asked, as if in passing, whether I could do with some more paper. It was rather as if the Captain of the *Queen Elizabeth* in its Cunard heyday were to inquire of a man on a sinking raft in mid-Atlantic if he could do with a lift. There could be only one answer; and, in reponse to it, a rapid-speaking, dapper and immensely alert Mr Wilfred Harvey came to see me from the huge firm of Messrs Purnell who then operated mainly as printers in Paulton, near Bath. They had done no work for us of any kind and were under no conceivable obligation to be even helpful. Harvey explained that they owned a publishing organization with a substantial paper allocation operating under the imprint of Juvenile Productions. They were proposing to close it down since they did not regard its publications to be particularly necessary to the war effort. Would I be interested in ten tons of paper in every rationing period? This would mean an increase to our quota of some forty tons a year on which could be printed a great many books. There were no conditions, but, reasonably, I was given to understand that Messrs Purnell would not take it amiss if we were occasionally to entrust to them the printing of a book. Wilfred Harvey did not look much like any conception of the Almighty, but he was offering us manna from the heaven of the Somerset countryside.

'Yes,' I informed Mr Harvey, 'such an arrangement will suit us very well.' 'Good,' he replied and went on his way. Nothing was ever in writing. The appropriate official forms were completed every quarter and I used to pray that the regulations would not be changed and that Mr Harvey and I had not misunderstood them.

Another little benefit came our way from the same source, which I was to enjoy even after Wilfred Harvey had devised the great British Printing Corporation, with its multiple interests. Paulton was deep in the countryside and became the herald of every spring. I hope it still remains so. On a morning of early spring every year would arrive on my desk a small cardboard box. In it, with the compliments of Messrs Purnell, would nestle a small bunch of primroses from the woods around the factory. Over the years Purnell were to print many books for us though I hardly ever saw Wilfred Harvey again. But the success of Michael Joseph Ltd owes as much to the consideration of this kindly man and his initiative as to any other factor. Great personal misfortune was later to befall him deriving I suppose from the illusions and follies that industrial tycoonery seems so often to engender.

Success and fame enveloped, but never altered, Richard Llewellyn following the phenomenal success of *How Green Was My Valley*. I recall meeting somewhere at that time the reigning Archbishop of Canterbury, who inquired how well it was selling and for how long I expected it to do so. 'Until kingdom come,' I said, and have felt a fool ever since. It was not a phrase I much if ever use.

Llewellyn's prolific generosity and eccentric liveliness did much to divert attention from the less pleasing realities of the time. He quickly propounded a view that taxation was immoral and that money unspent would rot away to worthlessness if not rapidly spent. How prophetic he knew himself to be I do not know. It was an engaging theory if one were on the receiving end of his generous hospitality. He somehow became immersed in the early days of ENSA under Basil Dean, whose autobiographies I was to publish with such pleasure over thirty years later. Richard acquired a singularly impressive flat in Upper Brook Street, which he naturally assumed would be immune against the destructive propensities of Hitler. He crammed its walls with paintings of great beauty, variety and value, and even attached them to both sides of the lavatory doors. In his bathroom I counted some forty toothbrushes. The prodigality of his entertainment became part of the mythology of the firm; and if at the last moment he could not appear he would request one to go ahead, alone if need be, and send him the bill.

I recall a summer evening when, as the office was closing, a charming little old man, full of character and immaculate in his best suit, arrived on our doorstep. 'Can you tell me where my little boy is?' he asked, with all the poetry of Wales in his lilt. 'Who is he?' we asked. 'Who else but Richard Llewellyn?' he replied.

In due course Richard left Basil Dean and ENSA to join the Welsh Guards, then in training at Sandown Park in Esher, where Joan and I had removed ourselves towards the end of 1941. Richard was supposed to be at work on a second novel, *None But the Lonely Heart*, which required, apparently, to be written in the meanest attic of the meanest dwelling he could find in London's East End. By night, he explained, he would be writing there and by day training with his Welsh Guards. From time to time he

would visit our rented house near Esher station. I never saw
him mount it, but he would arrive with an immense bicycle
attached to which was a searchlight possessed of a beam which
dissipated the black-out and illuminated the skies for miles
around. The bicycle would be wheeled into our hall to be less
readily available to any descending parachutist. The war was
always about to be won. He shared more than most Queen
Victoria's refusal to contemplate defeat. He would stay and talk
for hours enlivening every one of them.

One Sunday afternoon he telephoned to ask if he could come
to tea. Shining and immaculate as only a Guards officer can be, he
arrived. There was a certain conspiratorial air about him. He had
something to impart and it was deadly hush. Could Joan, by any
possible chance, let him have two hard-boiled eggs? We kept hens
in our disused suburban garage, and could. He explained that in
great secrecy the Welsh Guards would be entraining at Esher
station at four o'clock on Monday morning. They would be
changing trains at Clapham Junction and it was there that he
would hope to consume the eggs. We were given to understand
that the next stop would be Rome. He produced a revolver from
whatever part of a Welsh guardsman's uniform accommodates
one and swept it around our small sitting-room. 'Right through
to Rome,' he said looking fierce. 'I must be off now,' he added,
and with our two eggs and our blessing he departed.

At around four o'clock the next morning we, and I imagine
most of Esher, were awakened by a din through which no one
could be expected to sleep. The night air was full of the music
of martial bands. The tunes, undeniably, were Welsh. The
Guards, in the utmost secrecy, were entraining at Esher station,
our best-selling author among them.

I have felt always, and continue to do so, a sense of guilt at
so complete an avoidance of the war. Willy-nilly those who,
during it, lived in London and around could hardly avoid involvement, but participation is something different. In any of its services I would have proved abysmal.

It was not difficult at that time to become regarded as something of a success in publishing. Much of the competition was
engaged elsewhere. We were, at the beginning, a 'reserved occupation', but as things became more difficult each case was con-

sidered by the Publishers Association and anyone exempted on other grounds made possible an extra 'body' in the publishing arena. I was thus dispatched to Edgware for my 'medical'. At the end of this a sergeant looked sadly at me. 'Go home to bed, laddie,' he said. So great was the combination of relief and guilt that I fell from a bus and arrived much bruised for lunch at the Ivy with May Edginton, who had gamely put money into the firm and whose son Rupert was later to be an 'apprentice'.

Along with Peter Hebdon I was placed in Grade IV, lower than which we could not sink. The blitz and later the flying bombs and rockets confirmed my suspicion that heroism is an attribute of which I have never been conscious.

In 1941 I began to feel that there was a need in our list for what could be termed a 'Christmas' book. At that moment, mildly apologetic since it looked a small thing, Edmund Cork, the literary agent, sent me a short script of less than ten thousand words by the author of *The Adventures of Hiram Holliday*. We had an option on the author's next novel but neither he nor Edmund Cork thought that this short story should be regarded as fulfilling it. Nothing about Hiram Holliday had prepared us for *The Snow Goose* — for that was the title of Paul Gallico's unexpected submission. So far as we knew, he was a sports writer in the tough world of New York journalism. Both Peter Hebdon and I liked it; but since to publish so short a book even in those days was something of a dicey proposition, we wanted Michael Joseph's blessing. This we received with reservations shared by us all. We contrived an attractive production padded out to make as many as 64 pages, which we felt to be the acceptable minimum. It was priced at 3s. 6d. and we printed an edition of three thousand copies. Both the author and his agent were gratified by what they felt to be our understanding solution of a problem. We could, they were eager to assure us, look forward to a proper successor to *The Adventures of Hiram Holliday*.

Very little advertising was done for *The Snow Goose*, and had 'promotion' even by then entered into the vernacular of publishing, the circumstances of war would have ruled it out. It was not at all widely reviewed, but dear old Sir William Beach-Thomas in the *Field* could hardly restrain his enthusiasm. The little book started to sell almost entirely by personal recommendation which, as every publisher should know, is more effective and valuable than all the shouting and gadgetry cooked up by promotional ingenuity at its best and worst. The first printing of three thousand copies disappeared on subscription; and if anybody now possesses a copy, its value could be considerable. Mine, unfortunately, was 'borrowed' many years ago and never returned. I immediately had the little book made littler still and re-set to a 32-page format, thus making it, in every sense, one of the most valuable books in the Joesph list. Its consumption of paper was small and the revenue from its immense sales considerable. After the end of the war and the limitations of economy production, we issued an edition illustrated by Peter Scott which achieved an enormous sale that continues to this day. *The Snow Goose* remains far and away the best short book by Paul Gallico, some of whose later excursions into allegorical sentimentality required every now and again a certain editorial diplomacy.

A book which gave me a particularly personal pleasure during the war was Margery Allingham's *The Oaken Heart*. I had known her and her artist husband, Philip Youngman Carter, from almost my first day in publishing when she was published by Jarrolds. On the way to becoming one of the most distinguished crime novelists of our time, she possessed an enormous gusto and charm and a sort of gentle boisterousness, and a loveliness of feature never obliterated or even touched by the relentless acquirement of frame. Pip was a brilliant and versatile artist who contributed more to Marge's novels than many realized. They lived first in a tiny flat in Racquet Court off Fleet Street; but later, upon the scent of greater affluence, they moved to a large and lovely house in Tolleshunt D'Arcy in Essex where they were both to reign for the remainder of their lives. After the outbreak of war I suggested to Marge that she should write the story of a village going to war and *The Oaken Heart* was the result. It proved to be her favourite book and the signed copy she gave me is one of my greatest treasures.

When she died, the blow to Pip was a dreadful one. He was a quite different character, more reserved and less tolerant of the world and its ways. Quite how, after the war, he became editor of the *Tatler* I never knew, but it was an unlikely assignment and lasted for a shorter period than he thought it should. From time to time I urged him to write a book, and gave him the title *All I Did Was This*. He had the gift of writing and was a wonderfully versatile artist, being as well witty and pleasantly malicious in talk. He did not for long outlive Marge and he would have enjoyed his funeral. The winter wind of the Essex marshes was at its most devilish as the slow procession wended its way from church to cemetery. He was a heavy man at the end of his days and it took six strong men of Tolleshunt D'Arcy to bear his coffin. After it was over it required many whisky macs to restore the circulation of shivering mourners in Pip and Marge's bar, which all present had known so well for so long. Pip and Marge had lodgements in many hearts. Unaware, they somehow represented an element both poignant and gay in the contradictions of our age.

Early in the war Vicki Baum joined our list, and she remained one of its most popular writers. A new writer, whose first book aroused wide interest, was Mary Lavin. Another was Oliver Onions, whose *Story of Ragged Robyn* was one of the most enchanting novels we ever published. We seemed, in a strange way, to be attracting both those who had enjoyed success and those seeking it for the first time.

A major capture was H. E. Bates who, not altogether fairly I think, was disenchanted with Jonathan Cape. Already one of the most admired and dedicated writers of his age, Bates felt he had been treated less than generously in the publication of his stories, written at first under the pseudonym of Flying Officer X. These, with an extraordinary flash of bureaucratic imagination, had been commissioned by the Air Ministry. Their impact was immediate and immense and their authorship soon became known. He and his agent Laurence Pollinger, who looked after his interests with singular devotion and tenacity, thought the time had come for a change. At some time or other H.E. — as he was known by all — had met Joseph and liked him. Thus to me came *Fair Stood the Wind for France*, which it required no percipience to recognize as one of the best novels likely to emerge from the war. What seemed in those days to be the considerable advance of £750 was required for it and to this I agreed without demur. 'Rather a lot for Bates, isn't it?' queried Joseph when I told him. 'Yes,' I agreed, 'I suppose it is. But we shall get it back and be all right.'

'All right' we were and Bates remained with the imprint until his death. He never deviated in his loyalty, as some were to do in the extraordinary confusion of events which followed the death of Michael Joseph and the later sale of the firm by Illustrated Newspapers to the Thomson empire.

Joan and I were to see much of H.E. and his family over the years and particularly so when, in the early '60s, they found for us a converted orangery near their Kent home in Little Chart which we acquired as a respite from London. It was not, alas, long before the death of Joan; and their kindness to me at that time was beyond possibility of repayment. H.E. wrote of Joan in *The Times*; and when he died, it fell to me to deliver a brief address at the Service of Thanksgiving for his own life. He was, I think, the most dedicated writer of all who have illuminated our time. There was nothing else that he could conceivably have done. At one time he wanted to be an artist and he possessed a great affinity with the Impressionists, whose work he loved. He was, too, essentially a countryman with a distrust of sophistication and the ephemeral glitter that accompanied it. His garden too was an extension of his love of the Impressionists and the poetry of his prose style. As he gardened he wrote and as he wrote he gardened.

Rumer Godden was another acquisition of distinction. Some unkindly poltergeist attended my meetings with her. We met first for lunch at a restaurant in Greek Street on a day when its plumbing had been disturbed by enemy action. This, although I was not to know it until some years later, was painfully inconvenient for the distinguished newcomer to our list. On the second meeting, I was her guest at a small lunch party. I began some remark and immediately there was an explosion and a large glass jug of fruit-cup exploded over the table and everyone around it. On the third occasion, Rumer was to come to 26 Bloomsbury Street. That should have been safe enough, but as she arrived the ancient lavatory cistern shattered into small pieces and the hospitality of the house became limited.

In an occupation (whether for gentleman or not is doubtful, whatever Fredric Warburg has to say about it) that revolves around personal relationships and mutual confidence, one has inevitably to take the rough with the smooth. There are few disappointments more acute than to 'lose' an author from one's list. Whatever the reason, and there are sometimes good ones, it is somehow an affront. Rumer Godden left us for Macmillan when Spencer Curtis Brown, who headed the great agency firm, quite suddenly collected together a number of his most distinguished clients and moved them to that same imprint. It was an odd operation, but possibly a successful one for I think all who made it and remain alive have notably flourished ever since. We lost Pamela Hansford Johnson as well as Rumer Godden; Geoffrey Faber lost C. P. Snow; and there were others.

Towards the end of the war we published Michael Joseph's own book *Charles: the Story of a Friendship*. Its hero was not Charles Pick but Charles the Siamese cat who had accompanied Michael to the wars and home again and with whom he was probably in closer communion than with any human being. He seemed to enjoy an affinity with Siamese cats and their quirks of temperament. He wrote of them with great charm and sincerity. He made no attempt to impose his book upon us but submitted it in the ordinary way, accepting meekly such terms as I proposed. Its success was due to very much more than the circumstances of the time and it has become a minor classic. This I think he would regard with almost greater satisfaction than any other success to his credit.

An amusing autobiography appeared around the same time by one Albert Thomas, who had written a letter of considerable character to *The Times* on the subject of 'buttling' in the modern world. Albert, it appeared, was butler to the famous Dr Stally-brass, then Principal of Brasenose College, Oxford. I wrote and suggested he might care to elaborate his reflections in a book, and he came at once to London to discuss the possibilities. He was a perfect Wodehousian Jeeves but rather more advanced in age. He was impeccably respectable and from time to time deferential to the point of embarrassment; then would come a remark or comment of devastating perception which neatly reversed the whole procedure. I suggested he should adopt the title *Wait and See*, and he returned to his pantry in Oxford to get on with it.

At that time we were receiving a great deal of help and advice from Viola Garvin, who became our 'literary adviser' after her departure with her father from the *Observer*. Kind, generous and indefatigable in her enthusiasms, she was as ready to devote hours of her time to guiding such as Albert Thomas through his literary labours as she was to working with the most sophisticated of obscure poets. She was a most warm-hearted and loving friend, for ever tearing, with her slight limp, into the office with manuscripts enveloped around her, all brilliantly reported upon in pages of vivid and always helpful comment. She, and later Walter Allen as well, made enormous contributions to any success we achieved and they were certainly the best readers and advisers I have encountered in my publishing lifetime.

On the publication of his book, Albert Thomas invited Joan and me to dine with him and his wife in the pantry of Brasenose, and thither one Saturday evening we betook ourselves. Albert thought it proper that before our repast I should be taken to meet Dr Stallybrass above stairs. I felt I should apologize for having commercialized his butler and obtained for him a wider, if less enduring, fame than he himself enjoyed. Dr Stallybrass seemed hugely to enjoy the joke of it all and duly returned me to my host. The dinner was superb and so was the wine. Nothing like it had been seen, let alone eaten, in all the years of war. In a replete state we were taken to the cellars where the college had stored its treasures and in a corner of which Albert kept his own. From this corner Albert produced a beautiful set of fruit plates and dish which he presented to my wife and to me he gave a heavily decorated cigar cabinet reputedly a present from Napoleon to his brother Jerome.

Wait and See duly appeared and quickly exhausted all the supplies of paper we could make available to it. With the proceeds Albert eventually abandoned buttling and established a pet food shop in the Cowley Road not far from Brasenose College. Within a year or so the shop had gone; it was later replaced, if my geography is right, by some activity of that odd phenomenon known to me as Robert Maxwell. I never heard again of Albert Thomas and I fancy that he must now be buttling at greater heights.

Throughout the war and after it we were, of course, making substantial profits which no one in their publishing senses should have accepted as a likely norm. Our overheads were modest in the extreme and were annually around 19 per cent. Our list, although small, was respectable; and we appeared to have reached a stage none of us had ever thought attainable when we embarked in 1936. It was, in point of fact, a moment of great danger not only for us, but for the book trade as a whole. The immediate post-war policy of the book trade was disastrous: there was a euphoria to which I certainly subscribed. Michael Joseph was amongst those who did not. He thought that the price of books should be considerably increased in line with almost everything else and that the writing on the walls of public lavatories was a little lower than it had been. A view touched with cynicism, but in the longer term probably realistic. Certainly we would have been wise to increase book prices, despite the continuing imposition of the excess profits tax. In the end book prices rose at what appeared to be an excessive and unacceptable rate when in fact they were no more than catching up with other things.

But such reflections anticipate events. Suddenly, it seemed, the war, at any rate in Europe, was at an end. VE day was proclaimed and declared a Bank Holiday. Joan happened to be in bed with a chill and I found myself cycling slowly around Esher. It looked very much as it had done the day before when a war was being fought, and as normal as Bloomsbury Street had struck me on that Monday in 1939. But there was a totality of difference in the surge of reflections. Joan and I and indeed nearly all our friends and relatives had emerged unscathed. Our possessions had not been harmed and the firm of Michael Joseph, oneself included, had prospered beyond all expectation. With a sense almost of guilt one confronted a different day.

10
Mermaid Cavorting

THE sun, of course, was not for ever shining. There were times of storm and occasional depressions came in from the Atlantic and elsewhere. Not all our geese were swans, and some indeed of our swans became as less than geese. But retrospective reflection is gentle and I look back on those post-war years in Bloomsbury Street as probably the most satisfying of all my time. It was very likely the most smug and sometimes the most arrogant as well. Worse still. 'You're getting pompous, Bob,' said Joan when she thought necessary.

But the nag and uncertainty of war had gone. For the first time for years — indeed for an era — it was possible to look ahead; to anticipate with hope and not with doubt. For years, it seemed, life had forced itself through day to day, month to month, nightmare year to nightmare year. Dates had been important. Now suddenly they became much less so. It mattered very much that we published *How Green Was My Valley* in 1939. We might have published *Doctor in the House* in any of the years from 1945 to 1954. Exactness was no longer of importance. Those nine years are, for me, to be seen as a single span as no other period had or has been.

Michael Joseph seemed equally content during most of it, as he had been during the war, to operate in a relaxed kind of way in the country. Charles Pick returned from his warrior days and once again our small compact team was able to concentrate its attention on 'publishing good books well', which phrase I once hit upon in a bath and since have had no reason to regret.

The influence of hot baths on events both great and small could prove not unworthy of study. Looking at this point into a future still far distant, I know of three — or rather of two and a half — which quite radically changed the BBC. It was in a hot bath that Hugh Greene decided that the run of *That Was The Week That Was* should be terminated. It was in another that Lord Hill alighted on the plan to bring Hugh Greene's reign as director-general to its end. It was in yet another, and this could be my tiny contribution to the history of the BBC, that it occurred to me that what was being planned as BBC II might be better referred to as BBC2. The change from roman to arabic was approved and effected just in time.

Soon after the war Joan and I had found a potentially attractive semi-bungalow in what were then the more or less rural wilds of Cobham in Surrey, to be preserved for all time by virtue of the alleged sanctity of the green belt. There were rats under our floorboards and mountains of rubbish everywhere, but possibilities surfaced and for ten years I was to cycle through the Oxshott Woods to the station and commute to Bloomsbury Street well within the hour.

Among the first spoils of profitability and peace was a 'firm' car in the shape of a 1936 Wolseley, which, having accomplished 3,000 miles, had been laid up by its owner for the duration of the war with its maker's tabs still dangling from it. This became mine, or rather the firm's, for all of £365 and launched me into thirty years of 'company' motoring, the deprivation of which upon retirement is one of the hardest crosses a 'senior citizen' is obliged to bear. As soon as petrol permitted I would drive occasionally to London, and be able to boast to Philip Unwin at lunch that I had 'done Kingston Hill in top'. In London I would garage the car near the office for sixpence a day, erupting in fury when this was increased to an exorbitant ninepence and then to a shilling.

Opposite our home in Cobham lay a wild wood of some eight acres. It was reputed to be for sale at £500. We hadn't got £500 and in any event what value had an eight-acre wood in the green belt? Now it is a huddle of houses at goodness knows how much a quarter-acre plot and Cobham has become an unpleasing growth of multiple stores amid which, the last time I was there, a hair-dressing establishment proclaimed itself as of 'London, Cobham and Barcelona'.

Books were still enjoying the heady sparkle of success and only a few, who did not include myself until much later, wondered how long it could last. The problems of the '30s had been something of a myth, argued the optimists. Publishing was not really so much 'an art and mystery', and although the great part of its contemporary profits went to satisfy the demands of E.P.T., relaxation would one day come and, meanwhile, a flutter in overheads was an understandable expansion. Publishing on a shoe-string was a useful enough discipline, but was perhaps a little unseemly. Frugality and soft drinks were something to be left now with Stanley Unwin. It was obviously rather jolly to throw a party when a promotable book came out, and it enabled a lot of people to meet a lot of times. The circus had arrived in Bedford Square.

Others than Victor Gollancz now found the Savoy an agreeable place to lunch. Sandwiches round the corner had been all very well but the five-shilling maximum charge, with a modest surcharge for lushness, had opened up new areas of entertainment to expense accounts previously restricted to an occasional coffee and biscuits. As literary agents proliferated and prospered it was clear that the Ivy was more congenial to them than the local pub. And our friends the American publishers were beginning again their Atlantic crossings. During the war their parcels had been generous and welcome; it was only proper that some return hospitality should be contrived. 'I suppose you were bombed into this?' said a visiting American introduced to what we thought to be the elegance of 26 Bloomsbury Street. He, with most of his colleagues, was tottering on his feet within days.

Thus the pace was set for an era which was certainly agreeable, but which too soon was to carry the good cheer into corners of the City, where diversification was becoming a word in wide circulation. We ought to have a look at publishing, they were soon to say. It has a glamour we would like to share. Very interesting people you know, authors. It is a 'nice' business to be in. Thus in 'simplistic' terms the bait was laid which, in due course, was to entrap publishing in a world of alien values and into marriages almost invariably incapable of a progression beyond convenience.

But as yet such intrusions were no more than a wisp of cloud in a clear sky. We at Michael Joseph had managed to develop a list of considerable strength with authors who could be depended upon to produce a satisfactory procession of biggish sellers while all the time strengthening a back list which the limitations of war had so far made it impossible to exploit. We had C. S. Forester, H. E. Bates, Joyce Cary, Paul Gallico, Vicki Baum, Monica Dickens, Caryl Brahms and S. J. Simon, Gladys Mitchell and other occasionals contributing to an output still within the limits of around thirty new titles a year. The consequent turnover was around ten times that regarded by Victor Gollancz as minimal and our overheads were well within the confines of 20 per cent.

As urged always by Stanley Unwin, it was my responsibility to open the post of every day and this I was to do until the end of my time with Michael Joseph. It was an operation I regarded then, and regard still, as essential if a managing director is to retain a finger on the pulse of his business; especially in one so personal as publishing. Only thus is he able to know what is going on and how the climate stands. It would be possibly no bad thing if, in publishing at any rate, the size of a business were never to be larger than is consistent with its managing director opening the post. Sir Stanley was quite right. It enables a finger to be kept on every pulse and the ability to retain the 'feel' of things to an extent that nothing else can equal.

When, later, I was to consult Stanley Unwin about the wisdom or otherwise of 'taking on' the Hutchinson publishing empire afresh, almost his first words were, 'Open the post, Lusty. Open the post.' He was right, but when on the first morning I surveyed the sacks of it I recognized utter defeat. It was a moment of truth from which I was never wholly to recover.

It is customary to relate quips and anecdotes of Sir Stanley Unwin's eccentricities and puritanical frugality. He was never other than intensely kind, generous, helpful and considerate to me. Despite contrary views, I believed him to have a delightful sense of humour which he possibly owed, as other Unwins did, to the charm and lively wit of his wife. None the less it was there. I fell from grace for a while after conspiring with Edmond Segrave to expose his dealings with the BBC in the early '30s and, as I have written earlier, I am referred to in his auto-biography as a 'jealous competitor'. But I admired, respected and became immensely fond of the little man who fussed so effectively around the trade and accomplished so much for it and for the status of books and publishing throughout the world. The occasional embarrassment was his reluctance to let other people say this first.

Towards the close of his life I was a distant neighbour in Hampstead and would occasionally motor him home after a monthly dinner of the Society of Bookmen. He had not been well and I was especially glad to find him there on what I think must have been very nearly his last appearance. He looked small and a little uncertain and I felt suddenly afraid for the fragility of the old man. I went across the room to offer him a lift home and on the spur of the moment I almost embraced him, and knew suddenly that my eyes had filled with tears. Yes, yes, it would be very kind if I would take him home. Would it be convenient to call at Messrs Boots in Piccadilly where he had left a prescription? He sometimes went to Messrs John Bell and Croyden in Wigmore Street which was more convenient, but Messrs Boots were so very much cheaper. He had not himself a National Health doctor and thought it iniquitous that he should have to pay for his medicines ...

One year I was about to set forth to America and Philip Unwin had told me that proofs of *The Truth About a Publisher* were in the office. I asked if I might have a set to read on the ship. He thought this might be arranged but added, with true Unwin caution, that they were in short supply and great demand. However, round, post-haste, to my office came a set by hand with a note from its author. His 'nephew Philip' had informed him of my request. It was really most fortunate. Here was a set and would I write and give him my views after reading it. As soon as I set foot in New York would I deliver the proofs in person to Messrs Macmillan, who he hoped might publish an American edition. If I could deliver some enthusiasm with the proofs it might be very helpful. I gladly performed these duties with that admixture of pleasure and amusement which characterized so many dealings with Uncle Stanley.

The wrapper of the book was to contain a reproduction of the portrait by Oskar Kokoschka which had recently been completed and was on display in Uncle Stanley's room. At lunch one day after my return from America I asked Philip if I might return to his office to see it. Unexpectedly, Uncle Stanley was there, and I gazed with reverence on the portrait. 'I don't like the hands,' I said and I had the impression that the old man was not displeased. 'I have something here,' he said, 'which I think will interest you,' and he went to a small pile of what I saw to be advance copies of *The Truth About a Publisher*. 'My God,' I thought, 'the old boy is going to give me one.' Gravely he handed me a copy and gravely I inspected it and made some adequate comment. His hand came forward to relieve me of the book. 'I thought', he said, 'that you might like to be among the first to handle it.' The trouble was that to a business which is intensely personal he would make no concessions on any point which he felt was related to business. His determined exactitude became a legend embellished by anecdotes from every corner of the world. And yet, after a gruelling year as chairman of the National Book League, I received from Uncle Stanley a personal cheque equal to his generous annual subscription. 'I want, for this year,' he wrote, 'to double my subscription in this way as a token of gratitude for the work you are doing.'

One afternoon my telephone rang in Bloomsbury Street. 'Is that you, Lusty? Stanley Unwin here. I would like to come and see you.' 'Why can't I come and see you?' I asked. 'Because, Lusty, I am coming in the role of a literary agent and I do not believe publishers should visit literary agents. Literary agents should visit publishers.' He was round in five minutes and handed me a manuscript. 'I am here, as I told you, Lusty, in the guise of an agent. I am giving you the manuscript of my son David's first novel. I hope very much that you will want to publish it. No other publisher has seen it. When you have anything to discuss, kindly let me know.'

I felt greatly flattered; and *The Governor's Wife* proved to be a very good novel indeed, and by the grace of the providence that watched over Stanley Unwin was chosen by the Book Society as its book of the month. I explained to Uncle Stanley that agents liked to be taken out to lunch and would he come to the Savile Club with me. There we discussed reasonable terms and easily agreed them. I cannot recall the tedious facts, but within the next few days publishers were expected to insist on some territorial extension to their market and the principle of this had import-ance. 'Sir Stanley,' I ventured, 'what are we going to do about this new insistence of the Publishers Association? Ought we not to cover it?' He looked at me with those rather questing little eyes which did not penetrate quite so far as he imagined they did. 'Yes, yes, Lusty. I see what you mean. But it is Monday today and the situation does not arise until Wednesday. We will complete the agreement this afternoon.'

It was during my stint as chairman of the Society of Bookmen that it arranged a luncheon to celebrate its president's eightieth birthday. It had somehow not occurred to me that he would expect my wife, then fairly new to the book trade after twenty-five years or so in the world of medicine, to be present. He seemed a little put out. I explained that we were hoping it might be pos-sible to have a private celebration over dinner at the Garrick Club and this seemed to mollify him.

'Have you ever', I asked Lady Unwin as lunch proceeded, 'seen your husband in a loin cloth?' She said she hadn't and started laughing at the very idea. 'What, my dear, are you laughing at?' inquired Sir Stanley. 'Nothing to do with you, Stanley,' she said. 'Mind your own business.' I explained that high on the far wall of the Garrick dining-room is a not particularly attractive clock, borne aloft by Old Father Time in his loin cloth. There can be no doubt whatever that Stanley Unwin posed for the sculptor. It is a very precise likeness of countenance, little beard and all. And the Garrick evening was contrived.

It went well, Lady Unwin enjoying her sherry and her wine in total disdain of her husband's disfavour. We went down to dinner and Lady Unwin was placed to gain a frontal view of her husband's feat of strength on the far wall. 'There he is,' I said to her, pointing aloft. She burst into laughter. 'What ever is the matter, my dear?' 'It's you, Stanley. It's you in a loin cloth,' and she collapsed again. Sir Stanley had to peer for a view and he gazed solemnly on what he saw. 'Yes,' he said at length, 'yes. I see what you mean,' and for the rest of the evening, when he thought he could decently do so, he bestowed an admiring glance upon the Garrick's timepiece.

It was Stanley Unwin who propelled me into the larger world of the book trade and its politics. He supported my election to the Society of Bookmen, then, as it is now to a lesser extent, a sort of senior common room of the trade comprising a careful admixture of publishers, booksellers, librarians, authors and every now and again a literary agent. Membership is limited and there is an insistence upon fairly regular attendance which, allied with death, achieves a certain necessary turnover of members. With the proliferation of trade committees covering everything under the sun and the extension of the Publishers Association and the Booksellers Association into every nook and cranny, its practical usefulness has diminished. At earlier dinners were born such innovations as the National Book Council (later to become the National Book League) and Harold Raymond's brilliant inspiration of Book Tokens. I concede to no member of the Society of Bookmen a greater love for women, and that it has now opened its ranks to their intrusion is a trend which no man can withstand. But what I regard as insulting to women and puerile in men is the belief that their coming makes no difference whatever to the climate of its meetings.

Hardly had I recovered my breath after my first meeting at the Society than Stanley Unwin waylaid me to say that I was to represent the Society on the committee of the National Book Council. The chairman of the Council at that time was the great David Roy, the first man to convince me that the lilt of a Scottish voice in England is an incomparable commercial asset, while the lilt of English in Scotland is certainly not. I confessed as much to Joan. I began to revel then, as I revel still, in the gossip of the trade as it surges around the pump of a parish smaller than most suppose. I was fortunately placed to acquire it. From my first meeting with Edmond Segrave a short while after he became editor of *The Bookseller*, we contrived ever closer ties. Our affections and our hates usually conformed and we were similarly prejudiced. From time to time I would relay to him some useful and relevant item of news, such as the purchase by Walter Hutchinson of the World's Most Expensive Cow. Edmond could, and often did, write like an angel possessed, and the smallest paragraph he might compose for his own paper would shine from its pages as a jewel. He should, of course, have moved to higher spheres, for his talents deserved a wider world. But ambition was not his spur and he was content to remain where he was. In every crisis of my affairs I would make a bee-line to Edmond and had always instant access to his office.

There he would sit, in what he would regard as a decent, dark suit with a waistcoat and a gold watch-chain across its front. Rather slight in form, he was puckish of countenance, and his head would roll through greater degrees in laughter than any other I have ever seen. He would listen gravely from behind a desk whose considerable acreage was never less than a foot high in the greatest shamble of papers known to chaos. Should a letter be required his hand would burrow deep at an exact spot and emerge with it between finger and thumb. In due course he would pronounce with slow, careful diction as if anxious that his spoken word should achieve the perfection of his written. This tendency could, on occasions, extend anecdote to discomfiture.

His death in his mid-sixties was cruel, sad and utterly unexpected. Edmond and a few others one regarded as an integral part of one's own life and not to be removed. With Desirée his wife he had dined with Babs and me at the Garrick on the eve of our departure for Australia and Africa. He had been suffering considerable pain in a leg, but not, at that time, with much foreboding. At the close of our travels we had just left for home by sea from Cape Town when the first cable reached me saying he was desperately ill. Within a day came the second to say that he was dead and no day since has been the same.

It was through Edmond, after the war, that I again met Allen Lane and began an association and a friendship which became exceptionally close. A little while before he died we were talking of this and that when quite suddenly he looked at me. 'Bob,' he said, 'I think I would regard you as my closest friend.' There was a pause and he coloured a little as he realized he had not been completely truthful. 'In publishing that is,' he added. Allen excelled at gossip, gathering and dispersing it around by the bucketful. To him, too, I turned always at the first hint of trouble.

A more 'establishment' figure in the network was Jack Newth, the wise custodian of all the secrets of *Who's Who* for which he was responsible and a tower of strength to every good purpose that he touched. Within a year or so of Edmond's death he too was to die and I felt, and continue to feel, utterly desolated to have lost these three close friends, each completely different from one another in character and temperament and yet each eager to exchange all they knew of the quirks and eccentricities of the world around them, and to each of whom I turned whenever sense needed to be sought.

Happily still around, but now retired, is Philip Unwin. With Philip, whose *The Publishing Unwins* carries the message with an urbanity and distinction beyond my reach, I have in a sense grown up in publishing and in a friendship perhaps more domestic than the others. He is a more reluctant and less involved gossiper, restrained perhaps by the occasionally desiccated puritanism of the Unwins but miraculously saved, as his Uncle Stanley was, by the healthy rebellion of a wife who countenances none of it.

And then of course there is Juliet O'Hea, closer to me, and for longer, than any. I met her first when she was Michael Joseph's secretary at Curtis Brown and there was talk of her 'turning publisher' along with the two of us. But it came to nothing and agency retained one of the most acute minds in the business. For over forty years we have remained in constant touch and I think it can be said that only Juliet knows the whole truth and would not refrain from throwing any piece of it at me were she to think it necessary for my own good.

Here, then, was a network, contrived by chance and operated by accident, through which little that happened in the trade was likely to escape unnoticed. Thus it was that in those precious years which followed the war one's world somehow came together and attained a cohesion and a strength which was sustained by a home and a Scottish wife whose one dedicated purpose was to spread happiness wherever she might be without ever a thought for herself. She had also to ensure that the arrogance and self-satisfaction of a never easy publishing husband should be kept in check by controls applied with a precision so delicate that they were hardly ever felt but could never be evaded.

I have always believed that a development created by the problems of war could, if carried forward into the peace, have had profound consequences for publishing. Allen Lane had started his Penguin adventure in 1935. Many people prophesied a short life and disaster. It very nearly came, and Allen was contemplating retreat almost from the beginning. He, with many others, and certainly with Michael Joseph, was saved by the war and catapulted to success by its requirements. Allen was perfectly aware of this and it in no sense diminishes the value of the extraordinary contribution made by the enterprise of Penguin to the enrichment of our time. For a while he had the market almost to himself, until the initiative of Guild Books, formed as a 'publishers' co-operative' to publish paperbacks for the Forces on paper made additionally available by the rationing authorities. Dominant in the scheme were Walter Harrap and Jonathan Cape, who seemed never able to accept even the suggestion that such co-operation extended into normal times would be capable of stopping Allen Lane in his tracks and making virtually impossible the proliferation of paperback operations which in due course came about. The argument was invariably put forward that the paper would not be available. This was true enough, but it has always seemed to me that a way round or indeed a way forward could have been at least reconnoitred.

Our own Michael Joseph list had a great many titles ripe for exploitation in the paperback market with which we were not equipped to cope. We were not alone in this quandary, nor did we want to see our best-selling titles appearing as paperback editions under an imprint altogether dissociated from us. Surely, I thought, Allen Lane's problem will be to attract the best titles from the best imprints. An assurance of these will be valuable to him and worth some reciprocity. I discussed the matter with Segrave, who then knew Allen Lane much better than I did, and in due course went along to meet Allen. He liked the idea and thus around 1946 what came to be known as the Penguin group was formed. Its members, so far as I can now recall, were Messrs Heinemann, Messrs Faber, Messrs Chatto, Hamish Hamilton and ourselves. In return for a first option on our titles, Penguin Books agreed to publish their editions under a joint imprint and pay us a small additional royalty over and above that going normally to the author. It was an eminently satisfactory arrangement and was inaugurated by one of the first parties any of us had experienced since before the war.

Allen at that time had a spacious and attractive house with a large garden not far from Harmondsworth. Thither, for lunch, those of us who had negotiated the project were summoned, together with Edmond Segrave. It was prolonged, and alcoholic martinis of a strength and in quantities of unaccustomed prodigality were gravely delivered to us on some conveyor-belt system presided over by a Wodehousian butler acquired by Allen for the occasion. The talk was animated if increasingly incoherent. I suspect that no observer would have thought our business was to do with literature. We all made speeches; and to this day I can remember I began mine declaring that I felt 'always a bridesmaid and never a bride'. Edmond Segrave eventually woke up in a hospital; somehow realized it was *The Bookseller*'s press day and discharged himself. I clambered into the back of a car with A. S. Frere of Heinemann and we sang sea-shanties in unison all the way back to Bloomsbury. Somehow I found Oxshott Station and my bicycle which knew its way home through the woods. My macintosh was around me like a drunken Irishman's when Joan opened the door. 'Always a bridesmaid and never a bride,' I informed her before collapsing. Thus it was that the Penguin group got under way, and it greatly annoyed Alan Bott who was busily making plans for the launching of Pan Books.

In 1946 I paid my first visit to America where, over the next years, I was to enjoy so much exhilaration and acquire a great number of close friends. I am profoundly grateful that nearly all these periodical trips ('jaunts abroad' was the phrase still in use at Messrs Hutchinson when I returned there in 1956) took place when civilized transit by sea was the accepted mode of travel. Again, I am grateful that it was considered appropriate and proper in publishing circles that one should be accompanied by one's wife. This was, in fact, thoroughly sensible, for the presence of one's wife on an exhausting and intensive outing of this kind is invaluable. The change now is complete and dreary. An aircraft is boarded at Heathrow and there are probably never less than a dozen English language publishers in transit over the Atlantic. One is expected to accomplish a whirlwind trip in days and then fly home to be faced often with the necessity of reversing most of the decisions taken under pressure in New York.

In 1946 and for a number of years to follow the progress was more stately, more enjoyable and more rewarding. Flowers and telegrams would come to one's cabin and as often as not there would be champagne. It was still something of an enterprise. In the autumn of 1946, however, ships and their passengers were still within the control of the Ministry of War Transport and my journey was made in the *Aquitania*, whose major purpose was to ferry war-brides to Canada. This first expedition had its natural thrills and excitements, some of which were simple enough. Few of us had seen white rolls for years and to find them in abundance on the lunch tables of the *Aquitania* still alongside at Southampton seemed a little miracle. The cabin to which I was allotted was designed for two but contained fourteen. We were an oddly assorted bunch and, with a naturalized Russian who wrote poetry and manufactured skins for the containment of sausages, I rebelled after the first night. 'If', explained the management, 'you do not mind sleeping among the war-brides, we can put you both in a cabin for four but should we get other complaints we may be obliged to fill the other two places.' We had no objection whatever to sleeping with war-brides and since a steward was then persuaded to bring us tea and fresh orange juice every morning no additional complaints emanated from us.

I learnt a great deal about the manufacture of sausage skins, but little about the war-brides. In no part of the ship were we allowed to talk to them. By day their chairs lined the promenade deck, and so did the ship's considerable police force. Promenading males were not allowed to stop. 'Move along please; move along,' was the ritualistic cry. The ship was dry, but we were a congenial and happy bunch and enjoyed ourselves with gossip and Coca-Cola.

Halifax was our immediate destination and those bound for New York faced a mildly uncomfortable 48-hour train journey. A little apprehensive and a little homesick, I can recall now the inward thrill of finding myself detraining at New York's Grand Central at around half past one of an autumn night. I had been booked in at the Algonquin Hotel, so well known to the mythology of contemporary American writing. At that time a sternly enforced regulation forbade any visitor to remain longer than three nights in any one hotel. How quite I accomplished any useful purpose over the next month continues to mystify me, since much of each day was occupied in arranging where next it might be possible to sleep, and chasing laundry from where I had slept three days previously. But there was the glory and stimulus and exultant excitement of New York in the blaze and bustle of autumn sunshine. New York then had a magic not, I think, to be encountered anywhere else on earth. It seemed to emanate a galvanizing energy and there was time and enough for everything. My main contact was Alan Collins, then manager of Curtis Brown's New York office through which we sold such rights in our publications as we were free to handle. Alan Collins was endlessly kind and over the next thirty or so years was to become one of my closest American friends. He too was much preoccupied as to where I should sleep, and gave me to understand that I had narrowly escaped at least murder by joining my sausage-skin friend who had found sanctuary in some hotel in the far west of the seventies.

I galloped around the New York publishing houses as one possessed. The names of all, but the faces of few, were familiar. Within a few hours of arrival so prodigious was the hospitality that I had no vacant date in my diary either for lunch, dinner or weekends for the duration of my stay. It was reckoned then that an adequate visitation was hardly possible under less than four to five weeks. Six appointments a day were about as many as it was possible to keep. To accomplish these, to keep records of titles and authors which had been mentioned, to maintain contact with one's own office and somehow to consider a formidable deluge of books, proofs, manuscripts and projects was an exhausting commitment, to which were added social occasions which often proved a great deal more rewarding than an evening spent in one's hotel trying to read.

Shortly before this first American trip we had bought, and were soon to publish, an impressive first novel by a young coloured writer, Anne Petry, who lived in New York. *The Street* had been published by the great firm of Houghton Mifflin in Boston. It received considerable acclaim and sold widely. I thought I should meet Miss Petry and, with the dew of innocence still wet, suggested we should lunch together. No problem. But the faintest suggestion that there might exist a problem emerged

from the climate of New York after a very few days. I was on a
visit to meet Frank Morley, late of Messrs Faber & Faber in
London and now a vice-president of Harcourt Brace and both a
publisher of distinction and a wise man. I then knew him slightly,
but have known him very much better ever since both as the
author of *The Great North Road*, which I published while at
Hutchinson, and as a distinguished 'literary adviser' who has
saved me many mistakes and been more responsible than I for a
number of successes. Frank Morley has never fully recovered
from the shock of that meeting in New York. 'Perhaps you can
help me, Mr Morley? I have invited a coloured girl to lunch
tomorrow. There is no problem is there?'

No such conundrum had entered the experience of this wise,
sagacious and extremely human American. It obviously shook
him to say it, but how deeply I was not to know at the time.
'Well,' he had to say, 'I don't think I can tell you that there is
no problem. Will there be anyone with you?' 'No,' I answered,
'just the two of us.' He pursed his lips, as he often does when
wondering what to say. 'It might be helpful to have another
couple with you,' he said. 'Where do you think of going?' 'I
thought the Algonquin,' I said. 'Yes,' he replied, 'yes — that's
quite a good idea. But perhaps you should tell them what you
plan to do.'

How very odd, I thought, and in those days financially disconcerting, for visiting Englishmen were kept remarkably short
of dollars by the Bank of England responsible for doling them
out. I had to make a special application to pay a forgotten
laundry bill. But I thanked Frank Morley for his advice and left
him reflecting on it. I was able to add two of my travelling com-
panions to the party and confronted the management of the
Algonquin. It appeared slightly anxious. There was a consultation of a few moments. Yes, it would be quite all right. There
would be no objection, but a stipulation was necessary. It could
not be responsible for anything that might happen.

This was New York in 1946 and one of its most sophisticated
hotels. Miss Petry appeared. She was delightful. My other guests
appeared. We had an enormously interesting lunch and nothing
at all happened. I was not aware that we were even noticed.

On that first visit there was the additional problem of how to get home again. The Ministry of War Transport having shipped one out of the country accepted no responsibility for one's return to it. It so happened that whilst I was there the mighty *Queen Elizabeth* was to make her maiden voyage as a peace-time Cunarder intent upon providing Gracious Living At Its Best. I thought, naturally enough, that it would be agreeable to return within her commodious luxury. Every string that ingenuity could invent was pulled, but to no avail. She was full to capacity. Everybody had said so in England and everybody said so again in New York. Some of us who had travelled out together were determined that we should somehow travel back together but the *Queen Elizabeth* seemed elusive. On the spur of a moment I thought it might do no harm to ring Cunard's New York office with a casual inquiry. I did so. Could they possibly accommodate me on the homeward voyage? They were afraid all first-class accommodation had gone, but would I mind very much travelling cabin class? I would not mind at all. Yes, very well they can arrange that. Could I bring my friends with me? Well, how many? I thought around six of them. Yes, certainly. Perhaps my friends will each get in touch with them. My reputation as a wangler soared within the parish of publishing. I contacted the sausage-skinned Russian and the other chosen few. The modest return fare paid to the Ministry covered our journey however it might be made; and the World's Greatest Luxury Liner, anxious to reveal her paces, was a bargain acceptable to all.

In due course I was aboard as the appointed hour struck on Pier 90. During the morning I had rushed around New York on a spree of buying incense and myrrh, silks and tweeds for all at home. My cabin was for two, its other occupant an unknown quantity. My luggage and my packages accumulated with that remarkable efficiency which made the old Cunard company one of the wonders of our ancient civilization. I sped round the miracle of the ship, returning every now and again to my cabin, some ten minutes' walk from the sea, in the hope of sizing up its second inmate. There was no sign of such. A little before sailing-time an oddly shaped package arrived. Nothing more. Who on earth, I wondered, could be sailing to England with no more than this?

The light at the end of Pier 90, on the stroke of four o'clock, turned from red to green; and with marvellous precision and majesty we reversed into the Hudson river to move slowly down past that unforgettable skyline, aglow with its countless lights, soaring into the growing darkness of the heights. The *Queen Elizabeth* was on her way, for the first time travelling east in waters unthreatened by war.

The odd black box now looked slightly sinister on the cabin floor. It could be a bomb, I thought. I lay my one good listening ear bravely to it. It seemed clearly to tick and I rang for a steward. Did he know who was travelling with me? Yes, he did. A young American. 'Rather nervous I think he is, sir. He is travelling with his parents and keeping all his stuff with them. He only means to sleep in here.' That suited me admirably. When I went to bed he was already wrapped in his, but awake and clearly rather fearful. He hadn't seen an Englishman before. 'I am only sleeping here,' he said, 'I am living with my parents along the passage.' 'That's fine,' I said. 'What's in the package?' 'It's my trombone, sir,' he said. I never really saw him. He was asleep when I rose in the morning, and again when I appeared at night. He brought nothing but his trombone to the cabin, which I had virtually to myself. 'Are you still starving in England?' he inquired a little apprehensively one evening. I assured him that we were not nor ever had been. He didn't quite believe me. 'We have brought a lot of sandwiches with us just in case,' he explained.

I learned a valuable lesson during that trip, which led me to cultivate a habit that deceives quite a number of acquaintances into regarding me as more efficient than nature ever intended I should be. I thought it might produce pleasant results were I to notify the captain that he carried aboard the publisher of Hornblower, who would like to present him with a copy of the omnibus edition to commemorate so auspicious an occasion. Within the hour I was sought by a respectful steward. The captain's compliments, sir, and he would be glad if you would drink with him on Sunday at noon.

It was the usual sort of captain's party, that was to become a feature of every Atlantic crossing and must have been one of the most tiresome of crosses endured by Cunard's captains. But on this Sunday there was the innocence of innovation and here I was in the captain's cabin of the greatest ship afloat — and all for the glory of Hornblower and his author.

Most of the other guests were of that industrial calibre of power and authority which gives to their complexions a curious textural sheen which I have never observed on a publisher except when it came latterly to one who veered from course into commercial television. There was a gentleman of this ilk present who displayed a superb gold-plated razor he intended to present to the captain. I was not the only one promising gifts. 'Would you', he said to me, 'like a razor of this kind?' 'Of course I would,' I replied, wondering if I should offer a reciprocal book. 'Good as done,' he said, noting down my name and address. It never arrived and I have never since entertained anything but dislike and scorn for the famous firm he was paid to represent. From that time I carried around a small scribbling pad and jotted down, surreptitiously if need be, every casual undertaking I might give to anyone anywhere. It is a trick and a stratagem, but it has paid me well over many years.

Years later, after Sir Allen Lane had been made a Companion of Honour, I knew that he might be dead before he could receive it. Shortly after his death I was at a dinner party seated opposite Sir Michael Adeane, the Queen's private secretary. We had never met and I leaned across the table and wondered if he could tell me if Allen Lane had in fact received his c.h. before he died. 'I will find out,' said Sir Michael. The next morning, at an early hour, a message greeted me at the office. Sir Michael Adeane had telephoned. The message was that, yes, Sir Allen had received his award from the hands of the Queen before he died. It was a marvellous and most touching lesson in how such matters should be attended to.

One of the greatest men of books of my time was Fred Melcher, proprietor and editor of the American *Publishers' Weekly*. He was a man of pure gold and his whole long life was a dedication to books, to writers and to all concerned with either. I met him for the first time on that visit and for ever afterwards, until his death, Joan and I would make a bee-line from the ship to Fred Melcher for a first lunch in New York. He was enormous fun and had an acceptable enthusiasm which nothing daunted and which was never tiresome. He won in his lifetime about every award available to bookmen. His wife was a delight too. At the age of well over eighty her ambition was to own and drive a Jaguar car. On that first visit this wise, quiet and elderly American took me to a local football match where his own team was to be in combat. I understood but little of it, but watched, amazed and fascinated, Fred Melcher leaping to his feet, dancing around with arms flailing in the manner of a lunatic tic-tac man and bawling at the top of his voice.

He and his wife came to stay a night with us in Cobham and he was never to forget that he first heard the song of a nightingale at the bottom of our garden. He adored Joan and his face would always light at the sight of her. 'She had a little smile for me that was all her own,' he wrote after her death.

I think he was approaching ninety on his last visit to London. Still full of fire, he seemed a little failing and his head required the support of a massive and burdensome collar. He never so much as said so, but I had the impression that he did not wholly approve my return to Hutchinson. He was due to fly home and I had intended to bid him farewell, but when the day came I had not succeeded. I was in my office when I was told 'a Mr Melcher is asking for you'. And there at the entrance was Fred, rather frail and encased in plaster, with the rather lop-sided smile which had followed a mild stroke. 'I am on my way to Heathrow,' he said, 'but I couldn't go without coming to say goodbye.' I never saw him again and now all that he owned and made and lived with belongs to some mammoth enterprise of which it is only a part, but it is still making its doubtless viable contribution.

The Curtis Brown office in New York was always a blessed oasis of calm, wisdom, kindness and efficiency. The famous 'Zukie' was always ready to take over one's life and make every path straight. She possessed that special brand of enthusiastic kindness found almost entirely in American women. One of the happiest times of nearly every trip was its traditional weekend with Alan and Catherine Collins at Hunt's Farm in Hopewell, New Jersey, some fifty miles from New York. The countryside seemed never less than glorious in the autumn sunshine and there was always a sort of lunacy in the air when Alan was around. He was a man of nonsensical prejudice, but somehow knew it. 'God damn it,' he would say, thumping the table, 'you can't think that,' knowing very well that there was no earthly reason why one shouldn't.

Joan, Juliet O'Hea and I were once spending a short weekend in a small hotel in Marlborough. Drinking before dinner, we could hear a commotion in the hall. A familiar voice was in argument. 'Good God,' we said almost simultaneously, 'that's Alan Collins.' And so it was. He had somehow arrived in Plymouth and was motoring himself to London, spending this night en route.

Without hesitation the Collinses welcomed me to their family Christmas in the year that Joan died when Christmas at home seemed insupportable. I flew out in a blizzard not caring much whether we arrived or not. Their kindness was wonderful. Elizabeth Bowen was spending Christmas with them, too. Every morning she would write; and we scarcely moved from the house, for it was snowing most of the time. Alan taught me backgammon and fought with his brother and sister-in-law. Elizabeth Bowen was immensely wise and thoughtful and we would together exchange reflections on an American Christmas. We were still there on New Year's Eve. At midnight Alan unlocked a case containing a massive armoury of lethal weapons. From this he extracted a pistol and loaded it. 'An American custom,' he said, and opened the door. Across the valley lights twinkled in the village. 'Fire it,' he commanded, handing me the pistol. 'Fire it?' I asked. 'Yes, yes,' he said, 'quickly and aim upwards.' For the first time in my life I fired a revolver. 'How far has that gone?' I asked. 'Oh, I don't know,' said Alan, putting the thing away, 'about two miles I would think.' 'But could it hurt anyone as it comes down?' 'Very unlikely,' said Alan; 'have some more Bourbon.'

Alan too is dead, after a protracted and perplexing illness which he fought with great valiance. For a while he was in the London Clinic and one evening switched on his television to find himself watching the *Black and White Minstrel Show*. I was at home when the telephone rang. 'God damn it, Bob, you can't do that.'

'Do what?' I asked.

'Well, you are a governor of the BBC, aren't you?'

'Yes, Alan, I am. But why?'

'It's that Nigger Minstrel show I'm watching. You will have riots. You can't put on things like that. All hell would break loose in America.'

'We aren't in America, Alan.'

'I know you're damn well not in America. You would be in prison if you were. It's a disgrace. You are crazy and so is the BBC. It's asking for trouble.'

It was at Hopewell that we met Ogden Nash and his wife Francis, who we were to see much of over the years and who were utterly delightful. Ogden scattered inimitable verse in his wake and a collection of his impromptu pieces would make a rich anthology. On almost our last Atlantic crossing in the *Mauretania* they were fellow passengers, and Alan Collins arranged that we should have a joint credit in the bar. It was a voyage made memorable by their company and the oddities of the captain who, at his reception on the second evening, welcomed us all aboard the *Caronia* and read some execrable verse alleged to have been written by a passenger. The thought that such verse might be attributed to him caused Ogden Nash considerable agitation, which was not quietened by an even more painful outpouring from the captain as we approached home waters. On *Mauretania* notepaper before me are two verses from Ogden, 'not', he wrote, 'from the captain's joke-book, but for Babs and Bob':

A grinning tycoon of Fort Worth
When asked for the cause of his mirth,
Chuckled, Houston and Dallas
Will shore bust a gallus
When they hear they've just purchased the Earth.

A handsome young rodent of Basham
As a life-guard became a sensation.
All the lady mice waved
And screamed to be saved
By his mouse-to-mouse resuscitation.

In London he demanded to see the stage version of the Minstrel Show found so abhorrent by Alan Collins. Ogden revelled in it: 'All my favourite bath-tub ditties,' he said.

Ogden Nash was one of those rare creatures instantly to be recognized as almost wholly good. He played with words and their arrangement as an artist with a pencil when in reach of blank paper. I would have given much to be his British publisher and but for a moment of forgetfulness on the part of Alan Collins I could have been.

Ogden and Francis were in London a little while before the publication of Mary Wilson's poems. In a moment almost of fantasy I thought how agreeable it would be to contrive a dinner party in the Garrick's private room which would bring together Mary Wilson, John Betjeman and Ogden Nash. John Betjeman was an old friend of Mrs Wilson, but neither had met Ogden. There was not long in which to make arrangements and it never really entered my head that I would succeed. As wife of the Prime Minister, Mrs Wilson's commitments were extensive; John Betjeman's timetable is never other than crowded; and Ogden Nash was to be in London for only a few days. To diffuse the element of poetry with a vivacity of prose and glamour I added Lena Wickman to the party. She was, and remains still, the London representative of the great Swedish publishing organization of Bonnier, but I get sometimes confused as to whether Lena represents Bonnier in London, or Bonnier represent Lena in Stockholm. Her brother at the time was Minister for something-or-other in the Swedish government and a friend of Harold Wilson. I then included John Guest of Messrs Longman, who was well known to Mary Wilson. To my intense surprise all were not only free but apparently eager to be free. Mrs Wilson thought that she might be late as she was only arriving back in London at dinner-time on the appointed evening. She had a very full day in some provincial town, but would come straight from Euston Station. In point of fact, by exerting herself to an extent not expected of Prime Ministers' wives she was hardly late at all, which was just as well since the Garrick's chef refused to contemplate serving the main course until Mrs Wilson was ready to consume it. It was a hilarious evening; and in charge of the proceedings was Joan, then the Garrick's leading character-waitress, and herself a poet of some enthusiasm, who had contributed a talk to the BBC on What Poetry Means to Me.

Now scattered far and wide are the verses composed that

evening. Ogden fell heavily for Mary Wilson and wrote delightfully for her. Mary Wilson wrote a poem for him and John Betjeman distributed his favours. Joan the waitress went into a corner to compose a response to the tributes accorded her. Around midnight Mrs Wilson was delivered back to 10 Downing Street by Messrs Guest and Betjeman, and Ogden Nash expressed his conviction that there was not much wrong with this country.

I suppose that in total I must have spent some two years in America first with Joan and latterly with my second wife Babs. I only went twice alone. I know of few greater pleasures than Atlantic crossings in the great Cunarders, before a few hours in a flying cylinder achieved the same purpose. We crossed in nearly all of them, but as often as possible in the *Mauretania*. It may have been a lot of nonsense, but it was splendid nonsense. The value of such expeditions, and they were expensive, could not be measured in the terms required by modern accountancy. They were invaluable, and cumulatively so. But as old Ben Huebsch, one of America's most distinguished and beloved of bookmen, would often remind me, the most rewarding trip could be the one which added nothing to one's list, in which all temptation was overcome. There is, of course, a driving desire to return with a potential best-seller in the luggage. One of my luckiest acquisitions was a manuscript I heard about in Boston which existed with its author in Kensington. It became *Les Girls* by Constance Weeks and it added greatly to the gaiety of nations when it was published.

There have been two publishers whose achievements during my lifetime I admire above all others. One is Allen Lane, the other Alfred Knopf. The career of Allen Lane might with reason be regarded as more fortuitous than dedicated; but Alfred Knopf, greatly aided by Blanche, his first wife, devoted his whole allegiance to the quality of all that he printed, and he published and sustained with extraordinary consistency a list of brilliant distinction. They made a formidable couple; and Blanche, when in London, was the only American publisher who dared to hold court and not budge from her suite in Claridge's. Sustained almost entirely by a frugal nibbling of lettuce-leaves, she would summon the London publishers in turn and as one tottered exhausted from her presence, another would be waiting at the door. She would go through every list with meticulous care, expressing the utmost resentment and distress if something she favoured was not immediately at her disposal. 'But I thought you promised I should see that,' she would declare, knowing full well that she had never heard of it before. Her knowledge of 'goings-on' was prodigious and she kept the literature of every continent under review. I once made the comment to her that I thought publishing as we knew it might 'just see us through', and she never ceased to quote me. She and Alfred maintained separate establishments in New York and they battled with a verbal intensity which misled some. There existed in fact between them a most touching devotion which would unite in the most tender kindness to help any friend in need.

Towards the end of her life Blanche fought gallantly against increasing blindness, and when she died a sense of drama left the stage of American publishing. But Alfred remains still, supported by his marvellous second wife, Helen, who had never visited New York until she married Alfred and whose girlhood was spent in the saddles of the American west, shooting rattlesnakes from her hip. When I last saw Alfred he was supposed to have died from a stroke sustained the previous year. But this was not the intention of Helen, who removed him from hospital to his home and nursed him back to incredible normality. He was waiting to meet us on the station at Purchase in the loudest of gay shirts and a gaudy umbrella held aloft against the rain. 'I have just been reading a book, Bob,' he said almost at once, 'and it has moved me more than anything I have read for years. You should buy it from my office tomorrow.' I read it and did so, and for the first time in my publishing life contributed a short foreword to our edition. Its title was *The Day No Pigs Would Die* and it was hailed as a little classic. 'You and I', Alfred Knopf was to write to me, 'have never so far as I can remember quarrelled or differed about anything.' As a publisher this leaves me content.

It was not until I rejoined Hutchinson that I found myself the publisher of Eleanor Roosevelt. She was a most remarkable woman and while she was on a short visit to London we thought it might both please her and prove a useful public relation exercise for the new Hutchinson broom to hold a reception. She happily agreed and a day was set. She had arrived at Claridge's late the previous evening with a retinue of family, including grandchildren to whom she was determined to show London. I was to collect her at noon and conduct her to a Foyle's lunch at the Dorchester where she was to be the guest of honour. She was then to return to her hotel and at once set out on an expedition with her grandchildren. Within a few moments of her return from this she had to be ready for our reception, after which she had to attend a large dinner party in her honour.

She was at once entirely natural, relaxed and charming. Utterly lacking in pomposity, she was so alive, alert and amused that she somehow radiated a glamour which gave almost beauty to her features. She had not, I think, been in London since the war and I reminded her of the ferment which arose from her criticism of Brussels sprouts. 'That was terrible,' she said, 'and Franklin was dismayed. But the situation was saved by the wife of the British ambassador who prepared a quick cookbook on a hundred ways of cooking them. One copy was for me; a second for your King and Queen; and a third for Mrs Churchill.'

'I think', said Mrs Roosevelt after the Foyle's lunch, 'that you have in London a shop called Aquascutum? I want to buy a macintosh from them. I wonder if you can tell me where it is?' I obliged and left Mrs Roosevelt to gather her family, tour London and buy a macintosh.

I was to collect her from Claridge's just before six o'clock for the reception at Quaglino's, to which we were expecting some four hundred or so guests. We reached Claridge's almost together. 'The afternoon has taken longer than I expected,' explained Mrs Roosevelt, 'but I will be with you in five minutes.' And she was — having changed for her evening engagements. At our reception she welcomed every guest and then moved around the room speaking with those she knew. On the appointed hour she left for her dinner party. It was an extraordinarily impressive performance.

When we were next in New York she invited us to dinner in her apartment and it proved memorable and moving. There was but one other guest. It was a day or so after Dag Hammarskjöld, Secretary-General of the United Nations, had been killed in an air disaster, and his funeral was to be broadcast. 'If you do not mind,' said Mrs Roosevelt, 'I would very much like, after dinner, to listen to the funeral of my friend Dag Hammarskjöld.' The four of us gathered round the radio in the small sitting-room; and about the room were signed portraits of the world's war-time leaders. Here were the men who had led the free world through war to a victory from which had arisen the concept and existence of the United Nations on which so many hopes were pinned. In the centre of these events, and now America's representative to the General Assembly, was this wise and elderly woman who, with tears in her eyes, was listening to the funeral of the Secretary-General far away. It was an extraordinary moment of which to be a witness.

A few days later Mrs Roosevelt had us to lunch at the United Nations; but I have never ceased to regret the foolishness which made us turn down an invitation to spend a night at Hyde Park. It was ridiculously silly, but our schedule was a crowded one and a departure from it would involve many changes. Nevertheless, somehow we should have contrived it.

I do not know who told Mrs Roosevelt or how she became aware of it, but when a few months later my wife died, one of the first letters to reach me was from her in the most tender of terms.

Some of our later visits to New York were much enlivened by the BBC whose representative felt it necessary to ensure that a visiting Governor should receive adequate attention. With a stop-watch he would await us at Pier 90 and time our clearance through customs and our arrival at the Elysee Hotel in East 54th Street between Madison and Park Avenue. The Elysee had been recommended to us by Allen Lane with firm instructions not to tell many publishers about it. It was and remains a delight if an enigma. Its staff seems rarely to change and receives us always with the warmth of old friends. It is run by one Leo Quain and its side-show is the famous Monkey Bar next door. Its suites are individual and possess a certain glamour and if a fussy eyebrow is sometimes raised it is always a silly one. For me the Elysee at 60 East 54th Street remains the best hotel in the world.

*   *   *

Meanwhile, on the other side of the Atlantic, the Michael Joseph list continued to prove attractive to a gratifying strength of authors. Among those we happily recruited were Reginald Arkell, Gerald Bullett, Clemence Dane, Romain Gary, Geoffrey Household and a brilliant newcomer, Doris Lessing, whose first novel *The Grass is Singing* was a quite exceptional piece of work. Not long ago, on the publication of a new novel, I wrote wishing it well and hoping she was happy in her success. The rebuff was total. 'I do not think happiness is the business of grown-up people,' she wrote.

The economics of publishing then made much more practical the publishing of first novels than they do today and our 1951 list included no less than nine. One of these derived from my years at the Penn Club, where a resident, a little older than myself, was known to all as Harris. He was to remain there for almost the whole of his life. He had a certain amount of money, which seemed to make a 'gainful' occupation unnecessary. Thus he was at the beck and call of the other and busier residents and was an invaluable friend to have around the place. He did a certain amount of writing, but not very seriously nor, as far as one could make out, very successfully. When the war came Harris became a soldier — in the Signal Corps I think — and that bit of business over, he returned to the Penn Club again. Occasionally Joan and I would see him, invariably feeling a little depressed that a life agreeable enough in student days should be so long protracted.

One day in Bloomsbury Street I was told that 'a Mr Harris' was downstairs and would like to see me. In my office he handed me a manuscript. 'This is a novel I've managed to write,' he said. 'I don't quite know what to do with it and I thought you might advise me. It is not for you,' he added, as though horrified that I might think it was. He told me he was doing fairly well with science fiction short stories and the Penn Club, now in different premises, was doing fine.

I took the manuscript home. 'Old Harris has written a novel,' I told Joan, 'and he sends you his love.'

I read it with rising interest and excitement. It was not, as its author had prophesied, quite my cup of tea, but it was wonderfully good. I invited Harris to come again to the office. 'I know',

I told him, 'that you didn't think this was for us, but would you mind very much if we were to publish it?' 'Gorblimey no,' said Harris, which was a favourite phrase of his. And so we added to our list *The Day of the Triffids* by John Wyndham and thus introduced to the world one of the most successful science fiction writers of a generation. Whether on the strength of this success or not I do not know, in a short while Harris left the Penn Club with another of its long-term inhabitants, Grace Wilson, as his wife. Alas, their happiness together was brief for he died very shortly.

There arrived one day on my desk a rather flimsy and battered script from Spencer Curtis Brown. Its title was *Merrily, Merrily* and its author a Dr Ostlere whose only previous publication had been a textbook on anaesthetics. It looked of little consequence, but I sent it to a highly professional reader, Doreen Marston, whose son had recently experienced life as a medical student, which seemed to be the subject of Dr Ostlere's book. She reported with modified enthusiasm, thought that a good deal of editorial revision was necessary and that the title was dreadful. But she felt that it might be worth a certain amount of trouble. I relayed this to Spencer Curtis Brown, listing the changes suggested by Mrs Marston, requesting a new title and for good measure suggesting that some other name than Ostlere should be considered since we would want no confusion with the previous textbook. I suggested that he might drop Ostlere and use only his first two Christian names of Richard Gordon. If the author was ready to accept all this, then we would be glad to add his book to our list. Dr Ostlere was willing and would do his best to think up a new title. The revised manuscript, incorporating Mrs Marston's suggestions, eventually appeared and with no particular flourish went into production. No acceptable new title had come from the good doctor, but John Banbury in the Joseph office came up with the proposal of *Doctor in the House* and no one could better this.

After proofs arrived it slowly impinged upon us that we had an extremely funny book on our hands. A first printing of three thousand would reflect a mild optimism. Messrs Hebdon and Pick were in closer touch with the trade 'buyers' than I was and they both scented the sweet smell of success before I did. They came in a deputation of two to request the abandonment of caution and a first printing of ten thousand copies. By this time elements of uncertainty were creeping back into the book trade and rising costs required at last a new look at book prices. *Doctor in the House* was on the short side and a few years before would have been priced at around 7*s*. 6*d*. net. It appeared now that even on a print of ten thousand copies its price should be 10*s*. 6*d*. net and great was the lamentation among our sales-men.

When next in London and at the office, Michael Joseph expressed his doubts. 'That silly book by that young doctor' was his description and he could not understand how I had been per-suaded to print so large a first edition. *Doctor in the House* was published in March 1952 and by 1957 (when its price had to be increased to 12*s*. 6*d*.) had sold some 382,000 copies in thirty-three printings. Its genial author, who remains one of my closest friends, had become, as a very young man, one of the most successful writers of the post-war years. Anaesthetics were no longer necessary.

It was, I believe, the success of Richard Gordon and the consequential escalation of our profits that first produced in Michael Joseph's mind the reflection that we should somehow capitalize the growing prosperity of the company. Neither he, as the holder of 90 per cent of its ordinary shares, nor I as a 10 per cent owner had any capital and the acquisition of some would be a pleasing reward for our labours. Kudos was all very well, but hardly edible. The situation was not improved by the arrival in our list of a young officer of the Indian Army in search of a new career. He had already sold his first novel to the Viking Press in New York, and Ben Huebsch of that distinguished house brought it in proof form to Bloomsbury Street. He explained that its remarkable author, facing redundancy as a soldier, had with military precision prepared in outline thirty-two novels of which *Nightrunners of Bengal* was the first. Viking Press were confident that they had a winner to contend with and so, after reading it, were we. Thus John Masters took the book world by storm with a succession of best-sellers, to accentuate, pleas-antly enough, the problems and possibilities Michael Joseph had begun to contemplate. The eruption into our lives of Jack and Barbara Masters whenever they are around adds exuberance and colour. Success has left them both utterly unspoiled.

It is curious how, in publishing, a run of success somehow generates a momentum; the extraordinary sales of Richard Gordon attracted a succession of equivalent 'documentaries'. Good fortune and a certain diplomacy directed one of the most successful to Bloomsbury Street. Juliet O'Hea one day inquired if I knew anything about Henry Cecil, who had written a few novels of legal fiction which had been successful enough in a quiet way. I hadn't, but I said that it would be interesting if we could find someone to accomplish in the realm of law what Richard Gordon had accomplished in the realm of medicine. Of all things a tea party was being contrived by mutual friends and Henry Cecil, under his more impressive guise as His Honour Judge Leon, was to be there. Juliet arranged that I should sit next to him. All went very well. And if I were to start to relate the kindnesses and entertainments provided ever since by Harry and, later, his second wife Barbara to me in both trouble and serenity this book would never end.

On this Sunday afternoon at Chiswick over tea Harry said that he had been impressed by the displays everywhere of *Doctor in the House*. 'What a very odd coincidence,' I was able to reply, poker-faced. 'I have been thinking that you are just the man to do the same for the law. Indeed,' I added, 'I have the title for you — *Brothers-in-Law*.' Harry did not at once take to the title which had in fact come to me in my bath a few days previously, but he obviously was attracted to the idea, and being a meticulously quick worker it was not long before *Brothers-in-Law* became an accomplished fact and a best-seller, and Henry Cecil a writer of ever-increasing popularity.

Every once in a while, if a successful author has the wisdom (and the confidence) to remain with one publisher, a uniform edition becomes a possibility and few operations give more satisfaction to an author. It is interesting to wonder to what extent the popularity and standing of H. G. Wells as a writer is now influenced by his unwise and disconcerting perambulations around the publishing imprints of his day. It rules out the possibility of any uniform edition of his works until the time comes for all of them to enter the chancy arena of public domain.

It has been my good fortune to contrive five of these uniform editions, of which three contain the Michael Joseph imprint and two the Hutchinson. I like to think there is a certain aptness in their names. C. S. Forester has his Greenwich Edition; Joyce Cary his Carfax Edition; and H. E. Bates his Evensford Edition. All were alive to witness the event. Now they are not, but it is likely that these editions will carry them into the future more certainly than might otherwise be possible. In the Hutchinson list now repose the Danube Edition of Arthur Koestler and, in considerable contrast, the Lymington Edition of that pheno- menon which is Dennis Wheatley.

To continue in this abhorrent glow of righteousness, I always regret that we made less headway than we did with our Mermaid Books, which I designed with some care and I think a certain amount of ingenuity in the early '50s. There seemed then a need and thus a market for a midway stage between cloth and paper bindings. With the help of Lionel Darley and his minions at Messrs Burn we concocted, after a good many experiments, a binding of flimsy board on which was printed an attractive over- all design, the colours of which varied between title and title. The whole was then laminated and a book of some elegance and style emerged. 'And', proclaimed Charles Pick to all to whom he tried to sell them, 'they are washable.' Their price was 4s. 6d. net and I still rejoice when I come across a specimen in any library. They failed to make much impact against the increasing clamour of paperbacks and were soon overtaken by the twin demons of economics and inertia.

And so the cavorting years of the mermaid slipped by. We had no serious anxieties, except for those which every publisher is obliged to live with. The failure of a title induces an anxiety of one kind; the success, an anxiety of another kind, but still a very real one. Our record was enviable and had bestowed a certain glamour. Our list we kept to a size which permitted an attention to detail pleasing to authors and satisfying to ourselves. We lost the occasional author, but none much regretted. We did not remainder our books, but occasionally became obliged to dispose of 'copies surplus to our requirements', which conveyed a message much more acceptable to their authors. There was no reason to doubt the future and many even to welcome it. Could it be that an excess of confidence had come about? A complacency perhaps? Should I have earlier detected in myself an inclination to resent? If Michael was making plans, shouldn't we have been made more aware of them? Twenty years later it is easy to think up the questions and easy also to find their answers.

II

Extramural Activities

A RATHER premature propulsion into the wider world of the trade I owe first to Stanley Unwin and second to Geoffrey Faber. I was fortunate in my sponsors, who could hardly have differed more in either character or temperament. Sir Geoffrey Faber, as he was later to become, was too warm and sympathetic a man to be regarded quite as a father figure, but Edmond Segrave and I came to regard him as the repository of all good publishing principles, and their most enlightened spokesman as well. He possessed humour, wisdom and authority and an approach to life considerably less desiccated than that of Uncle Stanley. The Faber list was never other than distinguished, and so was the group of colleagues Geoffrey Faber gathered around him. Richard de la Mare—a son of the poet—set production standards of taste and quality which made any Faber book almost instantly recognizable. T. S. Eliot was a member of the board; and Faber's contribution to the publication of contemporary poetry was unequalled by any. There was a certain incongruity about the range of their massive list and there is some truth in the alleged comment by Rupert Hart-Davis that *How to Grow Moss on a Hard Tennis Court* a little typified what could be found only in a Faber list.

An obligation, acceptable in the book world generally, is that the trade which sustains one is entitled to some part of one's time and energies. Apart from that, my consistent experience is that a positive value is attached to any such involvement. It was in the early '40s that, on becoming a member of the Society of Bookmen, I was requested by Stanley Unwin to represent it on what was then the National Book Council. The proposed setting up of that organization had first been debated within the Society of Bookmen; and its purpose was to promote and further the wider use of books by every means it could. Its secretary was Maurice Marston, something of an anxious fusspot, but a dedicated enthusiast none the less. The funds made available by various sections of the trade were minimal and hopes of what they could accomplish have been never less than extravagant. But the National Book Council was at least a co-operative trade venture against a background of relentless individualism within which, it was said at one time, Macmillan spoke only to Murray and Murray spoke only to God. The prosperity of war and its aftermath of optimism was a heady time for such establishments as the National Book Council and a euphoria of optimism fomented plans and developments of all kinds.

The great David Roy of W. H. Smith was then chairman of the National Book Council. He was succeeded in a little while by Sydney Goldsack, aided and abetted by the authority of Geoffrey Faber who followed him. Sydney's gainful occupation was to sell the publications of Messrs Collins. He achieved this with a non-stop zeal and determination which would have exhausted most men by ten o'clock of any working morning. Sydney Goldsack was as irrepressible as he was inexhaustible, and he ignored with bland good humour the slings and arrows of occasional derision. He was an immensely kind man and I suspect a much more sensitive one than he appeared to be.

In due course the National Book Council became the National Book League, which it remains today. Whether this was good sense or good lunacy is still debated, but the doubts of those days made little headway against the enthusiasm of the enlightened. John Hadfield became the League's first director and it was he who, with Geoffrey Faber, stood within the war-time damage of 7 Albemarle Street and claimed it as the headquarters of the new League. The essence of the development from a Council to a League was to attract a public membership and a public subvention of its work on behalf of books and reading. It was a missionary activity and to be seen as such. At that time 'trade' was still a term of rather distasteful implications. The trade activities of the National Book League were routed through the back door — the tradesman's entrance; the more admirable, attracted to its charitable purposes, used the front. Inside they could find, for a pittance, many of the amenities of a club. Those whose responsibility it was to ensure that uncontaminated cash would flow to the upkeep of these new enterprises were hard put to convey to the trade on the one hand that its donations would not be devoted to providing luxuries for the members, and then to assure the public members that their monies would not be diverted to the dubious requirements of trade. The gradual acceptance of 'trade' and its contribution to the well being of 'society' has come almost by stealth. That the barriers should have existed for so long is an aspect of our century which one day will cry out for sociological investigation. Now—and it is significant as an indication—the appeals of the League, and organizations like it, can address themselves to the community at large with equal candour and conviction.

John Hadfield is almost an exact contemporary of mine. He was with Messrs Dent when Michael Joseph had to decide whom he should invite to join him in the creation of his new imprint. Not until many years later were John and I to discover that we were both contenders. John's talents are so wide in scope that for him to lose this contest was of no significance; for me it would have been catastrophic. It was the late Leonard Russell who devised and edited for Messrs Hutchinson the first *Saturday Book*, at once setting a standard extraordinarily intimidating to any successor; but in 1952, after Russell had produced ten brilliant issues, *The Saturday Book* was taken over by John Hadfield and for over twenty years, with extraordinary consistency and ingenious invention, he has produced an annual symposium which more exactly mirrors the quixotic eccentricities and fashions of our time than any other likely to be available to future historians. Indeed, it has often been John Hadfield and his *Saturday Book* that have led the way to a revival of interest in a wide variety of modes and fashions.

The National Book League could hardly have found as its first director in 1944 one who better understood its purposes and the difficulties of achieving them than John Hadfield. With panache, impeccable taste, the right contacts and discernment he entered the considerable fray.

As all these matters were pressed forward I was a rather subdued member of the National Book Council; later, under the requirements of an elaborate new constitution, I was translated into a member of the first committee of the National Book League. I remain today a vice-president and, so far as I can make out, am now the only relic with an association which leads unbroken from those formative years.

Until that time I had never, that I can recall, opened my mouth in public and was irrationally petrified by any prospect of having to do so. I remember vividly the misery and terror of my first faint utterance. It occurred to me that with plans for the League bounding forward at such a pace, it would be the moment to establish a Junior League for the encouragement of reading among children; television had not then taken hold. The moment came when this proposition required to be propounded. My presentation of the case was a complete failure. I ran out of both words and courage at the same moment. Geoffrey Faber was in the chair. 'I am sorry,' I said, 'I have forgotten the rest. Can I continue next month?'

Geoffrey Faber was followed as chairman of the League by Kenneth Lindsay, then a Member of Parliament and prominent in educational and cultural affairs. To my great astonishment Geoffrey Faber, who I rather assumed to be singularly unimpressed by my antics, contrived that I should become deputy chairman. Lindsay was the League's first non-trade chairman, which was of significance for the League because it enabled the League's public face to be seen as quite independent of the book trade and infinitely superior to it. It was not an easy period for any deputy chairman: I had to maintain the goodwill and support of an always sceptical trade, present some sort of public image in the naturally frequent absences of Kenneth Lindsay and occasionally feel obliged to remind the energetic director that funds were not inexhaustible while at the same time comforting an always anxious secretary that disaster was not in wait behind every door. I lacked diplomatic skills, was quick in irritation and thus added frequently to the frustrations of John Hadfield and to the fears of Maurice Marston, both of whom were to vanish during my term of office. John contracted a long illness and was obliged to give up his exacting and arduous responsibilities, and the pressure of events upon Maurice Marston, who was always to regret the development of the League from the cosier days of the Council, became in the end too much and he retired from the scene.

But it was during these years that I met personally and grew to know most of the publishers and a great many booksellers whose financial support it was a part of my duty to wheedle. It brought me in touch, too, with the many other cultural bodies and societies with whom John Hadfield had arranged affiliation and representation on our Council. It was a period of extraordinarily valuable experience not only for me but for the still young firm of Michael Joseph.

In 1949 I followed Kenneth Lindsay as chairman, with Sir Francis Meynell as deputy-chairman, thus achieving the alternation of a trade chairman and a public chairman which has been sustained ever since. My good fortune, although the work involved proved very great, was to be at the helm during the staging of the Festival of Britain in 1951.

This presented the League with its first great challenge and immense opportunities. It would have been readily seized by John Hadfield, but he had by this time left and we had not been fortunate in finding an adequate successor until the arrival of Herbert Howarth who splendidly bore the brunt of the Festival work. In the Festival of 1851 books had not been in evidence at all beyond a few which occupied a niche in the stairway of the great glass palace in Hyde Park. Gerald Barry was the new Festival's Director-General and he proved at once a forceful and faithful ally. There was much work to be done and endless consultations, but at the end of the day and rather to our own surprise we found the National Book League appointed as one of the four national organizations affiliated to the Festival's central authority. It represented a considerable triumph for books; and we set up a Festival committee, which I chaired, to organize and integrate the part which books were to play. The necessary funds were made available to us and I think it not unreasonable to regard the event as the League's finest hour to date. It was an immensely stimulating period and I think it must be difficult for those to whom the Festival of Britain is no more than a phrase to understand the jubilation and creative excitement which it engendered and the lasting triumph it achieved. For many years afterwards, until Sir Gerald Barry himself died, those who participated met annually for dinner on the anniversary of its opening and as the representative of the National Book League, it was always my privilege to attend.

In an event arranged during the promotional activities of the Festival I was one day invited to the roof of the Savoy Hotel to be photographed. The roof swarmed with Festival notabilities of all kinds. I was mooning around when I became aware of a gentle tapping of my shoulder. 'Do forgive me,' smiled an extremely obvious Sir Malcolm Sargent, 'but you are standing between me and the camera.' Years later, as vice-chairman of the BBC, I was the official host to a splendid orchestral party which followed an Albert Hall concert given by Russia's State Orchestra. Frank Gillard and I offered Sir Malcolm a lift in the BBC car from the Albert Hall to Maida Vale where the party was to be held. 'How very kind of you, sir,' said Sir Malcolm Sargent with almost deference, 'to be giving me a lift.' 'I am delighted,' I said, 'but I have always wanted to ask you a question and I now have the opportunity. How do you know that the third violin is actually playing?'

'By the light in his eye,' replied Sir Malcolm. 'There is no other way.'

The party was glorious and uninhibited. It was just as well that it followed and did not precede the concert. When I left, the orchestral musicians of the BBC and of Russia appeared to be exchanging shirts, as footballers do after a match. In every eye was a light.

It would be tedious to catalogue the events arranged by the League, but book exhibitions in great variety were staged up and down the land; and the finest exhibition of books ever devised was set up at the Victoria and Albert Museum as one of the main features of the Festival. By great good fortune, John Hadfield had sufficiently recovered from his illness to contrive and plan it and it remains a monument to his skill, his learning and his tenacity. The design was entrusted to Hulme Chadwick, a swash-buckling character of great ingenuity, not so well-known then but now one of the leading designers of our time and responsible among other things for a range of the extraordinarily effective garden implements manufactured and marketed by Messrs Wilkinson. Sir Norman Birkett was then president of the League, and he was unstinting in his help and encouragement. He had the slightly disconcerting habit of regarding me as his contemporary in age; but we established a close friendship with him and his marvellous Swedish wife. To see them together was a delight. He was a superb speaker and the only man I have known able to repeat a range of anecdotes in speech after speech without for a moment depressing any who had heard them all before.

The opening day of the Festival was not one to forget. There was first the Service of Dedication at St Paul's in the presence of the King and Queen, who were afterwards to make their way to the South Bank. In the evening Joan and I had been invited to the opening concert in the Festival Hall. On that morning the roads to St Paul's were closed to vehicles other than those conveying dignitaries of all kinds to the service. Joan and I had a driver; and on our way we came across a forlorn little group rather huddled on the pavement outside Bush House. One of the group was splendidly arrayed in mayoral robes and heavy-laden with chains and badge of office. The occupant looked anxious and harassed. An emissary stepped into the road and waved us to a halt. 'Can you', he asked in anxious concern, 'take the mayor of St Ives to St Paul's?' 'Surely we can,' we replied and the mayor clambered aboard. 'My town clerk lost his head,' he said. 'I've never known it happen before. It's London. The notice said "road closed to traffic", and he made me get out and sent the car away. Do I look all right?' We assured him that he looked extremely impressive and that nothing gave us greater pleasure than to have the mayor of St Ives in our care. 'All my buttons are undone,' he said, looking anxious. 'Can you, Missy,' turning to Joan, 'do up buttons?' Joan thought this might be within her powers but would have to wait until the mayor was able to stand upright. We drew up with a flourish at the steps of St Paul's. The mayor stepped out and so did Joan; she knelt, as if in an act of homage, on the pavement, and working from the bottom up safely enclosed the mayor in his robes. It made our day, splendid though it was in other respects.

On the next afternoon Gerald Barry was to come to the opening of our book exhibition at the Victoria and Albert Museum by Norman Birkett. At this ceremony the government was represented by the Lord Chancellor, Viscount Jowitt, who made one of far too many speeches. The assemblage was distinguished and the hall was packed. I was obliged to take the chair and make a speech of inordinate length, thanking all who had contributed to the occasion and announcing that both Leigh Ashton (then Curator of the Victoria and Albert Museum and as such our host) and Gerald Barry had been made Honorary Life Members of the N.B.L. for their pains. The proceedings would have been enlivened had I felt able to refer to the splenetic drama that occurred earlier when Leigh Ashton took violent exception to the splendid busts specially commissioned from the distinguished sculptor Barney Seale to adorn the exhibition. Leigh Ashton seemed prepared to throw the books, the busts and all connected with the N.B.L. into the Cromwell Road and it required much diplomacy to restrain him.

It seems a longish step from the Festival of Britain to a first meeting with Captain Robert Maxwell, but it is one that needs to be taken. We had all been enjoined, especially by Sir Stanley Unwin and Sydney Goldsack, to regard the gallant captain as a man of destiny with a mission to save the great wholesale book house of Messrs Simpkin Marshall then a-totter on the brink. Captain Maxwell not only wanted it, but knew what he wanted it for and what he could accomplish with and for it, if only recalcitrant publishers would agree to extend its credit and give it more advantageous terms. To this end we were picked off one by one until finally my turn came to be bidden by Mr Maxwell to lunch. I went alone to a lush establishment in Park Lane. With the captain was an old Simpkin acquaintance known to me as little Mr Minshull, an endearing book-trade character in perpetual battle with his false teeth. Mr Maxwell extended his hand and switched on his charm. 'With a name like yours,' he said by way of greeting, 'do you come from Eastern Germany or Poland?' I confessed that I came from neither. 'But your name is Lutski isn't it?' he asked. 'Not actually,' I said.

I hadn't then, and I haven't now, any objection to those emanating from either Eastern Germany or Poland, but I found myself unable to warm towards the personality of Mr Maxwell, and I fancy he detected a certain reserve. I had come to the lunch by bus from Bloomsbury Street. It was a good lunch but I felt somehow impelled to damn the consequences and return to the office by taxi. My letter of thanks was sincere, but I had to regret that we felt unable either to extend our credit beyond what was normal to Messrs Simpkin Marshall or to proffer terms more advantageous than in the past. A little while later they were bankrupt.

An interesting assignment that somehow came my way was an invitation from the Nuffield Foundation to investigate on their behalf the publication of the journals of learned societies, many of which were encountering difficulties. It was an area totally new to me and far removed from a sphere where less tutored minds were inclined to obey the promptings of hunch. Before me now are the yellowing pages of some sixty-seven paragraphs conveying the pith in pompous prose of my prognostications.

I looked into the practices and procedures of some thirty learned societies, and their disarray some twenty years ago was awesome. Costs even then were escalating in a way which made nonsense of publishing budgets, and little headway had been made in reproduction of material other than by expensive letter-press. The nature of the exercise, in most cases, required minimal printing quantities and yet the impact of such journals was often of the highest potential throughout the world. That the majority of journals were able to appear at all was due entirely to the dedicated clerical labours of some of the most brilliant minds in the land. 'It should be forgiven a commercial publisher,' runs paragraph 13 of my fading testimony,

> reared in the hurly-burly of jungle law, if he imagined it easy to discover in the world of learned journals, a vast inefficiency and extravagance in administration, production and distribution. In point of fact no assumption could have proved more false, and it is the commercial publisher who must bow in homage. Is it, for instance, necessary to pay authors? To pay rent? To pay editors? To pay anyone?

That was about the size of it; and as I groped my way into the fascinating highways and byways of learning I became increasingly aware that the latent possibilities had already found nourishment in the entrepreneurial fancies of another mind whose scent seemed somehow familiar. And there, sure enough, he was — Captain Robert Maxwell, with all his expansive competence, laying the foundations of his Pergamon Press and knowing well the quality of minds employed on the time-absorbing chores of keeping journals of the greatest importance in circulation.

At the end of the day I was to advocate the creation of some sort of co-operative administration or association of learned journals. I was never aware that the slightest attention was paid to any point that I made until literally the other day. Out of the blue from one of the newer universities arrived a letter from one eminent in his scholarly discipline, thanking me for the great benefits which had derived from my report over the years.

The publishing year is enlivened by its educative gallivants. Annually comes the conference of the Booksellers Association, to which publishers are personally invited, and the holiday towns in which they take place ring with the merriment of the book trade at play. It is the conviviality and the informal meeting with friends and acquaintances which provide as much, if not more, justification for the event than the solemnity of solemn resolutions solemnly arrived at. At least so it was in that span of years which followed the war and which may come to be regarded as the Years of Hope. To Bournemouth we went, and to Scarborough and Folkestone and Gleneagles and Thurlestone and Blackpool, in our hundreds, assembling at our hotels, pinning on our badges and ensuring that the allocated bundles of tickets would take us to this, that and the other. The reigning presidents would be seen in frequent consultation and harried organizers would ensure that Tommy Joy of Hatchards would know what was expected of him at half past three. It was then the annual lubrication of the trade, which produced little by way of agreement but ensured that disagreement would be pleasantly arrived at.

Rather larger and grander and very much more expensive, but properly 'allowable', were the International Publishers' conferences, held then every third year, but now less frequently. Sir Stanley Unwin was their advocate and their inspiration and none has been the same since his departure from the scene. Those involved are those in the main who wish to be involved and bestride the changing scene with declarations of great significance and in many languages. To Florence we all went in high festivity after the war and then Vienna, Washington, Amsterdam and Paris. State receptions, concerts, operas, outings, and all the rest, in company with hundreds upon hundreds of publishers with their wives, and their catalogues listing by the hundred thousand the books currently deluging the world or about to do so.

It was from Florence that the entire assemblage entrained for Rome to be privately blessed by the Pope. Privacy was not so accurate a connotation as the publishers of the world were led to expect. On the appointed hour we joined an excited and fervent throng of thousands. They clambered upon their chairs and shouted and clapped and stamped and cheered as if at Wembley waiting to be led in community song by Tommy Steele. His Holiness the Pope appeared on his throne, held aloft by stalwarts. Resplendent attendants seemed jostled by tough civilian thugs assumed to be conversant with the requirements of security. The Blessing appeared to be indiscriminate. The contest — for so it seemed to be — having ended, we embussed and presently Stanley Unwin came to the empty seat beside me. 'Well, Sir Stanley,' I asked, 'did you have a nice little talk with the Pope?' He looked rather sharply at me. 'No, no, Lusty, I didn't. You see, he knows me, so I pushed one or two of the others forward.'

The most resplendent figure in Vienna was Alfred Knopf. Always a clear replica of a Habsburg, he had on this occasion cultivated his side-whiskers to even greater splendour. He and Blanche had invited us to lunch and we were walking with Alfred back to his hotel after a morning session. It was an impressive performance. Various statues, apparently of Alfred, lined the route. Policemen on traffic duty paled and halted all traffic to enable so splendid an emperor to cross the road. Alfred would nod in regal acceptance of such tribute. We arrived at the hotel and there Blanche awaited us at a table in an open area around the entrance.

Loyal Austrians, thinking some lunch-time *coup* had restored the dynasty to power, would incline their heads and old-time courtiers would almost swoon. A stoutish little man would, every moment, or so, emerge from the hotel, obviously awaiting another regal guest. 'More royalty coming,' I said to Emperor Alfred. 'How do you know?' he inquired. 'Well,' I explained, 'that little man there, rushing in and out. He must be the manager and he is on tenterhooks.' Alfred inspected him. 'You bloody fool,' he said, 'that's George Weidenfeld.' I had never seen him before.

Later I was to see him again. On my return to Hutchinson I found that we represented Messrs Weidenfeld in Australia and marketed their books there. Bidden to a *Spectator* party one November evening, I saw George Weidenfeld standing there, for a brief second on his own. I approached him and introduced myself and hoped our efforts on his behalf in Australia were to his liking. 'Ah,' he said, 'it would be nice to meet and talk. Come and lunch with me in April.' I was reminded of a distinguished American publisher who was irritated by Victor Gollancz's habit of making a precise appointment many months ahead. 'My dear Victor,' he replied to one such proposal, 'I am very sorry, but I have to go to a funeral on that day.' Publishing is a way of life, a continual process of involvement which rules out the compartmental divisions so often regarded as civilized requirements. But I would not myself want it otherwise.

An outing which contained many characteristics of a Marx Brothers extravaganza, but which achieved none the less a most considerable success, was the publishing mission sent to Japan in the autumn of 1968. It was brilliantly led by John Brown, Publisher to the Oxford University Press. His previous experience of the Japanese had been as a prisoner of war, and it is doubtful if he then managed to envisage in his future (if any future at all could be envisaged) leading a deputation of fellow publishers seeking to promote the sale of British books in a territory considerably dominated by the Americans. It was as stern and relentless a test of courage and character as could be devised but none of us who knew his story and watched him could detect a hint of stress at any moment.

A major point in our briefing was the absolute necessity of taking as many bottles of whisky with us as ingenuity could find space for. It appeared that the presentation of a bottle was the prerequisite of every meeting. Laden with bottles draped in profusion around ourselves and our luggage and already assuming a monstrous nuisance, members of the mission assembled at London Airport for departure to Bangkok, where we would spend a night. As these things go we were a 'high-powered' lot. We had been advised to have formal visiting cards printed in profusion to scatter throughout Japan as for a paper-chase. 'They expect it,' we were told.

Our first overnight stop, some twenty-four flying hours distant, was Bangkok. Two members of the mission were in some trouble from the start. Alan Hill, then the ebullient managing director of Messrs Heinemann's thriving educational activities and now of the whole Heinemann group, had developed an overnight pile. His first, he confided. His doctor had prescribed as little sitting as possible which is an inconvenient regimen for a Boeing 707. Tom Rosenthal had gout and required a staff of immense proportions which he utilized throughout the tour. A large man with a determined gait, gout or not, he looked always to me as Moses leading his people into, rather than out of, the wilderness.

With our bottles of whisky pretty well intact, but with their cellophanic wrappings in disrepair, we arrived at Bangkok and its Oriental Hotel. The Floating Market required our attention and for half the mission I negotiated a price with the owner of a motor launch which seemed markedly cheaper than the rest. The moment of settlement, after a breakdown in mid-river, revealed the quotation as per head and not per launch. Graham Greene of Messrs Cape and Max Reinhardt of The Bodley Head had gone elsewhere for massage and refreshment and returned, as they were wont to do for the next fortnight, with lurid tales of the Orient and its ways. Alan Hill had taken an instant dislike to his allotted room, which again was to become a theme song over the next two weeks. It was not tiresome; it was simply a part of the life-pattern (so called nowadays) of Alan Hill.

Still with bottles intact we next morning boarded another plane for Tokyo by way of Hong Kong, Formosa and Osaka. The bombing over the Mekong Delta had stopped on that morning of November 1st. At Hong Kong a Mr Fuk Now attracted attention as one willing to exchange monies. André Deutsch, a member of the mission, was somehow and naturally in Tokyo ahead of us. He appeared at the airport waving a flag. By this time most of the whisky bottles had discarded their wrappings and required to be cuddled and coddled about us.

Still a governor of the BBC, news of my arrival had reached NBK, the Japanese equivalent of the BBC. Three of their officials took instant charge of me at the airport and bundled me into a car. It was as well, for the other members of the mission were soon in trouble. Alan Hill arrived at the hotel an hour late, clutching his luggage and very hot. He had decided to walk. His bottles had survived the ordeal.

The British Council then took solemn charge of us. They had not heard of the imperative necessity for whisky. Its presentation would prove difficult during the meetings and engagements arranged for us. Perhaps it would be as well to drink it ourselves? The Imperial Hotel was in the process of rebuilding. None the less its efficiency, service and facilities were outside the experience of most Westerners. A nightly massage became the requirement of every member of the mission. As long as such was vouched for by Messrs Greene and Reinhardt it was in order. At any hour a charming Japanese masseuse would arrive with a tin of Western baby powder. Her ministrations were gentle, deft and incredibly relaxing. The agonizing discomfort of Geisha parties required the alleviation of massage if nothing else. To sit cross-legged on the floor for some three hours, sipping *sake* and pecking at tidbits while playing footling games with matchsticks and a bespectacled Geisha girl in her late forties was as dedicated a service to the cause of books as ever I have made. Occasionally a host, overcome by an excess of *sake*, would be carried out. Its effect on us was not discernible. Communication was not easy. Unless in English, it was quite impossible. To become lost was easy and a thoughtful Embassy issued cards bearing their address and that of the Imperial Hotel. If lost, kindly return to one or the other.

They were in grievous error, but for some reason the Japanese retained a conviction that I was the oldest member of the party. They defer to the aged and treat them with the utmost respect and consideration. Were I to descend a step two Japanese would take instant possession of an arm apiece and would not relinquish me until descent was achieved. Each would bow and so would I. My staunch supporter was a delightful Mrs Kitamoura who worked with Hutchinson's Japanese agent. She was assiduous in attentions and conducted me with exquisite charm through the complications of shopping and the visitation of shrines she felt it necessary for me to see. 'Dear and beloved gentleman,' she was later to write to me, 'I hope you are still in the mood.'

There was an immense attractiveness about at any rate the superficialities of the Japanese way of life, so utterly different from our own. Their women I thought spectacular in their beauty, charm and grace. Their men much less so and but for the discipline of enforced courtesies at almost every turn, very much less so. We were made impressively welcome, and there was a clear desire to find an alternative English to that so assiduously purveyed by the Americans. I was fortunate to have the additional contact with broadcasting and spent a day of extraordinary interest with the executives of NBK. Their computerized programming of both radio and television was one of the most terrifying of Orwellian nightmares. 'What happens', I asked 'when some urgent change is required?' 'It does not like it,' they replied.

Imperturbable throughout, John Brown led the mission with tact and discernment. We met in his majestic apartment each morning for our briefing, often attended by anxious members of the British Council, a little apprehensive of apparent frivolity. Slowly we drank the whisky so carefully lumbered from Heathrow. A Geisha girl poured soup over Alan Hill's sock and this apparently threatened instant pneumonia. We sped in the luxury of the 'bullet express' to Osaka and Kyoto in which one was not surprised to hear by loud-speaker that Mr André Deutsch was wanted on the telephone. He had made careful arrangements with a friend in Tokyo. At a gigantic night-club some two thousand hostesses administered their charms until summoned by an electronic bleep concealed about them to report for other duties. Messrs Greene, Reinhardt and Deutsch returned from an evening of inquiry in chastened mood. They had been conducted to some doubtful club to be quickly surrounded by Geisha girls, who are normally of such impeccable propriety as to be unbearable, only to find that these were not girls at all but young men. Innumerable cups of tea were drunk in the cause of books; our visiting cards we showered around us; off came our shoes a thousand times a day; Alan Hill fell asleep during a briefing of remarkable candour by His Excellency the British Ambassador and nearly toppled from his chair. My own strange idiosyncrasy, which added to the Marxian climate, was to develop a previously subdued and unexpressed hankering for banana fritters which even the ingenuity of André Deutsch failed to explain to my night-club hostess. Her shrill 'bleep' soon summoned her to a less demanding client. After a fortnight we dispersed, many to further outposts of the English language, but I to Hampstead via Anchorage which persuaded me that, despite all, I would sooner live by books than by oil.

12
Days of Dilemma

I T is too easy for hindsight to suggest the wiser way of handling
a difficult situation. A glimpse just five minutes ahead would
so often be enough. The what-might-have-been is a continuing debate and a fruitless one as well. At the beginning of 1954
or thereabouts certain tensions began to become apparent in
26 Bloomsbury Street. Slow in coming, they were beginning to
affect all our attitudes. A greater wisdom would have detected
them sooner and then at least they could have been diverted into a
narrower channel. For many years Michael Joseph had been
only occasionally in the office, and in day-to-day executive activities had played little part. In the running of the office I had been
given a free hand and equally so editorially, although prudence,
if nothing else, required consultation on any major point. But
prudence can become lax and so can tact. We were doing quite
exceptionally well and it was understandable that a man of
Michael's temperament should develop some feelings of resentment. He never enjoyed publishing occasions or trade affairs,
but he liked recognition. He wanted, as do so many of us, the
best of both worlds. On my part I think it was understandable,
although not creditable, to feel an equal resentment when Michael
began again to assert himself. It was, however, 90 per cent
Michael's firm. That I could have owned a much larger proportion if Michael's instructions in 1939 had been followed was
never a factor. We had a first-rate staff, with Peter Hebdon and
Charles Pick running in harness as trade manager and sales
manager. The American publishers, now flocking over in
droves, in the main had known Michael better than they knew
me, but since he was so seldom in London they soon became

more accustomed to my face, as did others.

It was within this context that Michael brooded on what should be done and came to the conclusion that the obvious step was to sell the company. It was not a prospect I greatly cared for, but the acquisition of a modest capital benefit was as attractive to me as it was to Michael. This became his preoccupation and he realized that it was necessary for him to discard the image of a benign observer and assert himself in the owner's suite.

It was I, in fact, who put him in touch with Illustrated Newspapers, in due course to become our proprietors. Following the destruction of our Plymouth printers in the early part of the war I had been put in contact with Robert Paterson, who was at that time in charge of a firm of printers in Kent. It was a stroke of exceptional good fortune for both of us. Tonbridge Printers became suddenly assured of a substantial flow of work and, barring accidents, we could rely on a service far more efficient and rapid than would have been possible had we, as a consequence of the bombing, been obliged to farm our work around. Tonbridge Printers, from that time forward, were to print the substantial part of the Joseph output and I worked in the greatest harmony with Robert Paterson over the years. In due course Tonbridge Printers were acquired by the big London firm of Keliher, Hudson and Kearn and, on the retirement of Edward Keliher, Robert Paterson became their managing director. Among the larger of their customers were Illustrated Newspapers Ltd, themselves a part of the great Ellerman empire. The sun had begun its rise upon the age of takeovers and Michael Joseph had begun his explorations in it. One of his occasionally disturbing assumptions was that while rumour, gossip and speculation might attend the perambulations of others, he was accorded immunity from such. This was not so and our fears grew as the ogres about to devour us became ever more fearful. Michael was not a communicative man on such occasions but he would occasionally divulge some figure or other from his everlasting calculations which I thought greatly undervalued the company. Robert Paterson knew that Illustrated Newspapers were prowling around their world, and reflecting that the devil one knew might be more agreeable to work with than the devil one didn't, we agreed to put our 'principals' in touch. At no time was any sort of gratitude expressed for this initiative and as negotiations proceeded on their tortuous course I was hardly consulted at all.

It was around this time that other rumours began to circulate. They were to the effect that Derek Verschoyle was to join us to help Michael Joseph in his editorial labours. When this was put to me by my friend Graham Watson of Curtis Brown I flatly denied it. It seemed to me totally incredible that Michael should take such a step without consultation of any kind. But so it was.

Derek Verschoyle, who had once been in the Foreign Office, had floated around the periphery of the book world for some years. He had a certain dilettante charm, knew his way around and managed always to give the impression that few affairs of state were settled without prior consultation with him. He had worked on the *Spectator*, did a certain amount of reviewing and had just come to the end of a catastrophic spell of publishing under his own imprint. His most notable book had been entitled *Famous Balls*. There was no likelihood whatever that a Joseph/Verschoyle relationship would work much better than a Lusty/Verschoyle one would, and his presence would be much resented in an office whose senior members knew very much more about Derek Verschoyle than Michael did. I thus confronted Michael and we had a flaming row. He flatly denied at one point that I had any editorial standing in the office and it was time somebody came who knew a good book from a bad one. I thereupon rummaged around and by great good fortune managed to find Michael's original letter of appointment to me in 1935, which had been typed by Juliet O'Hea. I was to be the new firm's editorial and production manager. He gazed upon it for some moments. 'How extremely foolish of you to produce this,' he said. I was intensely angry, but realized suddenly that I was near to tears and to my even greater astonishment saw that Michael was too. At this point our fortune, taken rather literally at the flood, could have led on.

The one typical contribution made by Verschoyle to our list was the memoirs of the Duchess of Windsor. This may or may not have been a good book but it was never a Michael Joseph book and all my colleagues, with me, were both astounded and depressed. Verschoyle of course was exuberant and Michael, in his current form, much gratified.

The end of the Verschoyle affair came rather more quickly than even I had anticipated. Michael admitted his error and would I please be so kind as somehow to keep Verschoyle busy. There was little that I could do and within a short time Derek Verschoyle was on his rather melancholy way. He was a sad man, though likeable and with many talents. Success eluded him all along the line and continued to do so until he died.

Finally the sale to Illustrated Newspapers went through. Documents were signed, champagne was drunk, money was paid into the bank and a certain *bonhomie* was established. Our new masters were agreeable people but I had suspected that life would be different and so it was. Michael found it right to demonstrate the rigidity of his new control by a number of rather childish measures and these bothered me more than they should have done. They also disturbed Peter Hebdon and Charles Pick to the extent that they came in deputation to me and suggested I should leave and set up shop on my own, and they would join me. But this was not an acceptable proposition and I had no intention of doing anything other than riding out the situation which I thought would sooner or later and somehow become resolved between Michael Joseph and myself. It was the kind of campaign of which I knew Michael would one day tire.

It was at this unhappy juncture that I received a telephone call from one R. A. Holt of whom I had never heard. He thought that I might remember his father who was not only Walter Hutchinson's brother-in-law but his lawyer as well. Could he come and see me in confidence? I find it very difficult to resist seeing anybody in conspiratorial circumstances and Holt duly appeared in 26 Bloomsbury Street. As I knew, Mr Walter had died a few years previously and Mrs Webb was doing a quite remarkable job in keeping the still ramshackle empire in being. It had been widely assumed that some sort of collapse might come about and even before Walter died there had been anxious discussions within the Publishers Association of the implications to the whole trade of a possible failure by so large a member of it. What Mr Holt had to tell me was that the Hutchinson board, of which he was a member, were anxious to find a successor to

Mrs Webb who was nearing the age of retirement. He thought I might be able to tell them something about a Mr Verschoyle whose application was bing considered. Did I think that Mr Verschoyle could lead the publishing side of the business into the future? I still retained an affection for the place and felt that this as much as honesty required me to express my doubts. Mr Holt, who seemed to me a pleasant young man, did not appear surprised. As he rose to leave he said conversationally that he wished I was free to return. I laughed and said I couldn't do that and in any event I had a contract with my new employers. Would it be any good if they were to approach me, he asked; it's a free world, was my reply; and he departed. I gave this little further thought, but a certain new dimension was given to my current discontent. As a strategist I lack patience, and the more necessary that ingredient the less I have. It is a viciously destructive circle.

It was not long before Holt returned to battle. Would I care to have lunch at the Savoy with him and with Mr Walter's widow, who was then chairman of the company? Again a temptation difficult to resist, and to the Savoy I went. A rosy picture was painted and a flattering prospect. Far from collapsing it appeared that the whole operation was now booming — publishing and printing alike. The problems bequeathed by Walter had been overcome and what they wanted was someone who could reshape their pattern for the future and lead them further into the promised land. It was what can be properly termed 'a challenge'.

It hit me at a time of considerable anxiety; I was forty-five and if ever I were to make a change, now it could be done but in a year or so it would be too late. It was not the sort of challenge I wanted, nor had I sought it. But I knew well enough that if I were not to confront it, my future with Michael Joseph would be inevitably less easy. I would be in frequent revolt against my own timidity. Every molehill would become not a mountain but an Everest.

I should, of course, have put the whole problem to Michael. It was a chance to lay every card on the table. I think now that it would have brought us both to our senses, for there in fact existed between us a deeper understanding than either of us ever cared to admit. We could have reached a solution together within minutes. Of this I am sure. It was on my part a catastrophic error, from which almost certainly stemmed Michael Joseph's bitter campaign of denigration and hostility which eventually became demented and did far more damage to himself and to the one able lieutenant who aided him than ever it did to me. But even this hurricane of abuse would have blown itself out. Indeed, there were signs that it was doing so when quite suddenly he died. For all the time that I had known him he suffered from a gastric ulcer. Unfortunately no one who knew him ever took it over-seriously for it was as convenient an excuse for avoiding an unwelcome activity as could be devised. It had seemed always just a part of the Michael Joseph make-up. Anxiety in the main was awakened more by the consultants of one kind and another whose advice he sought and often conflicting treatments he followed. I once found him extracting wax from his ear with a hairpin. I have a respect for ears and inquired what on earth he thought he was doing. 'Doctor so-and-so told me to,' he said.

Michael Joseph was a brilliant and accomplished man, but never an easy one to know. Paranoiacally sensitive to his own hurts, he was curiously unthinking towards others. He quite seriously maintained that he had a more sensitive skin than the general run of mankind. He enjoyed the company of women more than the company of men. He was to some extent a lonely man and would brood for days on end, hardly speaking at all. He had a host of acquaintances but few close friends. He was married three times: first to Hermione Gingold; second to Edna Frost, a marvellously nice women of great charm and character who died soon after the war; and third to Anthea Hodson, who was his first secretary on his return to the office and upon whom fell the domestic brunt of all our problems. She triumphed all along the line and continues to do so still. Each marriage produced its off-spring and the complications of manœuvre would daunt any but Anthea's extraordinary clarity and warmth of mind.

Not long after the death of Edna, my wife Joan was ill, although not seriously. Michael was very fond of her and for some reason deeply disturbed. 'We have run parallel in so many ways, Bob,' he said, 'I hope you are never going to lose Joan as I have lost Edna.' It was a remark unlike any other he had ever made. I felt curiously apprehensive and was indeed to remember it when it exactly came about. We were so very nearly in accord.

Consultations developed with Hutchinson. Lawyers and accountants got together on a contract undeterred, it seemed, by one which already existed between the new proprietors of Michael Joseph and myself. I hired an accountant to poke his nose into the affairs of Messrs Hutchinson, rather hoping that he might emerge with red flags aloft. I consulted Stanley Unwin, who thought on balance I should make the move although he did not welcome it and I must be sure to open the post every morning. I put the problem to Geoffrey Faber over lunch. He had come from a wedding and was in full regalia. He looked solemn and worried and thought I should not go. 'I do not like them,' he said. The next day he wrote to say that he had confided in his wife Enid, who thought his advice had been bad. He too now thought I should go. I asked the view of Douglas Black, who at that time carried the great American firm of Doubleday upon his shoulders. He offered his help and later when I had launched the Hutchinson 'bull', he sent me a beauty in Lalique glass from Paris. With Edmond Segrave and Allen Lane I was in close touch. The terms of the contract looked fine at the time. It was just a pity that no one seems to have contemplated inflation with any seriousness. It was hardly surprising that rumours began to circulate in the village. Joan and I went off to an International Publishers' conference in Florence. It was almost the first one to follow the war and was splendid in the extreme. So splendid in fact that the Italian Publishers Association found itself in grave financial difficulties after it was over. There were more rumours in Florence and when we returned to London they had strengthened and were forcing the pace of events.

For better or worse the decision was made. I formally notified the new chairman of Michael Joseph Ltd that I wished to terminate my contract. It was a dotty way of doing it. There would still have been time for second thoughts had I gone instead to Michael. But the fat was in the fire and charity, if nothing else, requires a curtain to fall upon the unhappy scene.

But one final point requires to be made. It has been often put to me that I was not followed to Hutchinson by a succession of Michael Joseph authors. Firstly, I would not have so acted. Most of them were of course, and remained, close personal friends. I was sad to break my link with their writing. Michael Joseph and I never bickered over authors; neither of us claimed them as personal editorial possessions nor ever would. The operation of publishing is collective. The day of the editor has been the day of damnation. Only when an editor begins to say 'we' has wisdom entered his soul. Secondly, the terms of an agreement between my old and my new employers debarred Hutchinson for a number of years from publishing any author currently in the Joseph list. It was an unnecessary stipulation and would not, I think, have been sustained in any court of law. Thirdly, and most important of all, they were happy enough where they were.

For myself I felt as a professional footballer must on being switched from one team to another with a price on his head. From a point somewhere along the line I had ceased to be in control of events. I had very quickly to institute, as it were, a search for myself. I hoped very much that I was not so lost as I felt.

13
A Cold Plunge

THE details of the fifteen-year contract with Hutchinson I left in the shrewd and humane hands of Kenneth Ewart of Messrs Field Roscoe, then in Bedford Square. He was an admirable man and an admirable lawyer who operated always in high good humour, with common sense and a refreshing absence of legal pomposity. He retained always the right to be dogged and tough and his death within the next few years deprived many of a wise and shrewd counsellor. As contracts go it was a good one, although I am not convinced that hindsight would persuade me to sign another. If the climate is right, they should not be necessary; if it sours, they are seldom kept. I was to be managing director of the Hutchinson publishing enterprises and a director of the holding company which shortly came into being as Hutchinson Ltd. I wanted nothing to do with the Hutchinson Printing Trust, apart from the obvious requirement of being its best customer. Having watched Mr Walter in the early 1930s buy the next six manuscripts to hand when notified that his compositors were idle, I developed an early aversion to publishing being linked financially with printing. As with that footballer switching teams, a transfer fee was requested by the new proprietors of Michael Joseph which Hutchinson paid without demur. It had not occurred to me that I required a driver as well as a car, but Kenneth Ewart insisted that it was a necessary provision. It was to prove so convenient over the years that the deprivation on retirement is one of the most hard to bear. The only factor not much considered in 1955 was the possibility of serious inflation. My contract failed to take note of it and a salary which seemed attractive enough in 1955 had become less so when still adhered to in the 1970s.

Finally the formalities and discussions came to their end and signatures were applied to the documents which for better or for worse, for richer or for poorer, were to return me to the fold from which I had so thankfully escaped just twenty-one years before. Since that time I had neither entered a Hutchinson office nor read a Hutchinson book. Mr Holt, who had instigated and negotiated the solemnization of contract, invited me to Rules where champagne was consumed.

There was an early and amusing disappointment. It had not been considered appropriate during the negotiations that I should enter the Hutchinson office which I assumed still to be in that great mansion in Stratford Place, once called Derby House, but translated to Hutchinson when Mr Walter acquired it mainly to house his national gallery of sporting prints, but also to accommodate his companies in the bedrooms of the upper floors. My contract required me to live within five miles of the office and it occurred to me that a managing director's penthouse atop the servants' quarters would agreeably meet this requirement. 'But', said Edmond Segrave, rummaging about his desk to unearth a Hutchinson letter, 'they are no longer in Hutchinson House. I think they moved to Portland Place.' 'That's not too bad,' I said. Edmond took another look at the letter. 'No, it's not Portland Place. It's Great Portland Street. Now I come to think of it, they are in a block of flats over my bank.'

They were not, in fact, bad offices, occupying one complete floor of a substantial block of one-time flats. Edmond Segrave's bank was indeed below and so were a post office and a garage. They were, however, completely impersonal and not even a tatty collection of furniture salvaged from Paternoster Row was able to bestow character. My penthouse dreams faded in the presence of a reality both daunting and bewildering and yet shot with an excitement which could only derive from the morning, over a quarter of a century ago, when I had turned up at Paternoster Row to 'help Mr Lunn a lot'. Without the experience of those years I, at any rate, would have found the task now ahead utterly beyond my powers. Mrs Webb was retiring at the end of the year and her equanimity seemed never disturbed through what, for her, must have been a few difficult months of stress and doubt. I had not seen her in all the intervening years and in her eyes I must have seemed still the raw recruit she had once so kindly shielded from the wrath of her beloved Mr Walter.

In the month that elapsed between my departure from Blooms-bury Street and my immersion in Great Portland Street, Allen Lane loaned me his flat in Whitehall Court and to it, one by one, I summoned the current Hutchinson executives. A surprising number of them had been known to me in Paternoster Row. All I think were to some extent apprehensive but none the less warm in their welcome. Structurally, the publishing operation was much as I remembered it: an enormous number of imprints engaged in more or less competitive publishing; and those, such as Rider, which had possessed some identity, had lost it. Rider had at one time a unique list, dealing with the occult, Eastern religions and the like. Now it was publishing such titles as *I Was Monty's Double*, *Israel Thy Neighbour* and *An American in Europe*. Each imprint had its manager who dealt directly with Mrs Webb and had little converse with his colleagues. Indeed, I was able to effect an introduction or two. The production department was responsible to all imprints and for ensuring that some six hundred titles a year appeared in orderly, if not integrated, procession. In 1928 I had never been able to ascertain quite how it was all done and what sort of machine it was that on the whole seemed to work. I was even less able to find the answer at the end of 1955. There appeared to be no consultation other than with Mrs Webb; there was no planning other than that imposed by Mrs Webb; there was no authority other than that exerted by Mrs. Webb. There was certainly a relaxation in the climate obviously attributable to the absence of Mr Walter. I confided my perplexities to Edmond Segrave. 'I have always thought', he said, 'that somewhere at Hutchinson is the machinery of a Rolls Royce which has never yet found a driver.'

Many of the authors I remembered had died, but a great many had not and had remained with the firm through thick and thin with that curious brand of loyalty which somehow Hutchinson has always managed to inspire. The most shining star in their firmament was Dennis Wheatley, who only in recent years is becoming a little grudgingly recognized as one of the most extraordinary literary phenomena known to the English language. It has been a spectacle of the greatest interest to watch, and the warmth of his friendship to me over the years of his enhancing status has been one of the most agreeable aspects of the last seventeen years as his publisher. When I left Paternoster Row in 1935 Dennis Wheatley had published his first two novels. Both had proved highly successful. Over the next twenty-one years I hardly saw him, but was aware of a prodigality of output and an extreme loyalty to his publisher. No author with a continuing procession of best-sellers is left for long unaware that a welcome awaits him in other places. I knew very well that the path taken by Dennis Wheatley was strewn with proffered contracts of the greatest attraction.

I was, to be candid, a little alarmed by the prospect of Dennis Wheatley. I had heard that he was not all that easy to deal with and that his contract empowered him a voice in certain aspects of publishing where I think an author is better muted. I found that every novel he had written from *The Forbidden Territory* onwards was still in print and, what was more, still selling. It was incredible after twenty-one years but nothing like so incredible as it remains after another twenty. The same can still be said. Dennis Wheatley —virtually the whole of Dennis Wheatley—is never out of print and never stops selling. *Forbidden Territory*, written for readers of 1932, has the same appeal to readers of 1975. I think there can have been nothing like it during the lifetime of any author. He is a supreme story-teller. He has no illusions about his writing; no pretence. Those who for years derided, now cheer.

I need have had no fear. Dennis came early to meet me and bid me welcome. Rightly watchful and never hesitant to probe and question, some future historian examining the files might deduce that Wheatley was a troublesome and querulous author. Nothing could be more contrary to the truth, and few authors known to me have more readily listened to one's story and been more ready to accept it. Despite the glittering prospects dangled before him by envious competitors, Dennis Wheatley has never swerved in his allegiance to Hutchinson; and, although he has I think been wise, it cannot always have been easy.

August has been the traditional month for a new Wheatley. Around the close of every year he would call upon me, deliver two copies of his new manuscript and we would lunch together. His research is always meticulous and exacting. His references are voluminous in the extreme and always neatly filed. He is a collector of bits and pieces on every journey that he takes and he has tons of them against the day he needs one. Among all these tons he will know exactly where to look. He was not an author I wished to offend on my return to Hutchinson.

There were others. Philip Gibbs was still producing his novel every year; and Frank Swinnerton, mercifully still with us, was growing younger as his contemporaries grew older. Of younger writers there were Anthony Glyn and Gabriel Fielding and Dannie Abse. But I missed the climate of editorial excitement which persisted in Bloomsbury Street and which I thought should by one means or another become an ingredient in the metabolism of Great Portland Street.

By the beginning of September the first objectives were fairly clear in my mind and I thought it would be helpful all round if they could be achieved with some speed. Mrs Webb was to be in residence until the end of the year and I was given a small room equipped as no Hutchinson office in my recollection had ever been equipped before. There was a handsome new mahogany desk with a leather-coated swivel chair behind it. The floor had a carpet and there was a comfortable chair for visitors. Having assured herself of my comfort Mrs Webb left me to my own devices. 'What', I thought, feeling rather lonely, 'do I do now?' The only possession I had brought with me was my nine-inch ruler. It seemed somehow an inadequate instrument with which to control an organization publishing around three new books every working day. My brief-bag, I thought, should be stuffed with schedules and lists and graphs and balance sheets. It had nothing in it at all. The drawers of the new desk were locked and the keys were still with Mr Maple round the corner.

There came a knock on the door and a friendly face appeared. It was Mrs Webb's daughter Eileen whom I had not seen since the days of Selwyn & Blount. Would I like to be taken on a tour? From each side of the corridor which formed a rectangle enclosing a complete floor of the massive building, offices in a variety of sizes were arranged in no apparent order. A jam-jar label affixed to each door announced either the occupant of the room or the imprint managed within it. Feeling, I thought, a good deal more apprehensive than the natives, I made what I hoped were appropriate comments. The business of publishing went on around me. I wondered how long it might be before I again felt involved. The first day, when it came to its end, had not been eventful. I had waited for something to happen before being driven to the conclusion that nothing would unless I initiated it.

During the month, we had moved back to London from Cobham and had been lucky to find a 'duplex' apartment in Knightsbridge overlooking Hyde Park. The provision of a chauffeur to drive me thither provided a first lesson in the corruptivity of power. At first I was timid and embarrassed and crept into the car hoping not to be seen by any friend or acquaintance. I made polite conversation with my driver and apologized for any inconvenience I might cause him. 'Will it suit you to pick me up at five forty-five?' In less than a week I was bellowing from the pavement and cursing that silly so-and-so for not being around five minutes before I had asked him to be. It was a sad deflection. At least I avoided the back seat, the reverent handling of the brief-case and instant immersion in *The Times*. I sat always in front and chatted and learned much of life and its ways.

The first two drivers did not last long. The first had assumed that his salary was tax-free and the second was sinister. But then came Leslie Leveson, who was with me for years and is still my friend. He left when he married my secretary Anne Long, who stuck it out for more years than any secretary of mine ever has and who has nudged me gently into the self-service days of retirement. My next driver came to me after some years of driving the Beatles. 'If', ran the only reference I was able to obtain, 'you need a soup tureen in a hurry, he will get it for you.' After him came Dimas Gonzales, a native of Bilbao and deserving of a book to himself. His geography was as faulty as his honesty and decency were immaculate. 'Sir,' he one day announced in Park Lane, 'I am afraid I have lost Piccadilly.' He once recommended me to buy St James's Church in Piccadilly which he said was going for £10,000. 'Very cheap,' he said, 'and a garden too.' I was doubtful but intrigued and strolled across to investigate. There were two adjacent posters. One declared that

£10,000 (very big) was needed and a second a SALE (very big) of work. 'Ah,' he said, 'I am very silly.' He would confuse with sublime indifference Euston with Paddington and King's Cross with Victoria and this required an alertness in his passenger. After years of driving on a prescribed route to the office, a different landscape would one day become suddenly apparent. 'Where are we off to, Gonzales?' 'To Bilbao, sir. Ah, how silly I am. It is my holiday I am thinking of,' and we would turn slowly round. 'Gonzales, we seem to be heading north and going uphill. We should be heading south and going down.' 'That I know, sir, but I first have to find where we are.' 'Are you sure this is Heathrow, Gonzales?' 'Yes, sir.' 'But, Gonzales, I am going as a passenger not as B.O.A.C. freight.' He was once approached by a gang with an invitation to operate their getaway vehicle. He was much affronted, but a good time was missed by all since he would assuredly have driven into a cul-de-sac. As I left Hutchinson, his father in Spain acquired riches and Gonzales and his family returned there.

It was on, I think, my third day in Great Portland Street that Mrs Webb confronted me with a lady novelist of some popularity for whom I had better invent the name of Loretta Dubonnet. I had neither met her nor read any of her novels of which Hutchinson were about to publish one. She thrust a sheet of paper at me. 'Here', she said, 'is a list of my works in the order in which you are to read them. I would very much like you to come and lunch with me next week.' We arranged a convenient date. The lunch, when it came, was hardly a riotous success. 'The first thing you must do if you are to publish my books is to get that disgusting writer Karita Dubonning to change her name. She writes pornography as you probably know, and her readers confuse her name with mine and my readers do the same. It doesn't do at all.'

'It so happens', I explained, 'that at Michael Joseph we published Karita Dubonning with the greatest pleasure and satisfaction. I regard her first novel as one of the best with which I have ever been associated.'

'So you approve of pornography?' said Miss Dubonnet.

'No,' I said with such patience as I could muster during a bad lunch, 'I do not approve of pornography, and nor does Miss

Dubonning. I would not dream of suggesting to her that she should change her name.'

After lunch I was returned to my office in an immense limousine of some antiquity in the back of which a bookcase had been constructed. On its top shelf the complete works of Karita Dubonning seemed on parade. Each had been carefully annotated by my hostess and passages underlined in red ink. One by one they were brought to my attention. 'Disgusting,' said Miss Dubonnet each time.

She made it clear that our future relationship might be in doubt and in a little while I received an abusive letter from her husband who had gained some distinction in a quite disparate field. He wrote that he would like to horsewhip me. I wasn't quite able to gather why, but on meeting him subsequently at some dinner I offered my person to him for punishment. He seemed a little disconcerted and satisfied himself by upbraiding me for the ardency of my support of pornography. He thought that Hutchinson had always been a 'decent' firm and my clearly libertine policies were appalling. I promised that I would send him a copy of a novel which I had, at a late stage in its manufacture, withdrawn from publication since I thought it pornographic. This I did and when he wrote to say that he quite agreed with me he enclosed his account for twenty-five guineas. It was paid without comment and Loretta Dubonnet took herself off to the decencies of another 'house'.

My early encounters with the lady novelists of romantic fiction were hardly as Elysian as their stories. Denise Robins took almost immediate fright and persuaded Hodder & Stoughton to pay a substantial sum for the option contractually due to us. This I made use of to build a new reception area known as the Denise Robins Memorial Waiting Room.

With Norah Lofts I felt a good deal of sympathy. We had published rather successfully a number of her historical novels at Michael Joseph. But we somehow failed to achieve the always necessary accord and she left us for the Hutchinson list, explaining that she would feel happier dealing with Mrs Webb and her faithful ally Dorothy Tomlinson. To find, within a few years, that she was again to come within the scope of an alien soul disturbed her equanimity and she too removed to Messrs Hodder in whose firmament she shines with undiminished splendour. Messrs Hodder have done well by me.

Equally with reason for anxiety was poor Desmond Elliot, who now, as the presiding and ebullient genius of Arlington Books and other ventures, really has to decide how much he owes to me and how much to hanging upside down from his kitchen ceiling for five or so minutes every morning. In the early '50s he made a name for himself as the advertising manager of Messrs Hutchinson and had accomplished a remarkable transformation of their style. We, at Michael Joseph, required an advertising recruit and Desmond Elliot was encouraged to apply for the job. He got it, but it proved an unhappy venture. He found us as strange as we found him and it wasn't long before he returned to Great Portland Street. That in a short while the chief obstacle to his success in Bloomsbury Street was again to be his mentor impelled him to start up on his own account and he should never regret having done so.

It seemed to me necessary to demonstrate with cautious speed that a wind of change should be discernible around the group of imprints. It seemed sensible to propose the editorial integration of the whole group and to assign certain areas to specific imprints. Any superfluous imprint would be closed down. There was, of course, opposition and it was hard for a manager who had identified himself with a particular imprint to accept that he was an editor with as great a responsibility to the parent imprint as to the one he regarded as his own. Thus Hurst & Blackett, the original publishers of Hitler's *Mein Kampf*, assumed responsibility for romantic fiction and under the brilliant guidance of Dorothy Tomlinson soon became a leader in that field. The policy for the Hutchinson imprint was to be increasingly selective, but it was to add to its output a wider range of educational books, technical books and the like. Jarrolds was to be the imprint for the more ephemeral general book apt in the past to clutter the Hutchinson list. Stanley Paul was assigned to sports and pastimes, Skeffington reverted to its old speciality of religion, John Long took on 'crime in fact and fiction' and Rider slowly regained its lead in the fields of occultism, oriental religions and the like. Popular Dogs was to continue its successful life of dealing with Popular Dogs. The idea, in brief, amounted to the concept that if a book of any kind was worth publishing the new Hutchinson group was equipped to take it on. Even more important: it would be in the charge of an identifiable human being from its cradle to its long-distant (such is always the hope) grave. No single book in any category would become lost in the machinery of a large publishing organization. All of these imprints and all of the books would call upon the 'servicing operations' of publishing. There was to be one production department; one publicity and advertising department; one art department; one sales organization; one contract and foreign rights department. Publishing would be to an integrated programme channelled through a representative executive committee meeting weekly.

The impact of a publisher's imprint on the generality of readers is, I think, very much less than we like to believe. It is certainly minimal. What needs to be fostered, and is of the greatest importance, is what it means not only within the trade, but to authors, reviewers, literary editors and agents. The talk about publishers within the world trade of publishing is never-ending and it is within this circle of awareness and judgment that change has to be noted and talked about. I certainly underestimated the time required to 'change the nature of the beast' and I have since concluded that a far easier task, given the resources, would have been to start such a publishing organization from scratch.

After intensive labour a first comprehensive catalogue incorporating to some extent this overriding purpose, and explaining it, was achieved and distributed. 'Is it by chance', wrote Ben Huebsch from America, 'that the last title in that extraordinary list should be *Modern Kennel Management?*'

However large a publishing organization might be, I am sure there should somehow or other exist a demonstrable conformity. It may amount to no more than a matter of internal discipline even if evasive of definition. I regarded it always as 'the mark of the beast' and I established its need as much in my own interests as in others. By nature, I told myself, you are a small-time publisher. You have none of the inbred requirements of the tycoon. If you are going to succeed at all in the task you have chosen to take up, you can only do so by exploiting such talents as you possess. And so, along the line from the acceptance of a book to its publication, no matter under which imprint, I set up a series of checks requiring my attention. I found this of the greatest possible value: it permitted a final scrutiny of detail by the one person at the end of the day responsible and with the right to impose 'his mark'. By great good fortune this basic plan worked, although modifications became necessary. There had been no system of 'office' meetings of any kind and in the beginning I set up too many, and it was necessary to reduce them if the volume of work was to be achieved and delegation established.

Traditionally, for reasons obscure, the production of Hutchinson books lagged behind the standards of its competitors. It was hardly a question of economy since in those apparently halcyon days it cost no more to produce a book well than to produce it badly. There was no magic about it, but the application of taste, intelligence and discrimination. By the 'feel' and 'smell' of a book it was possible, until only a few years ago, to identify its publisher. Here, I thought, was an area in which the new Hutchinson could take rapid strides and it would prove of value not only to the publishing group but to the Printing Trust as well. Edward Young, whose contribution to good production over the years has been considerable and who devised the penguin colophon for Allen Lane, was fortunately available to come in for a while and devise a new pattern of production and new settings for note-paper, compliment slips, review slips, labels and all the para-phernalia of print used within the publishing group. To assist in this it was clearly necessary to adopt a colophon, something Hutchinson had never possessed.

From the early trials of the Michael Joseph mermaid I knew it would not be easy, and proposal after proposal was thrown out. And then one morning, from Dorothy Tomlinson's brother Charles, who was then working on publicity for the firm, came the suggestion of the bull. Taurus, it seemed, had been the watermark on the first paper used by Caxton in his printing of the Bible. This seemed acceptably relevant and a fine impression of a bull came from Charles Mozley the artist. It was at once pressed into service and proliferated wherever accommodation could be found. The Hutchinson bull could never perhaps achieve the playful gambols of the Joseph mermaid or Allen Lane's penguin, but he made an immense contribution to butting and shoving the Hutchinson presence more into the forefront than it had been.

It was some time since any unexpected best-seller had come from Hutchinson and nothing was more welcome than to find, within a few weeks, that one was in the pipeline. Raymond Anderson, then a Hutchinson editor, had read an article in *The Countryman* about a seal which sang 'God Save the Queen' and he had written to the author and extracted in due course a manuscript. The intention was that it should be published as a juvenile before the end of the year, and a number of illustrations had been drawn. There was some doubt around as to the wisdom of this policy and I acquired a set of galley proofs. I read them with that rare degree of increasing excitement which happens every now and again in the life of a lucky publisher. I was certain Hutchinson had landed a best-seller; I could hardly believe my good fortune; and I was convinced that it would be fatal to put it out as a juvenile. A certain amount of diplomacy was required and the progress of the book to production and publication was re-routed. Its title was *Seal Morning* and its author was Rowena Farre, who greatly aided publicity by disappearing at singularly inopportune moments. She had written an enchanting book from that strange hinterland between fact and fiction from which so many of the best-sellers of the contemporary scene have derived. At the height of her disappearance, and with the press full of it, she turned up to have lunch with me in Soho on the day of publication dressed in the somewhat exotic attire of all her press photographs. No one had spotted her, and I persuaded her to give an interview to Kenneth Allsop, then the *Daily Mail*'s literary editor, whose particular interest in the book had been aroused. It achieved very big sales and its fortuitous contribution to the façade of change within its publishers was very great.

While at Michael Joseph I had read somewhere a brilliant descriptive piece by Iain Hamilton who had recently become assistant editor of the *Spectator*. We met and I persuaded him to write *Scotland the Brave*, a book I have always regarded as being of exceptional brilliance which, for various reasons that ought not to have mattered, failed to make the impression it should have done. I took a great liking to Iain Hamilton and much admired his lively mind and his Scottish enthusiasms. It very soon became clear that the editorial strength of Hutchinson, from which everything devolves, needed a powerful injection of authority and strength and the accession of a 'group' editor able to hasten the integration. To my delight, Iain Hamilton jumped at the proposal, and his arrival on the scene achieved exactly what was necessary and provided me with a companion and colleague from whom nothing need be hidden. His contacts were wide and useful; his enthusiasms considerable; he made invaluable contributions to the lists of those early years; and it was a sad day for me when chance made available to him the editorship of the *Spectator* which he had always wanted and to which he felt he must return. The adjustment from journalism to publishing is neither an easy nor a natural one to make. Books are longer term at the best of times and, as production problems multiply, tend to be longer term still. The journalistic outlook is to the shorter term; the current problem; the contemporary sensation. It forgets that the 75,000 words of the book have first to be written and after that require some nine months for production. This is something altogether different from the quick piece of 3,000 words for tomorrow's paper or next week's journal. Some cannot make the transition, but Iain Hamilton saw it clear; and when he returned to journalism, publishing lost just that sort of talent it must be always ready to welcome if it is to keep pace with life. Much was to happen before his return to the *Spectator* in 1962 and the original winds of change had by then quietened. A certain excitement had left the air and the voice of the accountant was more loudly heard. Surely, it said, reasonably enough, all these changes should be more quickly reflected in your figures? What has gone wrong? In point of fact, not much had; but jam tomorrow is a difficult diet to put across month after month to those who prefer it today.

Iain Hamilton found his own successor in Harold Harris who also came from journalism — he was literary editor on the *Evening Standard* and, fortunately for us, had tired of it. He lacked, perhaps, the panache of Iain Hamilton, but he was better suited to the climate of plod which was to be the discouraging feature of the next few years. His strength lies in the amount of time and trouble and skill he is able to bring in detail to the assistance of authors in need of such attention. All three of the novels of

Frederick Forsyth were immensely improved by the attention given to their every word by Harold Harris. And many books of great value which have starred in the Hutchinson list over the last ten years owe something of their quality to his editorial skills.

The basic weaknesses of Hutchinson were its dependence upon publishing a large number of new books every Monday morning and the lack of a sustaining back list without which quiet sleep at night becomes difficult. These were its weaknesses in the 1920s and little had been done to rectify the situation during the intervening years. Definitions of a back list vary. Sir Stanley Unwin, I believe, defined it as turnover emanating from titles in the third year following original publication. Others have been known to interpret it as sales following publication, but their publishing lives have been short. Generally today it would be calculated from sales achieved after twelve months; and of the 35,000 or so new titles published each year by British publishers it would be surprising if anything like half of them aspired to back-list status at all.

To achieve a back list of any strength from general publishing alone is extraordinarily difficult. Normally it comes in the main from educational and specialist publishing; in these areas Hutchinson was deficient, and in the long term it was this deficiency which had to be corrected. At the same time a new zeal and excitement had to be injected into its current publishing activities. It proved to be a long, slow haul continually hampered by circumstances of one kind and another which prudence should alert one to expect but which none the less bring frustrations hard to bear.

I had not been long installed when the young man then in charge of contracts and rights wished to see me on a matter of some urgency. He was in a state of some excitement. From some source he had heard that a very extraordinary book about Hitler was being written by an aunt, who I was given to understand lived in Berchtesgaden. Word was beginning to circulate about its existence and apparently one or two plans for serialization were under discussion. James Clarke — for that was his name — thought that action was urgently necessary. I was not at all sure that we wanted a book by Hitler's aunt, but sillier projects had been known to succeed and I wanted an opportunity to inculcate zest, zeal and excitement. 'You had better', I said calmly, 'go and see her.' 'What, now?' asked Clarke, a little surprised. 'Yes, now,' I said. 'It is only three o'clock. It won't take you long. Come and tell me about it when you get back.' I felt mildly gratified by this new swiftness of decision. It was Big Thinking. An hour or so later I met James Clarke in the corridor. 'Not gone yet?' I inquired. 'Just off,' he replied, 'I will tell you about it in the morning.' 'Very quick work,' I said, 'will you be back by then? It's quite a way to Berchtesgaden.' 'I didn't say Berchtesgaden. I said Bedford Gardens. It's only a twopenny bus ride.'

I was to learn early that a change of policy and editorial direction can make little progress until its implications can be explained and assimilated right down the line and through every department. Even the look of the final parcel needs to reflect innovation if only by the application of a newly designed label. It enforced my conviction that the act of publishing is ideally indivisible and there must be effective publishing control of the whole operation.

During my first Hutchinson visit to America (the first in fact that had ever been undertaken by a senior Hutchinson executive) I was delighted to acquire the rights in the now famous book by Dr Seuss — *The Cat in the Hat*. Just published by Random House, it showed every sign of success and this, I thought, could be repeated within the British markets. It would certainly strike a new and, to me at any rate, a welcome note in the Hutchinson list. Furthermore, there was the prospect of a series of such books from Dr Seuss with all that this implied. We failed completely. Under our imprint *The Cat in the Hat* made virtually no impact. It was nobody's fault; at that time it simply was not a 'Hutchinson book'. Even three years later the story could have been a different one. I could offer no excuse. The American publisher and the author felt unable to entrust us with the successor and I could not blame them. In a little while we were ignominiously obliged to relinquish what rights we had in Dr Seuss's first book to Messrs Collins and watch it take its place in one of the most triumphantly successful series of its kind there has ever been.

None the less there was an encouraging sense of excitement in the air. A simple strategy obliged almost everyone to change their office from one part of the corridor to another. It made certain sense since it grouped the editorial imprints together, the production departments and so forth. But its chief contribution was to morale as an outward and visible sign of change. The inward and spiritual grace was not so easily discernible. Until that moment Brendan Behan would hardly have been regarded as a Hutchinson author. One of my abiding satisfactions is that a few years later it would have been difficult to imagine him anywhere else. A transformation had come about which enabled him to rollick drunk and almost incapable from office to office and find a warm welcome in each one. I was hardly ever to extract any sense from him at all. We smacked each other on the back and expressed undying mutual affection every so often until his death. It was Iain Hamilton and Rae Jeffs who somehow set alight the enthusiasm which produced *Borstal Boy* and its successors. The Brendan Behan story has been told often enough, in its humour, achievement and sadness. Rae Jeffs, occupying rather a difficult and diminutive post on my arrival, was soon to become one of the best publicity and promotional contrivers in publishing. She found in Brendan Behan a genius to which in time she felt obliged to devote the whole of her own remarkable abilities. I have never been quite sure that she was right, but Behan was an outstanding Irishman of his time and I am glad that he died of exuberance and excess before the madness of recent years took over. They would have been abhorrent to him, for he loved and respected all his fellow creatures and there was no hate in him.

An extremely welcome addition to the Hutchinson list at around this time, which has endured, was Arthur Koestler with his book *The Sleepwalkers*. It came to me by way of A. D. Peters, who was not an agent given to impetuosity and I was thus doubly delighted. I had always both admired and liked A. D. Peters. A strange man, he was never easy to know but was straightforward in all his dealings. 'We have had our battles,' he was to write to me at one time, 'and we have fought them, but without disturbing our relationship.' From such a man it touched me deeply. Arthur Koestler was reputed to be a 'difficult' author but at the same time one most publishers would be more than pleased to cope with. In the past he and Hutchinson, especially in the days of Mr Walter, would be regarded as an unlikely combination.

He has now remained with Hutchinson longer, I think, than with any previous publisher and with never a shadow of disagreement. Few more valuable additions to the now flourishing back list of the group have been contrived than the uniform Danube Edition of all Koestler's books. I lacked the intellect to deal with Koestler as I lacked the boisterousness to deal with Brendan Behan, but now within the office were people who could cope with either while I was content enough to be their friends and make noises of encouragement from time to time.

It was this kind of experience which obliged me to reflect on the role of administration within a large organization whose prime responsibility was that of communication in an increasingly complex society. Communication, as we now have to call it, is in one way or another an editorial problem and the creative minds from which it springs can achieve their best only if the climate in which they operate is congenial. If I accomplished anything in those first years at Hutchinson it was I think to create a climate in which sometimes dotty editors and dotty authors could work freely and with confidence. It might eventually be necessary to reach an unacceptable decision; but if the climate was right and there remained some degree of respect for the final decision-maker, then administration had come to terms with the infinitely more important role of the innovators of communication. I have had no reason to change this concept which in due course I was to find as applicable within broadcasting as within publishing.

The danger which exists, and to which there seems no answer, is that doubt and indecision can become evident at the top. Confidence can quickly evaporate and a decision which previously might be acceptable if rationally explained, becomes interpreted as an act of censorship. In a free society the exercise of editorial authority is not censorship and should never be thought of as such. On only a very few occasions over many years did I find it necessary to exert authority. There was, naturally, the occasional rumpus, but tranquillity would ultimately be restored and I cannot recall any incident which incurred lasting animosity.

We had, I thought, made a good deal of editorial progress; certainly the literary agents were putting forward authors and proposals more in keeping with the present than with the past. We arranged for an impressive series of encylopedias from the lively and ingenious operation conducted by George Rainbird, and in association with Alfred Knopf in America we launched Professor Jack Plumb into his *History of Human Society*.

It was still necessary to make some move which might possibly attract the young, new writers and to demonstrate the sense of partnership which should animate the relationship between publisher and author. It was this necessity which led me to devise the imprint of New Authors Ltd, in which I take a very particular pride. It was in some ways unique and it says much for the parent board of Hutchinson that, although contrary to all precedent, the proposal was accepted without question. The idea, briefly, was that from his first book, or rather with his first book, a writer would be in the closest relationship with his publisher and privy to all the facts and figures of the entire operation. It was, in a sense, an authors' co-operative, since any profit made by the imprint would be distributed among all participating writers. Only the author's first book could appear under the imprint. Contrary to established custom there would be no option clause in the agreement. Should the author become dissatisfied or disgruntled or in any sort of doubt he was free to take his second book elsewhere. In point of fact only one novelist was to do this of all who were published in my time. It was stipulated that the author should be informed of every cost associated with the publication of his book and its promotion, and he would receive a balance sheet covering all the activities of New Authors Ltd. It was a simple enough arrangement but an irritation to the computer whose convenience today has to be considered at an earlier stage than that of a mere human being.

A number of writers who have gained distinction were first published under this scheme; they include Stanley Middleton who has since become one of the leading novelists of his day and, in 1974, the joint winner of the prestigious and valuable Booker Prize. Indeed, the short lists of 1973 and 1974 contained three other New Authors writers, Elizabeth Mavor, Beryl Bainbridge and J. G. Farrell. Maureen Duffy was yet another New Author to gain prominence.

I would, myself, like to see the implications and purposes of New Authors much extended. It would be agreeable, for instance, to do away with option clauses, but the world of publishing has its jungles and its predatory inmates. I can see no reason at all to withhold from an author the fullest facts and figures. Much could be gained by revealing the detailed costs of production, of advertising and promotion. There exists the common purpose of finding as many readers as ingenuity can attract to listen to what the author has to say. A common purpose requires a partnership and not a squabbling gaggle for ever imputing motives of the basest self-interest.

It is impossible to be at all exact, but I would think that the generality of first novels published under the New Authors imprint sold something around a third more copies in their original editions than would otherwise have been achieved. They certainly attracted more widespread critical attention than first novels put out in the ordinary way. I think it a pity that Hutchinson have now abandoned the scheme, but I can well see its inconvenience to the efficiency of an automated administration and it could possibly make a more extended impact within a smaller, personalized imprint.

Over this period and from it the prospect looked brighter. No publisher can remain wholly unmoved when invited to publish the work of a competitive colleague, and that so fastidious and individualistic a publisher as Fredric Warburg should sign a contract for his autobiography was a decided encouragement. *An Occupation for Gentlemen* was its title, to be followed a good deal later by *All Authors Are Equal*. Neither dictum comes within shouting distance of reality, but they were good titles for excellent books whether read for what they said or what they concealed. To have published for Fred Warburg and his indomitable wife Pamela and to have retained the friendship of both is, even when said in the greatest possible humility, something of an achievement.

Fred Warburg very nearly had me thrown out of the Garrick Club, one of whose firmer regulations is that papers or documents or notes should not be produced during what is always assumed to be social conversation. Fred suggested he should lunch with me shortly after publication of *An Occupation for Gentlemen*. We had not been seated long at lunch when he pulled from his pocket a lengthy *aide-mémoire* of what he wished to complain about, together with a considerable batch of review cuttings. 'For God's sake, Fred,' I asked, 'put all that stuff away. It's against the rules here and you will get me thrown out.' 'Bloody silly rule,' said Fred and produced a further batch from another pocket.

Somehow, through the introduction of my father, by then in retirement near Shrewsbury, I received a manuscript from Lilian Beckwith which later was published under the title *The Hills is Lonely*. It sells still and was the first of a series of substantial and extremely popular sellers. A. D. Peters inquired if I would commission the autobiography of Kingsley Martin which I did with alacrity, and I enjoyed a friendship with him of considerable warmth until the day of his death. We had a minor line with royalty and arranged to publish *Lonely But Not Alone* by H.R.H. Wilhelmina, Princess of the Netherlands, after her abdication in favour of her daughter. She obligingly signed a copy. His Imperial Highness the Shah of Iran entrusted *Mission to my Country* to us, which would have pleased Mr Walter.

The time had gone quickly since 1955. It had been a period of considerable strain and many tensions. Quite what the financial heights had been expecting I do not know, for it was never revealed. I recollected quite often a remark made shortly after I had assumed responsibility. I treasure it still. 'Now,' said the voice in tones of well-meant congratulation, 'now that we have had a good review in the *Sunday Times* and publishing has turned the corner ... '

14
Old Bogy Man

I SEEM to remember as a minor monster of my childhood the sinister, looming figure of Eamon de Valera on whose ninety-second birthday I am writing this. He seemed then to be threatening one's safety and one's possessions. 'If you are not a good boy, master Bobby, Mr de Valera will come and take you away in the night.' He wore a romantic cloak around which the wind seemed always to swirl.

I never quite brought myself to record this memory to Mr de Valera himself, but I wish I had. He would have gently smiled, serene in the depth of wisdom. I have met but two men on any terms of friendship who seemed to me from the first encounter to be in a category above ordinary mortals. The first was Eamon de Valera and the second John Reith. It was consoling after a while to discover that Reith was also capable of remarkable silliness. I daresay de Valera was too, but I was never on terms to discover it.

Shortly after Iain Hamilton joined me at Hutchinson as editorial director we made a journey to Dublin together. Like so many ardent Scots he had a special love for Ireland and the Irish and he had many associations there which sooner or later added powerful Irish writers to our list. There was Edna O'Brien, whose first novel, *The Country Girls*, we were shortly to publish; Brendan Behan was another whose books and characteristics were to enliven the Hutchinson scene; Michael Farrell yet another, whose great novel *Thy Tears Might Cease* was long in coming and published alas after his death. His friend Monk Gibbon had completed the editorial revision the author had not lived to do. Had it been published a year or so later than it was, I have always felt, its impact would have been stronger. In all such affairs there is a shifting climate difficult to discern, especially when one is planning a year or so ahead. None the less, *Thy Tears Might Cease* has achieved its stature in Ireland, if more slowly than James Plunkett's *Strumpet City*, which also began its preparation around this time.

It was thus Iain who suggested we might begin a manœuvre to extract an autobiography from Mr de Valera, who was then Prime Minister. Another purpose of the journey was to meet Edna O'Brien, who was then married to Ernest Gebler, another Hutchinson author. She had undertaken to provide us with breakfast, for we travelled in the proper manner, by train to Liverpool and then by the overnight Dublin ferry. An enchanting young woman welcomed us to her suburban home. All the charm of Ireland was in her smile and in her gentle ways. The lilt in her Irish voice turned words into jewels and her breakfast achieved a wonder all its own. She seemed to retain the innocence of childhood, and there was a freshness in her questioning wonderment of what life was about. We took a particular pleasure in publishing *The Country Girls* and naturally hoped that we should be entrusted with its successor. Alas, before that was ready we had rejected a novel by her husband which we found rather objectionable. In high dudgeon Edna flounced from our presence to another publisher and shortly afterwards her marriage came to an end. Not unnaturally we felt a trifle bruised, since her only criticism of our activities was the rejection of Gebler's book.

Such events, however, were not in contemplation when on the evening following our breakfast with Edna we presented ourselves to the Prime Minister's office. Mr de Valera stood to receive us and one was at once impressed by the grandeur of his figure and the immense dignity of his bearing. One knew that his sight was failing. He did not move from behind his desk, but his hand went instantly and directly to your own. He never fumbled or faltered. No light had been turned on in the room. As we talked the autumn darkness gathered, but the old man was not conscious of it. We talked of the purpose of our visit and he listened with patience. His debt to history; the extraordinary range and drama of his life; the need for his own version of events; the importance of his outlook on world affairs; and so forth and so on.

For most of the time he sat very still, but occasionally his hands would play with a desk ruler, which they found unerringly. But he was adamant and remained so. He talked quietly of the problems such a task would present: his failing vision and the burden that would be placed on others; the necessary examination of records; the time required. No, he was afraid that an autobiography was out of the question. We turned then to the suggestion, less attractive, of an authorized and definitive biography. Would he co-operate and make available his papers? Would he allow complete freedom of comment? Yes, he thought after a few moments of reflection, this might be more of a possibility. He could see the need for such. Who might we have in mind? What would be required of him? It would not be easy while he remained Prime Minister. He talked slowly with great humanity and immense courtesy. By this time we could barely see him. The only light came from the courtyard beyond the window. It was agreed that the proposal would be considered. We thanked him for receiving us and gravely he thanked us for coming. He rose from his chair and without hesitation in the dark walked straight to the door and opened it for us. There was no fumbling for the handle. Again he shook hands. And so into the poetry of a Dublin night we went, leaving the old man in his darkening room, with the memories our talk must have stirred.

We were fortunate in persuading Thomas O'Neill to undertake the formidable task, and he was to work closely with Mr de Valera, ably supported by the indefatigable and always helpful Miss Kelly who appeared to divine on any instant precisely what it was Mr de Valera required. O'Neill was Assistant Keeper of Printed Books at the National Library of Ireland and was later to become a lecturer in history at University College, Galway. He was given leave of absence in order to devote more time to the necessary researches, but even so the going was hard and in due course Lord Longford was recruited to give impetus to the completion of the work.

Within a short time Mr de Valera became President, and my next visit was to his official residence, Phoenix Lodge. His greeting was always warm and friendly and I received in due course the accolade of a drink, which I was told was rare and denied even to visiting ambassadors. But it is the recollection of my final visit in 1970 which remains. The biography had just and at last appeared, and I was anxious to talk again with the President, to thank him for all his patient help over so long and to ascertain his feelings about the outcome after all its delays and anxieties. I hoped, too, that he might inscribe a copy of the book for me. The presentation copy we had prepared for him had been taken to him a week or two earlier by Lord Longford and O'Neill together. But not without alarms. The leather-bound copy had disappeared en route. Lord Longford thought that sinister designs might be in operation. However, it was returned to him intact at the last moment. He had left it in a lavatory.

My appointment was an early one on a Friday morning. I had flown over on the previous evening to be host at a small party to launch the publication of a new Arrow paperback of Irish significance. It contained the diverting irrelevancies of all such Dublin parties, which give a character unique in the world to Dublin, where the priorities of life seem more ridiculously sensible than anywhere else. The inevitable drunk in a mackintosh with a bottle of Guinness protruding from each pocket, wove his uneasy course from group to group. Someone's old mother had insisted on her right to come and, secured for safety in a chair, sang ditties at the top of her rasping voice. No one seemed to know what the party was about. There had been one last night and was to be another tomorrow. They would all be meeting again, if indeed they ever separated. I told some of my appointment for the morning and was reminded of the bitter hostility the very name of de Valera could evoke. 'Spit in his eye,' said one with fierce relish; 'the devil take him,' said another. But many wished that I would take their love and respect.

The taxi-driver was young and at once excited. He had never driven to Phoenix Lodge before. I explained the purpose of my visit, and thought that I had sold a copy of the book. The taxi-driver was a great admirer of the old man now living in Phoenix Lodge, awaiting retirement and the inevitable close of his long and extraordinary life.

We were stopped at the Lodge gates. There was a telephone conversation before we were sent on our way. It seemed a sad and lonely place. Beautifully kept, immaculate, but with little sign of life in the wide, undulating grounds. At the great door an officer of the Irish Army, polished and correct, received me. I gave him the book, and asked if he thought the President might sign it for me. 'I will take it to him,' he said. 'I think he will.' For a few moments I waited in an immense, impersonal but impeccable reception room. Nothing was out of place. It utterly lacked character and again life had slipped away.

I seemed to remember that this room led to the President's own. The soldier appeared in the doorway and took me through. The President stood, very tall and very still behind his desk. He always seemed to me to emanate a great quality of 'stillness'. Few men possess it and it conveys an impression of composure and effortless authority. I could see that my copy of the book was there on the desk. The soldier left us and the old man took my hand in both of his. He spoke a sentence in Gaelic, as if it were a prayer, and smiled. 'You don't know what I am saying,' he said. 'I am wishing you a hundred thousand welcomes. It is the Irish way.'

I thanked him for receiving me and said how many years it had been since we first discussed the book together. 'I hope', I asked, 'that you have no regrets and are pleased with it?'

'It is not my book,' he replied. 'There are parts of it I do not like. Some of it even I had not seen.' This I thought was doubtful, for I believe Miss Kelly or Thomas O'Neill had read its every word to him.

'Of course you cannot be pleased with it all,' I said. 'It is not the book we really wanted. It is you who should have written it. But it is a good second best. You would not want a sycophantic exercise.'

'I know,' he replied, 'I know. You are quite right, but I hadn't the time. Without my sight it would have been too difficult. But there are things in it I do not like. It is not always accurate. And', he added with something like vigour, 'you have left out the picture of my Granny. I am very sad about that.'

'Have we?' I asked, rather appalled. 'Did we have a picture of your Granny?'

'I don't know,' he said, 'but I thought so. Have you not seen the picture of my Granny? I owe so much to my Granny.'

'I do not recall it,' I said, 'and will certainly look into it. In any new edition', I assured him, 'the picture of your Granny will be added.'

'I shall be glad of that,' he said, 'I want you to see the picture now. Miss Kelly will have it,' and he pressed the bell on his desk. He knew its exact position. The efficient and devoted Miss Kelly appeared and we exchanged greetings. 'I want Sir Robert to see the picture of my Granny,' said the President, 'can you find it for him please?' Miss Kelly departed and he turned to me again. He knew exactly where his sightless eyes should look. He smiled faintly. 'You were not Sir Robert when last you came to see me. I was very glad to hear that news.'

'Thank you,' I said, 'but it's a silly business. You do not have such things in Ireland.'

'No,' he said, 'we don't, but I wish we had. It would have helped me very much ... very much indeed. It is a useful system and a good one.'

Miss Kelly returned. 'Here', she announced, 'is the picture,' and gave it to him.

He gazed upon it and his face softened with affection. He was seeing it in every remembered detail. With a smile he handed it to me; it was a splendid Victorian portrait of an old Irish lady, strong and fearless and loving. 'My Granny', said the old man, 'was wonderful. She told me stories of Ireland as I sat on the kitchen table of the farmhouse. I loved to hear them and to see the country.'

'If', I asked, 'you had written any part of this book, which period would you have chosen?'

'Oh,' he replied without hesitation, 'of my boyhood in the country. Of my life there with Granny and of the stories she told me.'

'And if', I asked, 'you were to live your life again what would you choose to do?'

'I would teach,' he said. 'I would teach.'

'I have been told', I said, 'that you are the only man in Ireland who understands Einstein.'

He seemed not displeased and there was no denial. 'I will tell you a story,' he said. 'I have always been interested in mathematics — pure mathematics, and I know about them. It has always been a pastime of mine, a hobby, to work out mathematical formulas. Since I have been blind I have been obliged to learn them by heart. Not long ago I had a little operation, and as I was coming round from the anaesthetic the doctors got worried. I was repeating phrases unintelligible to all of them. They thought something had gone amiss. The old man seemed, they thought, to have gone off his head.'

He smiled. 'All I was doing', he went on, 'was to repeat mathematical formulas over and over again. And I was doing it in Gaelic. I well understood their anxiety.'

'They tell me', I said, 'that your wife has not been well. I am very sorry to hear this and I do hope she is better.'

'It is a sadness,' he said, 'but it is not very much. She is old you know, older than I am, and her memory is not quite what it used to be. But that is all.' He paused. 'After all,' he went on, 'I am old too and my memory is not what it was. In my younger days I would drive my car a lot around Ireland. I knew every village and every town and every road between Dublin and Cork and Dublin and Limerick. I knew every turn and every corner. When I became too blind to drive I would sit and enjoy the journeys in my mind. I could visualize every inch of the way. Now I am afraid my memory misses some of the turns. It is not very safe.' He paused. 'Will you take a drink?' he asked.

'Are you taking one?' I said. 'If you are, I will have a little of your Irish whiskey.' He rang the bell and the soldier came in. 'Some of our whiskey for Sir Robert,' said the old man, 'and a drink for me too,' he added.

'Tell me,' I asked, 'what you think of the reviews the book has had? They have been very good on the whole, but nearly all of them refer to that night during the war when Winston Churchill telephoned to offer you full membership of the British Commonwealth. Is that true? Can you tell me about it?'

He smiled and the soldier returned with my whiskey — of lethal proportions — and a glass for the President, which he placed with great precision on the desk. The old man's hand went straight to it. 'Brandy,' he said. 'It's what they tell me I have to have. Good luck to you,' he said and took a sip. 'Yes,' he went on, 'it's true enough. I thought the old gentleman had had a bit too much of this,' and he motioned to the brandy. 'It was three o'clock in the morning,' he said, 'and I was asleep. But I had a telephone at my bedside. Churchill was on the line. He wanted me to see an emissary at once. I thought it must be an ultimatum. "Won't the morning do?" I asked Mr Churchill. "No it won't," he said and that was that. It wasn't going to solve any problems.'

There was a pause. 'The world doesn't get much nicer,' I said.

'No, no indeed it doesn't,' and there was a sadness in his voice. 'It is all very worrying.' He seemed somehow very much alone at the big desk in the huge, beautifully maintained house and far removed from the whirling events outside. We had finished our drinks and the talk was coming to an end. He reached for the book. 'Here you are,' he said. 'I have gladly signed it for you.'

I thanked him for it and for receiving me with such kindness and at such length. I had been with him for well over an hour. He rose and came away from his desk towards me. There was an instinctive acceptance between us that this goodbye would almost certainly be the last. He again took my hand in both of his. 'I have enjoyed your visits,' he said. 'May God bless you and everything that you may do.'

I turned and left him standing there. The bogy man of childhood seemed very far away.

15
Gloom Days

A SPAN of years around the 1960s I could well expunge
from my memory. One redeeming feature was to enliven
the close of 1960, but that was almost obliterated at the
outset and only rescued by a hairsbreadth.

The Hutchinson scene was proving intractable and I was still
smarting from the revelation, not discovered by my investigating
auditor of 1956, that the publishing 'profits' derived in the main
from substantial subsidies from the more flourishing Printing
Trust. There was nothing wrong in this, but it presented its
problems when, almost immediately after my arrival, it was decided that these grants should come to their end and every activity
of the group should stand on its own feet. It was an entirely
sensible decision which I fully supported, but I anticipated that
the effect on my publishing responsibilities would be more widely
appreciated than I found them to be. The board had given full
support to the overall policy of 'planned plodding' which I had
outlined often enough. I had no recipe for any short-term transformation, nor indeed the capability of achieving it by entrepreneurial skills which, boiled down, usually means the entice-
ment, with sacks of wallop, of authors from the lists of competitors.

Progress had been slow but I was not altogether dissatisfied
with it, although I felt quite unable to communicate this to my
colleagues of the parent board. The overall quality of our production had been transformed not only to our own benefit but to
that also of the component members of the Printing Trust responsible for the great part of our output. The publishing imprints had been rationalized within an integrated editorial policy
and the publishing staff had become not only of a much higher

calibre but much reduced in age. I felt, too, that for the first time in its existence Hutchinson operated within the mainstream of the book trade throughout the world, was more respected and played a much larger part, through representation on a number of committees, in trade affairs. From a wall in the boardroom a large oil-painting of Mr Walter looked upon me with astonishment and distaste—almost everything I thought I had accomplished would have been repugnant to him. He had no use at all for the Publishers Association, to the council of which I had been elected while with Michael Joseph. My switch to Hutchinson meant for the first time there was a spokesman for an organization which in the past had aroused many anxieties.

I had worked hard and had enjoyed doing so; any exhaustion, frustration and humiliation possibly derived from the need month after month to be on the defensive when explaining 'progress' to the parent board, whose perfectly proper requirements were facts and figures. There was never a member of that board who treated me other than with kindness and friendship. I took no great pride in the fact, but I had confessed at the start my inability to talk in terms of financial sophistication, which requires future projections almost totally impossible for a publisher to supply. Any such projection, however elaborately dolled up, must take a publisher into a future more distant than his list makes possible. It cannot be more than guesswork and dangerous guesswork at that.

I had at last managed to find a supremely efficient secretary, calm, attractive and amusing, who assured me that she had no intention whatever of getting married. Since I had stolen her from another department she knew Hutchinson and required no instruction. Within a couple of weeks she was, of course, engaged to a young doctor and became Priscilla Madden, and now has at least five children, including one godchild of mine, and lives in a Somerset manor-house with a lavatory in the garden that appears to belong to the National Trust.

At the beginning of the November of 1960 I had an unpleasant bout of flu and felt more than usually knocked about. But more worrying was the sudden deterioration of hearing in my solitary ear. This had happened once before in the 1930s, when I was warned that it might not recover and that it would be a sensible precaution to learn lip-reading. I did not find it a cheerful occupation and I made little headway. However, after an anxious few months, a recovery came about and I had experienced no further problem until this moment. It was judged, however, to be a part and parcel of the flu then in vogue, and we went off for a brief holiday in Cornwall. During it my hearing seemed subjected to wide variation; at one moment it might be the normality I had learned to live with, and in the next almost disappear in extremely unpleasant distortion. It was otherwise an agreeable holiday, enlivened by news from Old Bailey that Sir Allen Lane and Penguin Books had been cleared of the charge of pornography thought by a ridiculous prosecution to be contained in *Lady Chatterley's Lover*. It was from the proceeds of the vastly inflated sales that were to follow that Allen built his attractive villa at Carvasal on the Costa del Sol which he named, appropriately enough, El Phoenix. It was to play quite a part in my future, for it was to El Phoenix that Allen took me with his family after Joan's death; and it was El Phoenix which he loaned me for a honeymoon when I married again.

At the end of a week we returned to London and my hearing appeared to be restored. The usual pile of mail and problems had accumulated, but 'nothing really has happened', reported the lively Priscilla, by this time, if I remember rightly, preoccupied with her damned doctor. Towards the bottom of a pile of letters was one from the Post Office which looked somehow grander than the usual communication from that establishment. It had been sent in the first instance to an old address, and at some time during its wanderings had been run over by a bus, for tyre marks were clearly on it. None the less, it bore the signature of Reginald Bevins, then Postmaster-General, and it stated that with the Prime Minister's approval he was inviting me to become a governor of the BBC. If the prospect was agreeable, would I please let him know at the earliest possible moment and keep quiet about it until 'Her Majesty's pleasure has been taken'. Various relevant documents were enclosed containing the BBC's charter; its articles of association; the Beveridge Report and the most recent edition of the Corporation's *Yearbook*.

I was not unnaturally greatly elated although alarmed that

the delay in response might already have proved fatal. I doubted if Her Majesty had lost much sleep over it and telephoned the Postmaster-General's secretary to explain the delay. He seemed undisturbed too.

Before sending a formal acceptance I thought I should perhaps clear matters with my aurist. He seemed well satisfied with what appeared to be a return to normalcy and thought that all should be well. I thus informed Mr Bevins, who replied that the next meeting of the Privy Council must be awaited after which an 'announcement would be made from Downing Street'. It was a normal five-year term of office and payment was at the rate of £1,000 a year. I had already consulted Hutchinson's chairman, by this time Mr Holt, and received his permission which was afterwards ratified by the board. The fee was to be deducted from my pay-packet; and as by the end of the subsequently protracted day they received something like £10,000 of subsidy and a number of books we would never otherwise have published, it wasn't too bad a bargain for them and I was freed of any conscience about the demands upon my time.

In due course I was informed that the announcement would be made on a Friday morning; it was accorded a good deal more publicity than such announcements are given today. Another appointment at the same time was that of Sir David Milne, as national governor for Scotland. It seemed to me courteous to thank Mr Macmillan for so considerately appointing a one-time publishing colleague and he replied very nicely, saying that he had felt proud to be able to do so. On that Friday evening Joan and I had a celebrationary dinner at the Caprice and received the ever-tactful homage of Mario. Life, we tended to think, was looking up.

My first meeting at Broadcasting House was to be on the first Thursday of November. I looked up my fellow governors and found none that I knew. There were seven of them, which would mean that, round a table, I could probably manage well enough for sound. But, alas, it was not to be. A day before the meeting my hearing quite suddenly plunged to a new low. By some miracle it had sustained itself for exactly the short period needed to justify my acceptance of the BBC. But for that I would have had no alternative to a refusal. It was a depressing blow, and the very day on which I should have reported found me prostrate on my back in the Royal Free Hospital under the acute gaze of a bevy of female medical students while John Groves, by this time a rather worried aurist, injected disturbingly long needles into my neck. 'Watch his eyes,' he said, and the pair I chose to gaze upon in return were the most beautiful I have ever seen; they haunt me still. Consultations and examinations and deliberations of all kinds were deployed. Nothing looked hopeful. It was decided that I must have an immediate operation to ensure a greater flow of blood to my failing ear. This was unpleasant and no one warned me that my countenance would no longer remain as I or anybody else had known it. An eyelid, somewhere along the line, dropped for ever. 'Do you always look like that?' inquired a rather formidable field-marshal I happened later to meet at dinner. I explained. 'I thought you disapproved of me,' he said.

There was no immediate improvement in my hearing. It varied between bad and abysmal and there developed in my right arm a curious agony which I was obliged to endure for three unending months. 'It happens about once in a hundred times,' explained the surgeon. I was just able to attend a BBC meeting before Christmas. They had prepared for my disability with great kindness and had placed me next to the chairman, Sir Arthur fforde. I must have made a singularly odd impression. I could not even hear Sir Arthur's kind words of welcome, and thus made no response at all. The first I knew of their existence was when I read them in the minutes.

I have written of all this not to indulge in any dissertation on infirmity, but to record the quite extraordinary benevolence which restored my hearing for just those few days necessary to justify my acceptance of a BBC governorship which was so profoundly to affect the future years of my working life. Without the new interests which came, and the many new experiences which derived from them, and quite apart from a great number of new friendships gained, I could not have confronted the publishing anxieties which were to come, still less the death of Joan which was to follow within the next eighteen months. She became desperately ill with a virus pneumonia as soon as I returned home from hospital, although she seemed to make a remarkable recovery from it. My father also died at the beginning of the new year.

My acute deafness continued, with minor intermissions, for another year or more. I came slowly to the conclusion that faced with the choice, which no one is, I would on the whole prefer blindness to deafness. A disability in hearing disqualifies from participation to an extent which frighteningly chills one's soul. But a complete loss I never sustained; slowly improvement came and finally much of the ground was recovered and has now been held for a decade. It remains often a nuisance, but one to be shamelessly exploited from time to time if one is shameless enough to do so — and I am.

It was not until later that I found myself involved in a publishing problem of a most unpleasant nature: I was immersed in a controversy most tendentious and distressing and came within a hairsbreadth of resignation from the Hutchinson scene. It can well find its place in a chapter so full of woe. It needs to be told and it was most curiously paralleled by an affair of some significance within the BBC.

In 1933 the Hutchinson imprint of Hurst & Blackett (now devoted to an output of romantic fiction) was in the charge of Cherry Kearton, who had recently joined the firm from the foreign department of Messrs Curtis Brown. He had been recommended as 'a likely lad' to Walter Hutchinson by Michael Joseph, at that time Curtis Brown's manager. Kearton's publishing nose had sniffed out a book by one Adolf Hitler called *My Struggle* which was 'enjoying' some success in Germany. Cherry Kearton, through Curtis Brown, acquired from the author the right to publish an English translation throughout what was then referred to as the British Empire market. Its author decided that the English translation, made by a Captain E. S. Dugdale, should be shorn of some of the more violent passages in the German edition and to this procedure Cherry Kearton agreed. It is, of course, easy to be wise after the event but one cannot help speculating on the possible consequences of this expurgation. Would a complete version in English have awakened a greater foreboding? My friend Cherry Kearton is happily retired and grows roses in the Caterham valley. Will any historian of the future, fumbling around for the causes of the Second

World War, find its source in the tiny office of Messrs Hurst &
Blackett in that Paternoster Row which the author of *My Struggle*
was to blow to smithereens?

The imprints of the Hutchinson group of those days were not
enamoured of bibliography and Walter Hutchinson refused always to date the publication of his books. Their records too were
subject to frequent destruction by fire or war or both. Thus no
evidence exists of the sales of *My Struggle* in its expurgated form,
but it would seem that a cheap edition was brought out in 1936
and reprinted in both 1937 and 1938 — still in expurgated form.
The original contract, signed by Adolf Hitler, required a royalty
of 25 per cent, but at some time between its signing and the
present day one with an eye for such things neatly cut the signature of Hitler from the document.

In 1939 Messrs Hurst & Blackett, no longer under the juris-
diction of the author, reissued the book under its title of *Mein
Kampf*. This was translated by James Murphy and was un-
abridged. Thus for the first time its demoniacal nature became
evident to those reading only English. During the war this
edition was reprinted six times, the last being in May 1943. It
would seem that this edition lasted until 1944 and for the next
twenty-five years *Mein Kampf* was not available in English within
the British Commonwealth in which Messrs Hurst & Blackett
had the exclusive market. It was, however, available in America
and its market in an edition translated by Ralph Manheim,
thought to be a better translation than those prepared by either
Captain Dugdale or James Murphy. *Mein Kampf* was also continuously available in a number of foreign translations.

The problem of what to do about *Mein Kampf* was one which
only slowly impinged when I became responsible for Messrs
Hutchinson's activities after 1956. From time to time it was
suggested that a demand awaited it. There was no doubt that the
original contract remained valid. Technically, its author or his
heirs and successors could have obtained a reversion of the rights
during the many years it remained out of print. In due course
the Bavarian Government were to claim the rights as theirs, following their sequestration of Hitler's properties. Only very slowly
and after some five years of inactivity did I find myself reflecting
that an editorial responsibility of an extraordinarily unpleasant

nature rested with me. From time to time I put the problem to others and there seemed almost unanimity of opinion that new adult generations had the right to know from what hideous source derived the vile oppression of Nazi Germany and why and how it led to the obscenity of the Second World War. In those early days of private inquiry there arose no hint of the intensity of opposition which in due course became manifest. In various languages, and in English in American territories, *Mein Kampf* was in circulation as a fact of history. The wickedness of it and its total obscenity were plainly to be seen.

With some deliberation I at no time consulted the parent board, of which I was a member, on any question or problem of publications. At no time had I been asked to do so and on no occasion had I been questioned as to the whys and wherefores of any title published by any imprint of the group however contentious. It at no time entered my head that I should acquaint the board with any of the problems which were confronting the reissue of Hitler's miserable *Mein Kampf*.

After consultation here and there, it seemed to me wise to use the translation made by Ralph Manheim for the American publishers, Messrs Houghton Mifflin of Boston. It seemed generally accepted as the best that had been done. Messrs Houghton Mifflin had, in fact, to some extent profited from the absence of any other English version and a considerable number of their copies had passed across the frontiers of our territory over the years. I thought that the lapse of time, and the justification for a reissue after it, required an explanation more authoritative than that of a publisher, and we were fortunate that Professor D. C. Watt of London University agreed to provide this. His long introductory essay and his annotations to the text were masterly and provided a commentary which brilliantly exploded every point made by Adolf Hitler as it arose. Publication was scheduled for the early autumn of 1965 and it was announced at some length in our relevant lists, which I had hitherto assumed were at least glanced at by the members of the parent board, who automatically received them.

I was already aware of doubts, and indeed antagonisms, among the publishing staff. Far the most serious came from Harold Harris, himself a Jew, who was outraged by our plans.

He had, of course, every right to be outraged if he felt that way, but I found his attitude difficult to understand although it prepared me to some extent for the onslaught to come. Almost simultaneously I found we were under attack from what I would have thought to be two altogether disparate bodies — the West German Government (acting on behalf of the Bavarian authorities) and the Board of Deputies of British Jews. The Germans were protesting on legal grounds, denying our right to publish property which they had sequestered and which they thought would arouse old antagonisms best forgotten. More astonishing to me, and to others to whom I talked, was the relentless fury of the Jews that the record of their dreadful persecution under Nazi Germany should again be illuminated. Both they and the German government had one objective in mind: the whole episode of *Mein Kampf* and its consequences should be swept under the carpet and forgotten — so far, at any rate, as the English language prevailed throughout the Commonwealth.

Normally doubts crowd in upon me, but on this occasion I had none. I thought that a letter to *The Times* outlining the problems would prove of value and I submitted one in draft to the editor, who agreed that, when appropriate, he would hope to print it. I further acquainted the then Foreign Secretary, Michael Stewart, of our intentions and of the implications which seemed to loom. He was grateful for the information but hoped that we would not in fact publish until after the Queen's projected visit to West Germany. Reasonable enough.

In all these to-ings and fro-ings there had been no concealment. It seemed to me an editorial matter and especially so in the overall climate of 'overlordship' which appeared to be gaining ground in the whole arena of 'communication'. The scene was set; the plans were made.

On Wednesday, July 18th, there was a routine meeting of the parent board; and on the Friday I was to begin my annual holiday which, with my wife and stepson, was to take me on a Russian liner to Leningrad and back. I had nothing much of consequence to report to the board, and being short of material I launched into an account of the problems which had confronted our reissue of *Mein Kampf* which, I had explained, had been in our seasonal catalogue for months. I seemed to hold their attention which was more than I could normally hope to do. Not a word was said, not a funeral note, and so far as I knew the meeting came to its end.

Hindsight and the charity of age require me to accept a certain blame. I have to admit that I would have been wise to paint the picture at an earlier stage, and that had I done so every action that I had taken would have received support. It was the affront of ignorance which did the damage and not the facts of the matter. However, I went happily off to Leningrad. Half-way through the Baltic Sea on our return came a cable from Holt requesting my attendance at a special board meeting two days hence. As I could neither swim nor fly, this was impossible; nor was I going to have yet another holiday interfered with by Adolf Hitler.

On my return I was informed that all plans to republish *Mein Kampf* had been halted. I was in dire disgrace since I had incurred great expenditure and even more embarrassment. The press of course reported abject surrender to the pressures of Jewry and the Germans.

I wrote the drafts of many furious letters of resignation and consulted my trade stalwarts, Allen Lane, Edmond Segrave and Jack Newth. They were appalled. Allen Lane wanted at once to publish *Mein Kampf* as a Penguin and was ready to damn the consequences of breaching Hutchinson's rights, which Holt had prudently reserved in his ill-fated communiqué. But they counselled against resignation on an issue so unpleasant and so did my newer allies at the BBC. 'Wait until you are sacked,' advised Hugh Greene.

A little while later, Hugh Greene, as director-general of the BBC, faced an extraordinarily similar situation which brought him too within a hairsbreadth of resignation. The occasion was a meeting of the governors which for some reason I and another governor were obliged to miss. Hugh felt that his report to the board had been dullish and on the spur of the moment told of a proposed *24 Hours* interview with Baldur von Schirach after the completion of his sentence as a war criminal. This plan, he said, had his full support since it was an exposure of the deep corruption involved in a man's surrender to Nazism. To his intense surprise Lord Normanbrook was at once questioning and doubtful, but at least he expressed his opposition in the director-general's presence, which was more than my board had done. Hugh Greene thought instantly of my recent experience in a similar situation and wished I were in my place. Certainly I would have come to his aid, and so I believe would that other absent governor; and between us we might have tipped the balance. But the decision went against Hugh Greene and he was instructed that the interview should not take place. Greene was deeply angry and upset and came, he told me later, closer to resignation than ever he had before. After the meeting he expostulated with Norman. 'It's your own silly fault,' said the chairman, 'you should never have raised the issue.' Hugh Greene and I decided we had each learned one lesson. Neither director-generals nor managing directors should ever attempt to fill up time at board meetings.

Nothing more was said about *Mein Kampf* for some two years and then it arose in more or less casual conversation with Mr Holt, who had never been other than scrupulous in leaving editorial judgments in my responsibility and in fact was to remain so until the end of my days with Hutchinson. The mistake of the board, in my view, was to allow its indignation with me to deflect it from calmer consideration. In the July of 1965 no public controversy had arisen, and there remains no doubt in my mind that if we had then proceeded with our plans to publish, the subsequent outcry would have been considerably muted.

I had very nearly had enough of *Mein Kampf*. It was never a book I would want to publish and it was a wretched dish to find on one's plate. I knew very well that the attack, when it came, would be levelled against me. One of the oddities of the contemporary scene is that the more impersonal groups, agglomerations and conglomerates become, the more pertinaceous is the search for a human scapegoat in time of trouble. I suggested that as an alternative we might wash our hands of the damned thing and let Penguin take it on since they were so keen to have it. No, this would not do at all, it would be an abnegation of our responsibilities. I rather agreed but with a reflection best described as wry.

The assault when it came was this time more vicious. In the normal course of publishing routine I had explained our plans. Harold Harris maintained a consistent view throughout. He was deeply opposed to publication and shared entirely the view again put forward by the Board of Deputies of British Jews, which sent a deputation to see me. Others in the office junior to Harold Harris were disturbed, and a note in which I stated our plans was 'leaked' within a matter of hours.

A worrying factor was the deterioration during the past years in the world situation. Violence was on the increase; so were racialism and terrorist activities. This added argument to the serious doubts of responsible sections of the Jewish world. The West German Government made new approaches and made new threats, but not, I felt, with any intention of carrying them out. The price of the book was fixed at a high rate, which was indeed necessary since I insisted that the contractual royalty of 25 per cent should be paid willy-nilly. This would go to Curtis Brown and the problem of getting rid of it was theirs and not ours. The onslaught from the Jewish press and various Jewish organizations continued. It was even suggested from one quarter that 'as money seems to be your chief objective' a body of Jews would be ready to purchase our rights. I dealt with all these matters as best I could and received at the end of the day most powerful support from the Council of Christians and Jews, which included many of the highest distinction. As I suspected, the criticism was levelled almost entirely against me in person; and when that year I visited that horrific nightmare of publishing known as the Frankfurt Book Fair I was told that a bomb threat against me had been made.

Publication took place in 1969, under the Hutchinson imprint, of course, and not that of Hurst & Blackett. The book was reprinted towards the end of 1969; and three years later an expensive 'softback' edition was done. This created another protracted outcry and further visitations from the Board of Deputies, who reminded me of an assurance that we had no plans for any paperback issue — by which I had meant an edition put out as a popular paperback at the cheapest price. Our 'softback' edition was in the original format but with a stiff paper binding and at a relatively high price. On this occasion the *Jewish Chronicle* took a course which I greatly admired. They were adamant in their view that publication was wrong and especially so in this cheaper form. I was under considerable attack from them. On publication they sent copies to a number of leading historians, some of whom were Jews. There was no dissenting voice. Each one of those historians was fully in favour of publication and felt that the book should be readily available. Each opinion was printed in the *Jewish Chronicle*, despite their completely opposite conviction.

I was much touched by a conversation with a young German student. The book was not then available at all in the German language (and this ban on it is still, I think, maintained) and I told him of the difficulties we had encountered. He thought we had been quite right and was angered by the suppression in his own country. 'I have a right to know', he said, 'what it was that sent my father mad.'

16
A Curious Case of Plagiarism

A<small>N</small> always fascinating conjecture is to what extent plagiarism in books operates without detection. The risk can often be very slight and I frequently wonder how far a publisher could proceed in the publication, as a new book, of an accepted 'classic' before the dawn of a truth which can prove disconcertingly diverting as well as costly. The strange case of James Collier's novel *Fires of Youth* was certainly unique within my own experience and probably the briefest exposition of it is wisest and best.

In the spring of 1962 Arthur Koestler announced the establishment of funds to be administered by Trustees which would seek to alleviate the desolation of culture for those languishing in one or another of Her Majesty's Prisons. It was an admirable, imaginative and liberal scheme and warmly accepted by the authorities. A sum of £400 a year as prize money was guaranteed by Mr Koestler, and one of £100 a year, to cover general expenses, by A. D. Peters, the literary agent. Administration of the scheme was undertaken by Mr Peters, who became a Trustee, together with the Hon. David Astor, Mr C. H. Rolph (C. R. Hewitt) and Mr John D. Illsley.

Prizes were to be awarded in arts and crafts, music and literature, and a distinguished panel of judges undertook to assess the entries and determine the winners. The members of the literature panel were Henry Green, J. B. Priestley, V. S. Pritchett and Philip Toynbee.

A number of manuscripts (how many was never divulged) were submitted and after due examination and deliberation a manuscript (written in hand and only subsequently typed) entitled *Young and Sensitive*, by Don Robson, was awarded the first prize. In selecting it the judges wrote: 'We were unanimous in awarding the first prize to Don Robson's novel. We believe that it will be recognized as a work of outstanding merit in its own right, independently of the special circumstances in which it was written.'

I had for some years been privileged to publish the works of Arthur Koestler and was thus glad to have the first opportunity of considering Mr Robson's prizewinning script. As soon as it arrived I read it personally and at once shared the enthusiasm expressed by the panel of judges. At this time I also met Mr Robson (who had completed his prison sentence) and was much impressed that a not altogether articulate young man should have been able to write so sincere and moving a story. Thus, through his agent, A. D. Peters, who undertook to act for Mr Robson in a voluntary capacity, a normal publishing agreement was signed.

We contrived our publishing plans with considerable care, not only because we felt the novel to be a major achievement, but also because we thought that the Koestler Award should be made widely known.

During the process of publication we were in frequent touch with Mr Robson and arranged that, as decorative endpapers to the book, we should reproduce two pages of the novel in his own hand-writing upon the designated paper of H.M. Prison, Dartmoor.

The book was published on September 28th, 1964, and received wide critical acclaim:

'The judges remark that it is a work of outstanding merit irrespective of the special circumstances in which it was written. They are right.' John Higgins, *Sunday Telegraph*

'The novel has a primitive drive, a crude jagged sort of veracity, like a Sunday painting in which the sharp observation and visual gentility are oddly mingled.' Iain Hamilton, *Daily Telegraph*

'The best account of an adolescent affair I have ever read. ... It is not an elegant performance, but it is the kind of honest recreation of experience that renews one's faith in fiction.' Irving Wardle, *Observer*

'He *has* written a work of outstanding merit ... the bleak story of a boy's first flirtation, a really perceptive look at the youngster's relationship with his father, is strongly reminiscent of the best of Sherwood Anderson.' Mordecai Richler, *Spectator*

'Intense and absorbing.' David Hughes, *Sunday Times*

'A very good book.' Peter Lewis, *Daily Mail*

'One of the best, most poignantly written novels for years.' *Vogue*

Don Robson himself was interviewed on television and the book was accorded much greater publicity than could normally be anticipated for a first novel. Paperback rights were quickly acquired by Messrs Penguin and rights in both the German and French languages were taken up.

The scene was set for a modest but distinguished success and Don Robson informed us that he was at work on a second novel. He had meanwhile married an admirable young woman and found regular employment in the north of England.

So far so good, and there was nothing to disturb the equanimity of the scene or to suggest that the casual reader of a copy borrowed from a public library in Swindon was to reveal a quite astonishing deception. In September 1965 a letter reached my desk. It was a civil and courteous note from a gentleman in Swindon pointing out that the reading of *Young and Sensitive* by Don Robson had seemed somehow to strike a chord of familiarity. He had reflected on this and had subsequently discovered a strange similarity between this novel and an American paperback, *Fires of Youth* by Charles Williams, which he had acquired from a local bookshop.

Hardly daring to breathe I requested the loan of this paperback. It came and an examination proved disconcerting in the extreme. Apart from trifling changes the novel *Fires of Youth* was identical to *Young and Sensitive* by Don Robson, and had been published in 1961.

It was clearly necessary to proceed with caution and, if at all possible, to trace the Charles Williams of *Fires of Youth* and also the American paperback publisher. Mr Robson had, at the same time, to be confronted with the situation and the French and German publishers, together with Messrs Penguin, warned of these dicey developments.

The dilemma was one of considerable delicacy. A very worthwhile scheme had been clearly subjected to damaging abuse. The gentleman in Swindon, equally clearly, had in his possession a 'story' capable of creating a considerable sensation, which sooner or later was bound to explode. In addition to this the Home Secretary was shortly to open a public exhibition of the work submitted for the third year of the Koestler Award. A number of red faces seemed a certainty but the decision was at once taken that a public announcement should be issued with as little delay as possible and in such a manner as to do the least possible harm to the Koestler Award scheme.

All my efforts to trace either the American publisher or the real author at first proved abortive. So, too, it proved impossible to ascertain if *Fires of Youth* by Charles Williams had ever been in circulation within Dartmoor Prison. Mr Robson's explanation sounded plausible and once confronted with the accusation of plagiarism he never sought to evade the consequences. His story, which he continued to maintain, was that in Dartmoor with him was a fellow prisoner who 'fancied himself as a writer'. Mr Robson, anxious to participate in the 'literary' contest, alleged that he 'purchased' a script from his fellow prisoner for fifteen ounces of tobacco. He then copied the script in his own hand but made minor changes which he thought made the story 'more proper', and indeed he claimed that he 'turned it into interesting literature'. In point of fact the changes were negligible, as any comparison revealed.

No proceedings were instituted against Mr Robson who indeed continued to his best ability to minimize the financial losses his admitted deception involved. He in time refunded in full the money received from the Trustees of the Award.

A careful, but frank, statement was prepared for publication on behalf of the interested parties. It read:

The following statement is issued by Messrs Rubinstein, Nash, for the Trustees of the 1963 Arthur Koestler annual award for creative work by prisoners in Her Majesty's Prisons, and Messrs Hutchinson.

A novel entitled *Young and Sensitive* by Don Robson was selected by the appointed judges to receive the 1963 award for creative writing. In the following year the book was successfully published by Messrs Hutchinson.

Within the last weeks it has been ascertained that the novel did not in fact represent the unaided work of the winner of the award but derived largely from a paperback novel previously published in the United States entitled *Fires of Youth* by Charles Williams of which neither the author nor the publisher has it proved possible to trace.

Young and Sensitive has thus been withdrawn from circulation and plans for any further editions have been cancelled.

The Trustees of the Award and the Publishers deeply regret this incident.

This note was to be released on a certain Tuesday morning towards the end of 1965 and all concerned were vastly relieved that no premature leak had taken place. An explanation put out before the story became known was clearly better than one seeming only to be prompted by an injurious disclosure.

The race, in point of fact, was won almost by minutes. Ten minutes before the statement was issued a newspaper telephoned me to say it had heard a story and could I or could I not authenticate it.

Many will remember the wide publicity which followed and the remarkable absence of blame or of doubt as to the wisdom of the scheme as a whole. There was no disclosure of the whereabouts of Mr Robson and no exploitation or distortion of an incident which, however serious, certainly held a considerable element of humour. 'The bloke should be given the Duke of Edinburgh award for initiative,' commented a prison warder on duty at the Charing Cross exhibition referred to.

The story was widely repeated in other countries and finally, almost by chance, the real author was discovered to be James Lincoln Collier of Croton-on-Hudson in New York State. Mr Collier behaved with great magnanimity and with his agreement the novel was republished by Penguin in the form in which he wrote it with the addition of an explanatory foreword.

17
Reithian Heights

WHEN in 1960 I joined the Board of Governors of the
BBC, the Pilkington Inquiry into broadcasting was
well under way, and the Corporation was producing its
voluminous papers for consideration. Each or these was scruti-
nized by the board and it was a fortunate moment for any newcomer to become involved. The various papers covered every
aspect of broadcasting and the BBC, and when assimilated provided a nourishment of knowledge which might otherwise take
quite a few years of the five-year term to acquire. It was naturally
a moment of some anxiety for the BBC. It was for the first time
up against the submissions of a rival authority and had to sub-
stantiate its claim to pre-eminence in the world of broadcasting,
and sustain the philosophy of public-service broadcasting as
first proclaimed by John Reith. In the final outcome the BBC
was to emerge from Pilkington so much whiter than white that
it proved to be positively embarrassing. But this could not be
foreseen and it was part of Hugh Greene's wise strategy to enlist
the support of Lord Reith, which it was never wise to assume.
He was predictably unpredictable and capable of hurling a
thunderbolt against the citadel of his own making.

Shortly before my arrival on the scene a Beerbohm cartoon
of Reith in his early BBC days had appeared in a Sotheby catalogue, and it was shrewdly thought by the BBC that its purchase
would agreeably flatter the old man when he came to hear about
it. I had never met Lord Reith, but regarded him as one of the
great men of our time. Some years previously I had read his
rather appalling autobiography *Into the Wind* and now thought
that I had an opportunity to present myself to his notice and

possibly extract another book from him. I thus invited him to lunch at the Garrick Club. There was no conceivable possibility of not recognizing him. That 'wuthering height' as Winston Churchill had called him, was unmistakable and immensely powerful in its magnetism. The great scarred face, the erratic assemblage of fierce eyebrows, the curiously unexpected gentleness of the smile which removed all impression of ferocity, the mobility of his hands, the dramatic artistry of even his conversational voice and the odd search for what to say with it.

He was extremely affable and I made what I hoped to be the right noises about the BBC, the impact of his continuing presence and how delighted we all were that he felt able to support our evidence to Pilkington. It seemed that Hugh Greene and even more his wife Elaine had won his friendship and admiration. All seemed well. He knew nothing of the BBC's acquisition of the Beerbohm cartoon until I told him that it was now in a prominent position in the third-floor boardroom. 'Yes,' I explained, 'it was spotted in a Sotheby catalogue and the BBC dispatched an anonymous bidder to its auction who was successful in obtaining it.' Rather good going, I thought to myself, gratified that so new a governor could talk in such terms to so great a being.

Lord Reith looked at me with that expression of astonishment he so well cultivated. Both his hands were on the table, and he was leaning slightly back in his chair. 'The BBC bought that?' he asked.

'Yes,' I said, 'and very glad they were to do so.'

'My boy,' said his lordship, 'my boy, I was the other fellow bidding.'

Some months later, by which time I had enjoyed other encounters with Reith, I was deputed to take the chair for him on an occasion regarded as of some importance. In those days, and I think still, the BBC organized occasional residential seminars for senior staff at Uplands, near High Wycombe. Various courses were run and various speakers of distinction in a variety of fields would be invited to address the assembly. Lord Reith, in this period of patriarchal benediction, had consented to speak one evening. The BBC was to be his chosen subject. 'Put a foot wrong,' I was helpfully admonished, 'and you will undo the good of years.'

I arrived early, Reith arrived late. We were to dine with one or two of those attending the course and the dinner, naturally enough, was of institutional mediocrity. Reith seemed a little tetchy. The business of the evening followed immediately. I was to make an introductory remark or so with appropriate genuflection, Reith was to follow and there would then be some sort of discussion. I thought I could just about relate the Beerbohm story without disaster. Keeping a wary eye upon the architect of our destinies beside me, I launched into my account. I was unnerved by the impression that Lord Reith was turning slightly pink, but I couldn't be sure; and had I been, there was nothing to be done about it. The story caused a good deal of amusement, and after a few other remarks I sat down. Lord Reith rose slowly to his greatest height. He looked towards heaven as though in the role of a prophet who had just left it and would shortly return. He had no notes of any kind. 'That story', he began, 'which Mr Lusty has just told you, happens to be true except in one particular. And an important particular. I have never in all my life called a governor "my boy".'

And then some magic was wrought in John Reith which made for every person in that room an evening to remember for the rest of a lifetime. It was spellbinding. For nearly an hour he talked about the BBC and broadcasting, about its past, about its future, about the problems it had surmounted and those it had still to face. It was inspired and so was the theatre of it all.

Quite suddenly he sat down and for a moment there was silence and then applause, a little restrained as if it was, perhaps, not quite the proper thing to do. Clearly it was not an occasion for questions, let alone discussion, and I ended the meeting. An excited young producer, coming up to me with a drink, was ablaze with enthusiasm. 'I have heard Caruso sing,' he said, 'I have seen Pavlova dance and I have now heard Reith talk about the BBC.'

Reith was to take me back to London and we clambered into the rear of an enormous Rolls-Royce to be driven away. He was rather quiet, but towards the end of the journey he put his hand on my knee. 'My boy,' he said, 'I do not know what came over me tonight. I said things that I have never said before and will never say again. Very curious. I am glad that you were there.'

An early visit I made within the BBC was to its impressive library, one of Reith's early essentials, then in the charge of Robert Collison. He was a Reithian and asked if I knew that Lord Reith had in his possession a complete but unpublished manuscript dealing with his experiences in the First World War. I did not, and wrote to Reith telling of this talk and suggesting that if in fact there was this script, would he consider letting me read it.

Almost by return of post arrived the manuscript of *Wearing Spurs*. This, apparently, had at one time been seen by Jonathan Cape who turned it down much to its author's chagrin and bewilderment. He would be much interested to hear my views. It was not a long book and I read it at a sitting. I found it of intense and curiously moving interest. As a revelation of the young Reith its main fascination would be for those who at some time had come within range of his strange and contradictory character. But there existed quite enough of such people to ensure a modest and comfortable sale and it would be a nice book to have in one's list. It was certainly authentic Reith from the start. The arrogance; the uncertain certainties; the conviction of what should be done and when and how. As a young officer he is sent with a dispatch to a meeting of allied generals. 'I came away', he declares, 'convinced of how much better I could wage this war than they.' He was clearly gallant and a man of action. He managed somehow to acquire the best horses and charged fearlessly towards any destiny he felt was beckoning. He won his spurs; and while he occupied his flat in Lollard's Tower within the precincts of Lambeth Palace they hung from a hook on a lavatory door. His pride in them was very great.

I knew that he would want and expect news more immediately than was reasonably possible and I thus telephoned from my home late one Saturday evening to tell him of my enjoyment and of the pleasure it would be to publish the book. 'I am sitting here with my wife in front of a little fire after a simple supper, wondering what news you might have for me,' he said as if he were some old-age pensioner soliciting fuel. 'It's very good news for me,' he added. 'We will not discuss terms this evening,' I said, 'but I will be writing you on Monday.' I proposed, in that letter, an adequate but not excessive advance. 'I can only imagine', he retorted 'that a nought has dropped from your letter.' I explained, as best I could, the facts of publishing life and he seemed mollified.

In due course *Wearing Spurs* was published and was widely and favourably reviewed. I proposed that on the day of its publication he should again join me for lunch at the Garrick. He was in lively form and explained his regret at not earlier indulging in and enjoying some of the good things of life. Yes, thank you, he would take a little sherry now and perhaps a little wine with his lunch. It was a warm day and he chose some cold meat and salad. A new, rather inexperienced and obviously nervous waitress appeared before his lordship and placed before him a full carafe of white wine and another of red. His great eyebrows rose in some astonishment. 'All this for me?' he asked. 'No, I am afraid not,' I had to say, 'she thinks them oil and vinegar for your salad.'

Lord Reith, like most authors, followed with zeal and interest the sale of his book. He discovered, as most authors do, that not every bookshop seemed familiar with it. With the famous spurs it made a brave display at Messrs Hatchards in Piccadilly, but this hardly compensated its author for the lack of copies elsewhere. But it did well and one of the reprint book clubs acquired it for later issue. The sales figure none the less continued to appal him. Surely they should be multiplied by ten? Into what grave error had we fallen? All of his friends who were able to run a copy to ground were reading the book with the greatest interest. Many more were complaining of their inability to obtain it.

His faith in me began to wane. There was a certain petulance which arose in part from my disinclination to purchase outright for an immense sum the vast personal diary in which he recorded the activity of his every day. He placed in *The Times* a rather sad note asking for suggestions as to what he might do with this. Oddly enough, at a much earlier date when still working for the *Evening Standard*, my colleague Harold Harris had examined it on Lord Beaverbrook's instruction but had concluded that neither was it publishable nor was it worth Lord Beaverbrook's acquisition for his massive archives.

Lord Reith was also again becoming disenchanted with the

BBC, and he did not approve all of the activities and innovations of 'that fellow Greene'. He hoped I was exerting my influence against him. I had to tell him that I was doing no such thing. I was in close agreement with 'that fellow Greene' and so were my fellow governors.

Lord Reith was, of course, invited to the Guildhall Banquet in celebration of the BBC's fortieth anniversary. A personal letter from the chairman, Sir Arthur fforde, had accompanied the invitation. His lordship had been good enough to accept 'on the absolute understanding that he would not be called upon to speak'. This he was given. On the morning of the feast he telephoned the director responsible for arrangements. 'It is clearly understood', he said, 'that I do not have to speak tonight.' The director confirmed that this was so. There was a pause, only to be described as pregnant. 'But why', then thundered his lordship, 'am I not to be allowed to speak tonight?'

Not long after *Wearing Spurs* was published, Lord Reith was to fulfil Her Majesty's command to be her High Commissioner at Holyrood House in Edinburgh for the annual Assembly of the Church of Scotland. It was an honour well deserved and one which enormously pleased him. In a theatrically staged production he fulfilled the leading role to perfection and enjoyed its every moment. When the honour, contrary I believe to all precedent, was accorded him for a second year he confided to me, quite untruthfully, that he had accepted only for his wife's sake. 'I was greatly astonished', he said, 'that my wife should want the experience for a second time. She is a remarkable woman, but only from her ankles up.'

He was kind enough, on the first occasion, to invite Babs and myself to one of his formal banquets in Holyrood House. In a letter accompanying the splendid invitations he hoped I would see to it that *Wearing Spurs* would be well in evidence in all Scottish bookshops and particularly in Edinburgh 'where the interest will be very great'.

On the evening before the banquet I had been the BBC host at a supper party following a concert, and the Lord Provost was my guest at a centre table accommodating Edinburgh's highest dignitaries. There was an attractive display of candlelight, and after a while I was conscious that something appeared to be falling as if from the heavens above. No one else seemed to notice this, but I became aware that something quite extraordinary was happening to the Lord Provost's eyebrows. They were slowly solidifying in white candlegrease. So was I, and our suits were a mess. I drew the Lord Provost's attention to our condition and conveyed the appropriate apologies of the BBC. What had happened was that a candle had in some way exploded. It was fortunate for us that the blast was upwards and not into our faces. The Lord Provost had other suits to call upon, but I had none and was due to accompany Lord Reith in the morning to the opening session of the Church Assembly. Repairs were not beyond the ingenuity of the BBC.

Lord Reith's banquet was splendid and impressive pageantry. No monarch alive or dead could have played more perfectly the role of Reith. Emblazoned by decorations and glory, he moved around his guests escorted by court dignitaries of Scottish tradition. The son of the manse was enjoying his rightful heritage.

I had an odd, small link with Reith. My first wife, Joan, had attended Park School in Glasgow and so, in his day, had Reith. The Reiths' manse was adjacent, and Joan remembered that when Reith's father lay dying the morning singing of hymns was stilled. I told Reith of this. 'I will tell you what really happened,' he said. 'My father was a long time dying. He was conscious that he could hear no morning song from Park School. "Why are they not singing?" he asked and was told that it was on his account. "Send across a message," he commanded, "telling them to sing louder than ever they have." '

The evening progressed with slow stateliness at Holyrood. At a certain hour, after many guests had left, formality was a little relaxed and those remaining removed to a rather less imposing room on the floor below. In due course Lady Reith, escorted by her entourage of ladies-in-waiting, departed for bed and again the guests had dwindled. I had been told that Lord Reith wished to speak to me and thus, with others, we were ushered to a lower room still. It appeared to be a room for equerries and others of that ilk who could be summoned to the presence by serried rows of dangling bells. Formality had almost departed, although Reith shed none of his festooned and shining armoury.

He came across to me. 'I cannot see any copies of my book in the bookshop windows,' he said in reproachful tones. 'You are losing me many sales. It is a great disaster. The book has been a lamentable failure.' To the best of my ability I tried to assure him that it had not been any such thing. The High Commissioner turned sorrowfully away.

It was around this time that I contrived the only meeting between Lord Reith and Sir Allen Lane, and I felt curiously privileged to do so. It seemed to me that their impact on awakening minds has been incalculable and surely something which historians will note as they survey other less agreeable activities of an era. I think too it can be argued that their achievements have been orchestrated into some symphonic splendour beyond comprehension, and certainly unknown to them. Reith, at the BBC, preceded Lane and his Penguin books by a dozen years of radio in a formative period. His conception of public-service broadcasting was a great deal more liberal than legend suggests. He determined not to undervalue the intelligence, perception and curiosity of its audience. He saw more clearly than most the capacity of radio to awaken minds, especially young ones, to wider interests and compassions.

It was the same conception, less deliberate perhaps, which determined Allen Lane that a public existed for good books in paper covers at a cheap price. In the main, this had been a market for the exploitation of popular fiction. Nothing wrong in that, but Allen Lane had other ideas which were, at first, derided by the trade. It could well be that Allen Lane, in 1935, was furthering in the world of print the purposes set by Reith for radio. Even towards the end of his life he never really was able to comprehend the magnitude of his own achievement, and was bewildered by the acclaim and honours accorded him. When he learned of his knighthood he took to his bed for twenty-four hours of disbelief. 'I felt bloated', he declared. No two men could be accorded temperaments further apart, but I was fascinated to witness that their recognition and understanding was instant.

Allen Lane was quick in decision on almost everything except the destiny of Penguin Books after his departure from the scene. The thought of ultimate delegation was one he could never bring himself to countenance. The pen would almost be poised over final documentation only to be thrown away at the last, often to intense embarrassment. He discussed the problem with almost everybody he met and he received proposals for its solution in great variety. He was fearful for the editorial independence and integrity of Penguin if, after his death, it should fall into an alien financial control which, in point of fact, was very likely. One day I suggested to him that it might be possible to place Penguin Books within a control similar to that of the BBC and which would give it a unique status in British publishing. 'Why not', I suggested, 'have a word with Reith?'

Thus it was that I came to take Reith to lunch with Lane at the Penguin headquarters at Harmondsworth. Reith at that time was chairman of British Oxygen, whose offices stood at the beginning of the Great West Road and were a little complicated to approach. We had received minute instructions from Reith as to how this could be overcome and he would be awaiting us at half past twelve.

It was a vile day of driving rain and we messed our approach. I could observe a great figure striding up and down a covered entrance. We finally made it. 'You are late,' said Reith, 'and you did not follow my directions.'

We drove in more or less silence to Harmondsworth, and presented ourselves to Penguin's reception desk. I explained our purpose. The girl made inquiries. 'Sir Allen will be with you in a few moments,' she said. Lord Reith looked unhappy. 'Would you do this to me?' he inquired. 'I don't think I would,' I replied, feeling craven. 'No, I don't think you would either,' he said a little grimly. And then Allen, full of cheer, came down the stairs and it was at this moment that recognition was immediate. There was no doubt about it at all and Reith was at once transformed. All tetchiness disappeared.

We toured the Penguin operation, Reith clearly impressed. 'Most wonderful,' he said. 'I had no idea. I am enthralled by this.' And so he continued throughout. We had an agreeable and convivial lunch. Lane talked about his problems and Reith understood them. He could recognize the similarity with those which he had solved in broadcasting. He would give thought to the matter. 'And no doubt, Sir Allen, I shall be hearing from you?'

They parted on terms of great cordiality, and during the run back to his office Lord Reith enthused about Sir Allen and all that he had seen. I drove on to my office and on arrival a message was awaiting me from Lord Reith. He wanted to express his warmest thanks for an experience which had deeply impressed him. Allen, of course, did nothing at all. After a few weeks I received a pained letter from Reith. 'I have heard nothing further from that fellow Lane,' he wrote. 'I thought he wanted me to take it over.' And in these few words lies the explanation for so many of the frustrations which bedevilled all his years.

It was while I was vice-chairman of the BBC that the Reith–Muggeridge conversations made such superb television and especially for those with any experience of Reith. Again was revealed the range of his theatrical ability. I wrote him a line of appreciation, but by this time I was losing favour in his sight. The 'negligible' sales of his book bewildered him. He replied thanking me for my kind words. He himself was doubtful of his wisdom in agreeing to the conversations and then launched into a blistering attack on the incredible parsimony of the BBC over the matter of his expenses. They had behaved abominably and would I kindly attend to the matter. I replied that if the vice-chairman of his time had interfered in a point of this kind, he would not have been best pleased. I felt sure that his accusations were groundless, as indeed they proved to be.

Alas he was unable any longer to understand the BBC or that it could not conform to the simpler pattern of his day. I asked him once how he would run the BBC today with its television channels, its proliferations of radio commitments and the inevitable complexity of its administration. He had thumped the table. 'I would run it today exactly as I ran it yesterday,' he declared.

I was in touch with him once or twice again and sent him books when he was in hospital. But there was little response. I had failed his hopes and was associated with, if not indeed responsible for, the imagined failure of *Wearing Spurs*. Within a little while he went home to Scotland and before long he was dead.

He had decreed that there should be no memorial service, but left instructions as to the form one should take. A great congregation attended one in Westminster Abbey. At its close a lone Scottish piper marched the aisles playing a lament. It was an intensely moving farewell.

18
To Russia With Love

MY first involvement with the Russians arrived in 1959 when we announced our publication of Dudintsev's novel *Not by Bread Alone*. There were the usual complications of copyright and the ever-present risk that some other translation might beat us at the post. The book had caused something of a sensation, implicit in its title, and it was then impossible to establish any link with its courageous author. That we had it at all was due to the initiative of a young editor, James Clarke, at that time in charge of our contracts and foreign rights department. This is a key position in any large publishing organization for it enables its occupant to establish personal contacts with publishers all over the world. As events developed the author was able to hear of our plans and to express his pleasure, but there could be no formal agreement.

From an obscure agency in Czechoslovakia we were notified that the novel had been made copyright in that country and that any unauthorized translation would be proceeded against. We took no notice and the translation continued at top speed. Within a short time I received a call from the Russian Embassy and was requested to receive two emissaries empowered to discuss with me the problems of *Not by Bread Alone*. A date was arranged and promptly upon the appointed hour two very large Russians presented themselves at my office. At that time most large Russians looked astonishingly like Mr Krushchev and these were no exceptions. They exuded a vaguely sinister impression and a certain emanation of threat. 'We do not wish', one said with no beating about the bush, 'that you should publish *Not by Bread Alone*.' It would have been a wise precaution to have Iain Hamilton with me, but I had not thought of this and to have summoned him at this stage would, it seemed to me, concede pusillanimity. I thus expressed my regret and said that we had a contrary intention and were well ahead with our plans. 'But', they protested, and they seemed throughout to speak in chorus, keeping perfect time, 'the novel, it is copyright. It has been registered in Czechoslovakia. They can stop you.'

'If it is as simple as that,' I replied, 'we would protect our own copyrights in like manner. It is a pity', I went on, 'that we still have this big problem to settle. It means that so much which should be published in both our countries cannot be.' They seemed to agree and then started on another tack. 'Mr Dudintsev has changed his mind,' they said. 'He does not now want his book published in your country or translated into English. He has changed his mind.' I again expressed regret but added that if the author had indeed changed his mind or wished to correct any impression his novel might make, I would be most willing to print at the beginning or the end of the book any apologia Mr Dudintsev might write. This seemed slightly to deflate them, but only for a moment. 'No,' they said, exchanging a glance, 'that would not do. It would not help at all. It is a pity that you cannot understand. It is not good for the relationship between us.' I made no reply and there was a lengthy silence as they appeared to reflect. The climate, in a curious way, had improved.

Consultation appeared to be conducted by telepathy and after a moment or so was concluded. 'You are', they said, 'determined to proceed with your plans. You will publish *Not by Bread Alone*?'

'Yes,' I replied, 'that is exactly so.'

There was again a pause and their eyes seemed to search the room. For the first time a certain humanity became evident in their looks. And then with total irrelevance and total unexpectedness they looked at me and smiled. 'What nice wallpaper you have in this room,' they said. They rose, I thanked them for coming and escorted them to the lift.

From the strangeness of that moment the Russians became completely co-operative and actively so in our publication of *Not by Bread Alone*. No reference was ever again made to their displeasure. I was able to correspond with Dudintsev in Moscow, and somehow it was arranged that royalties should reach him. When a little later I was in Moscow, Dudintsev was put in touch with me and we had a long telephone conversation.

Publishers at that time were not including Russia in their perambulations around the world and Iain Hamilton argued most persuasively that I should go there. It wasn't a prospect that greatly excited me, but in the spring of 1960 there appeared to be a slight breeze of liberation in Russian policies. Iain had been in touch with MezhKniga, the huge Russian organization at that time responsible for all Russian publishing, and ascertained their enthusiasm for such a visit and their assurance that they would make all arrangements for it.

I had little idea of what to expect or what I might achieve. Nor could I suppose that I would arouse much enthusiasm as Dudintsev's publisher. On the other hand it would be worth while if some continuing liaison were to be contrived, for there must be many books of value on both sides available by other than fortuitous whimsy. Neither would it come amiss if the Russians could be persuaded to pay royalties to British authors other than a chosen few. I was certainly not willing to make the expedition alone, nor did I feel it was exactly a jaunt to which I should subject my wife.

Thus I invited my friend Tom Girtin who, in return for the free ride, would come along so that to the best of our abilities we could ensure one another's safety. It was not then the casual flip it has become today and neither of our wives entertained much hope of our return to them. The necessary visas and documents were arranged with the minimum of formality and on the evening of May Day we had what our wives assumed to be a last dinner together before entrusting ourselves to the care of B.E.A. and its midnight flight to Moscow.

I felt a little hesitant about going without a more specific purpose than seemed apparent and thus on the spur of a moment I drafted a rough agreement between Hutchinson and Mezh-Kniga under which we would respect one another's copyrights and undertake the payment of normal royalties. It seemed a little grandiose in conception but would at least serve as a basis for discussion at the various meetings being arranged.

The whole progress of the visit acquired a kind of lunatic

quality and a year or two later, while crossing the Atlantic, I recorded some of its events in the style of J. D. Salinger, whose novel *Raise High the Roof Beam, Carpenters* was much in vogue. I sent it to Iain Hamilton, by that time editor of the *Spectator* and its publication seemed to arouse some amusement. I venture thus to quote it:

PRESS LOW THE STOP-COCK, PLUMBERS

Tom Girtin it was who came with me on the trip to Moscow. The one who lives in Montpelier Square and has the swell pictures. He writes books, too, and appears in the odd film as a smash hit.

We set out, after a poshed-up dinner and too many brandies already, from Cromwell Road in the bus. Only one other geezer on it, apart from the driver, and he wore a deerstalker cap but kept his ears free. So Tom and I whispered, going as we were to Moscow and at that time of night. At London Airport Tom and I sink another brandy, for it isn't every midnight that we take off by jet to Moscow.

Then we get into another bus, still along with the deerstalker bonzo, and drive out into the night to the plane. A whopper it is. As soon as we are aboard and cosy in the bright lights a very shapy dame offers us another brandy. We need it by then and before we know what is what or where it is, we are zipping the sky with a hell of a shoving in our backs and on our way to Moscow are Tom and I.

The shapy dame then gives us another dinner and offers us a bottle of champagne all fizzy. Tom thinks we'd better have it, and so we do and I agree. We are licking along at a pace a chap says over the mike, and Germany is down below. I look out into the moonlight and see one great straight ribbon of a road running true as a rule across miles and miles. All lighted up it is and broad and endless. Where, I wonder, and call up the guy in the white jacket.

'Look at that great road,' I tell him, and he looks at it and then at me — a bit of an odd look. 'That', he says, nice and kind, 'is the edge of our wing,' and I fall into a sleep.

'Moscow,' says the chap on the mike, 'we are getting there,'

and very funny Tom and I feel about it. We've both read a lot
and heard about it all our lives. And here we are over it at half-
past five on a Tuesday morning. Only half-past three it is at
home. Funny and strange it was, and we didn't like leaving our
shapy dame and the plane and the guy in the white coat. It
looked just like Moscow somehow. Great pictures of Lenin and
red stars all over the shop. No doubt where we are.

Chaps seem very civil. Find us on a list and push us through
everything very quick and nice. Before we would have had time
to say how d'you do to a reception lot in London, Tom and I are
bowling along in a cab to Moscow. No doubt about it; flat and
muddy-looking it all is one minute and the next great sudden
blocks of flats. Block after block after block all looking the
same.

But if you want a guide book to the place that's not my intention at all. Tom would be better at that. He walked around
with a street map and didn't lose himself or me and I didn't
lose him. Wanted a Catholic church Tom did before he wanted
anything and gets himself to a circus instead. No funny business
but sounds the same in the lingo and Tom gets his church all
right and does all he has to do the same as at home near Montpelier Square. Our hotel very large and very plush and very
heavy. Must have weighed a lot with all the bits. We each have
a room with a bath and all. Silly nonsense this no plug business
told around. The Russians just like washing their maulers under
running water, so their basins just don't have plugs and that's
all there is to them bar the holes. They haven't just lost them like
some nuts say. They have them in the baths like you and me and
they fit too. The hot water comes out of a hot tap and the cold
water comes out of a cold tap and a lot of daft nonsense Tom and I
had read a week or two back in a paper that ought to have known
better by a chap who never did know much, we soon proved to
be poppycock.

However, this is a literary piece. What I want to arrive at is
the celebration they celebrated for old Dan Defoe. Tom and I
knew of old Dan Defoe, but not that he had a celebration on. It
was all very kind. We had spent an afternoon drinking tea with
the Union of Soviet Writers. A nice lot who talked very civil
if they did now and again take a peek over a shoulder. Tom kept

his eye on me for I had said a thing or two that made him shiver and he wanted to get back to his pictures and things.

'You will be missing', they said, 'the celebrations in London on the tercentenary of Daniel Defoe?'

'Yes,' I said, 'and very sad we are. Especially Tom. London won't half be having a night out.'

'Well,' they said, 'you come along to our do. Right glad we will be to see you,' and so along on the Saturday night we went to a theatre about the size of Drury Lane belonging to this Union of Soviet Writers.

They met us in the hall and took us to seats in the front row, very civil.

'Sorry,' they explained, 'we're not quite full. Saturday night, the telly and all,' and Tom and I felt at home all of a sudden. Old Dan would have got a lift. First a smashing dame, very well cut, took on as compère and swell she was. As swell as any dame we saw in Moscow where dames don't seem to be too swell. Tom and I kept in mind those goings-on at Glebe House in Chelsea — PEN — where the faithful gather around that old tree that grows in the hall.

This dame announced a string quartet and four old gaffers in dinner-suits came on and gave it to us. Seventeenth-century English music — the whole lot. After that, believe it or not, a fine figure of a woman retired from the Bolshoi opera gang, but still in form, came along to sing 'No John No' in Russian. Tom looks at me and I looks at Tom and, Dan, he looks at both of us from the programme. This big dame she sang and swelled and sank and floated again something impressive and although it was Russian you could tell easily that it was John. After that a big chap with a little flute comes and flutes. Very pretty, but it looked funny with the bigness of him and the small flute and the stage all empty. But he played away until going out to let on another chap who gave a dramatic reading. Very dramatic it was, from *Robinson Crusoe*. He read on for quite a while and then walked in a real big-sized star from the Bolshoi. Got an ovation from all the Union that was there and he sang 'Annie Laurie' in Scotch. A very big voice he had and very handsome and the applause was something for a Saturday night with the weekend and the telly. He sang it again and I think again.

Well, we got on celebrating Dan's tercentenary for quite a time until the smart girl comes on and announces an interval to it all and that the next part of the programme will be a film about London. And what a film it was, but this is literary and to keep it literary a chap comes suddenly up to me with a mike and says you will now record for Moscow Radio who you are, what you want here and what you think of these celebrations. Luva-duck, I thought, and Tom just sits and giggles without showing it.

'What,' I say, 'now?'

'Yes,' he says, 'now — a recording for the Moscow Radio,' and through my nut runs a thought of all those blokes that might be listening somewhere waiting to pick something up.

'Me?' I ask, playing for time. 'Me on Moscow Radio?' 'Yes,' he says again, ever so polite, 'you and now — and then some supper.' What I put out over that mike I never heard and never know. All about how nice it was to be there, what I was taking a dekko at and how nice it was that we all thought so high of dear Dan. That seemed to satisfy them, although poor Tom was gone a bit pale. So they took us off to supper, past the cold ham and the beer along to the tea and the biscuits in a more swagger room.

We sat with a lot of members talking of writers and that. One of them comes up to me and says, 'I want you to meet our angry young man.' 'Angry young man?' I say as best I could with biscuits in my mouth, and they took me along to see him. A nice young man, very tidy. 'This', they said, 'is Mr Yevtushenko,' and we greeted one another as if we were members of the same union. 'And what', I ask, 'are you angry about?' He looks at me. 'The system,' he says, 'the system,' and I can hardly wait to get back and tell Tom who is still getting into the biscuits.

He goes a bit paler than before and thinks it is time we are off. So we shake hands all round the Union of Soviet Writers and find a car waiting to take us back to our hotel, which is more than I've ever found outside Glebe House (PEN). And that's a bit of what happened on the literary front when Tom and I went to Moscow and we reckon it's a contribution, for no other English delegation turned up to celebrate Dan Defoe's tercentenary that night. No sign of George Weidenfeld who gets around and

Captain Maxwell wasn't there either. Just Tom and myself and the Russians.

Before leaving London I had become committed to an enterprise which Joan viewed with the utmost Scottish caution. The brother of a friend of mine had at some distant date defected, and I was asked if I would ascertain the state of his health and deliver a small present. This I readily consented to do and was given a cellophane container enclosing a colourful collation of expensive ties. 'There are probably all sorts of things in the linings,' warned Joan. 'Of course not,' I declared, with an inward spasm of alarm, 'you must really not be so ridiculous.' I had inquired how the gentleman was to be contacted. 'Do nothing,' was the answer, 'he will get in touch with you.'

Thus with my cellophanic package we arrived at Moscow's airport in the appallingly early hours of May 2nd. The bunting of May Day was still festooned in tired abundance. Our passports were cursorily examined and a list was consulted. Clearly we were on it and rooms had been reserved for us at Hotel Leningradsky. Thither we were driven at once in as normal a taxi as could be envisaged. The fare was modest and no tip was expected. The hotel was new but its interior decoration and design was clearly from plans deriving from Victorian England at its most lush. The place was barely awake, but our rooms were ready and contained every facility for gracious living at its best.

Upon every floor, adjacent to the lift, was a desk presided over by a rather matronly lady supposed, by all who supposed such things, to be an active informer to N.K.V.O. Her motives may indeed have been sinister, but she was in effect the floor's hall porter and performed a singularly useful function.

At a still early hour we were in some need of breakfast, but Intourist were not yet awake and our meal vouchers were thus unobtainable. None the less, we were given a most hearty breakfast. The waitress was delightful; and her uniform was the black frock with neatly starched white cap and apron no longer known to capitalist Britishers. She had one English phrase which was 'Okey-Doke'. She somehow made it clear that we had not consumed enough breakfast to expend the coupons allocated to it, which she would accept from us later in the day. The deficiency had to be made good and unwanted cigarettes cascaded upon us. Okey-Doke.

At the appointed hour Intourist awoke and our needs were quickly and efficiently catered for. We could eat off our vouchers in almost any restaurant in the place; a car and an interpreter would be at our disposal for six hours a day. Our interpreter proved to be a charming young woman named Lena, who was perfectly prepared to operate as a secretary as well. She confirmed all our appointments, bought for me a toothbrush and some toothpaste and suggested we should book seats for the Circus, for the Bolshoi Ballet and for the Puppet Theatre. For all her services Lena would accept no present, nor would she join us at any meal. She did feel able, however, to accompany us to the Bolshoi in order to 'translate the ballet' and explain which was Madame Ulanova.

With or without Lena we were free to wander as we wished. Tired one afternoon of culture, we at the last moment abandoned plans to visit yet another Art Gallery. Lena found it hard to understand, but what would we like to do instead? Motor into your countryside, we said, and have a look at life there. And we did, touring areas certainly not referred to in the glossy literature of Intourist. At the enormous University of Moscow I wearied of the endless lecture halls. I would like, I said, to see how the students live if it is possible. I think it can be arranged, said Lena and it was.

Our first formal meeting with the hierarchy of MezhKniga achieved some success after a highly alarming start. It was the later morning of May 2nd. The conversation, as throughout our stay, was entirely in English. 'It is a pity about the plane we had to shoot down yesterday,' said the chairman as an opening gambit. 'What plane?' I inquired with a slight weakening of the knees. 'The American spy-plane,' explained the chairman as to a child. 'The Americans — they sent a spy-plane on May Day. It is very bad. We were obliged to shoot it down.'

I looked at a paling Tom and he looked at me. Years in Siberia stretched ahead. 'They should not send a spy-plane on May Day,' complained the chairman with some bitterness; and the incident passed, nor was it ever referred to again in any place. But clearly it was May Day that rankled. Spy-planes — Okey-Doke — but not on May Day.

As a conjuror produces his rabbit so I produced my draft treaty between Hutchinson and the Russians. I read it through in silence, clause by clause. The listening appeared to be intent. 'But this', said the chairman when I had finished, 'is splendid. It is exactly what we would like. Why has it not happened before?' Feeling much like a Foreign Secretary arranging Peace in Our Time, I confessed that I did not know. Tom was gazing at me with some pride. And well he might, I thought. 'There are a few small points to consider,' said the chairman. 'We would not be quite certain about the Canadian position' (thus revealing a quite astonishing mastery of a fairly technical point significant to the Commonwealth market) 'but we will examine it with care and tomorrow we all sign. Yes?' I explained that I felt much gratified. I would be very glad to sign but there would of course have to be a reciprocal agreement and I had no facilities for preparing it. 'Overnight we will turn it inside out,' they promised, 'and we will clarify a few points.'

A further meeting was arranged for the next morning. By this time my original draft had been rendered into perfect legalistic English; the points clarified were sensible, necessary and impeccably phrased and the reciprocal document most scrupulously drawn up. It was not possible to fault a comma. My mind boggled when wondering how a similar exercise might be attempted in London. They were ready to sign. There remained only one small hitch. They could not sign their agreement. This would have to be done by Mr Chuikoff of the Foreign Publishing House with whom I was to meet on Saturday. Mr Chuikoff, it seemed, was a very important man indeed. I put my pen away. We would all sign on Saturday. There was full agreement about this.

Mr Chuikoff, on the Saturday, was very formidable but equally delighted with the proposed agreement. There was, however, one small hitch. Money was involved and this required the authority of the Minister of Culture. A trifling point, but there it was. Perhaps we could all sign on Monday? 'But we go home on Monday,' I said. 'Ah yes. But you sign in London and we sign here. Yes?' Of course, no one signed anything anywhere. A brief telegram to me in London greatly regretted that it could not be done. I never knew why, for the prospect most clearly appealed to them.

Through all our stay we went with our driver and Lena where we wished when we wished. We lost ourselves in the magnificent complexity of their underground while on our own. Our only clash with authority was an extremely courteous request by a policeman not to photograph some area of the Kremlin when he spotted Tom about to do so. We shared tables in crowded and gilded restaurants and swilled vodka with loud gentlemen from East Germany who had no good word to say for anything Russian and damned them loudly. A Russian major begged our pardon, but he would like to instruct us in the art of drinking vodka. The sight of our foreign ways was more than he could bear to contemplate.

At a party I became worried about the ties in the cellophane bag which awaited collection. I was passed from hand to hand until I was assured that I would be contacted. I was, at crack of the next dawn. It was the defector himself, very calm and very assured. He would be at the hotel in half an hour. How would I recognize him? I look an obvious Englishman he said. Tom and I planted ourselves in the foyer. The obvious Englishman came in. We approached, exchanged polite greetings, handed over the ties and he left. An odd and tragic instant.

We met publishing house after publishing house and with the 'house of children' enjoyed a particularly hilarious afternoon of which again I plead the liberty to append an account which in due course I wrote for *The Bookseller*:

AN AFTERNOON ON A SOFA

We had adjourned from the sombre committee room with its solemn table and chairs and the hour-long talk with rather face-less executives on the problems of publishing in Russia. It was the headquarters of a 'house' dedicated to a field of publishing with which I was not much familiar and discussion had been desultory and in very general terms.

And now, in an inner sanctum, the charming lady of the party was seated beside me on the sofa; as animated and delightful a member of her sex as Moscow had so far produced. There was brandy on the table and sweetmeats at half past three in the afternoon and expressions began to supplant the faceless countenances so far revealed. There were some eight of us gathered around. Tom Girtin was in animated conversation but managing, I could discern, to exercise his watching brief for any incident in which I might find myself involved.

'You 'ave in Loondon, Mr Loosty, a little man, very old, with a beard. Hees name it is Sir Allen Lane. He was shortly here.' Madam Smallwoodski, for so I named her and not with complete irrelevance, was ready to chat.

'No,' I said, and I found that in Moscow it was possible to respond with a frankness that would be much less welcome in many more acceptable quarters, 'you are once again confused. It is not Sir Allen Lane you have in mind. He has no beard. It is Sir Stanley Unwin of Messrs Allen & Unwin. I can understand your confusion, but you should get it right as they would hardly welcome it.'

'Ah, Mr Loosty, you are correct in what you say. It was Sir Unwin of Allen & Unwin. He was here and he was sitting on this sofa with me as you are. Mr Loosty,' and Madam Smallwoodski moved closer as though to reveal a confidence, 'I thought Sir Unwin was a gentleman. He is not.'

No member of the book trade in any part of the world will fail to comprehend the sensation upon me of this revelation. And so far from home. Brandy, I thought, quick and in quantity while I order my thoughts. At least on one occasion alcohol must come to the salvation of Sir Unwin.

'And what', I inquired after what can only be described as a pregnant pause, 'did Sir Unwin do to you?'

Madam Smallwoodski searched her vocabulary. 'Mr Loosty, Sir Unwin he was very naughty. He was as I say it, sitting here, next to me. We talked about publishing. It was very interesting. He talked much. And then, Mr Loosty, do you know it, Sir Unwin he promised to send me his catalogue. He never did. It shaked me very much. Sir Unwin is not a gentleman.'

'I will', I said, as relief, if a certain disappointment, overtook my speculations, 'convey the message to Sir Unwin. I am sure that he will send you his catalogue. I am, as a matter of fact, sure that he did send you his catalogue. You do not receive all that is sent you.'

'Mr Loosty, I want something to know.' Clearly another train of thought was disturbing Madam Smallwoodski and she edged again a trifle closer. 'Mr Loosty, you own Ootchinson and you are a capitalist.'

'No,' I replied, 'I do not own Ootchinson and I am not a capitalist in the sense you mean.'

'But, Mr Loosty, you must own Ootchinson. You are its chairman and its director. You must own it. Mr Loosty, I do not believe you.' It was evident that Miss Smallwoodski was again losing faith in her English contacts.

'I cannot help', I told her, 'whether you believe me or not. All I can explain is that I do not own Ootchinson. I have hardly any financial interest in Ootchinson. I am not thus a capitalist beast.' I could sense that Tom had one ear cocked.

'Mr Loosty, you cannot be telling the truth. You must own Ootchinson.'

'Miss Smallwoodski,' I said, determined somehow to prevail, 'I no more own Ootchinson than your Mr Blatoviski (which was not his name) over there owns this house of which he is manager. He is paid a wage and so am I. He has his overlords, and so have I.'

More brandy, I thought, for Tom had caught the word 'overlords' and was making gestures akin to despair.

'Mr Loosty, is it the truth that you tell me? It is hard to understand.'

'Indeed it is the truth,' and I fixed the lady with as stern a glance as I could summon. 'Indeed it is so. And if you do not believe me, let us,' I said — too late aware of a general silence in the room — 'let us, all of us, drink to the damnation of overlords.'

Good God, I thought, what have I done. Tom was obviously muttering prayers and thinking of his home never to be seen again. There was a silence. And then every man to his feet; me to mine and with Madam Smallwoodski smiling beside me. All glasses were replenished and upraised. 'To the damnation,' we said in unison, 'to the damnation of overlords.'

Back in London the man in the macintosh who had come by appointment mysteriously made, looked at me with some suspicion. 'We understand', he said, 'that you have been to Moscow. We know that the Russians are anxious to contact you.'

'Well,' I said, 'that's fine. They promised to let me know about a copyright principle. All they have to do is to telephone.'

'We understand', he said, 'that you got on rather well there.'

'I'm very glad to hear it,' I said. 'That really was the purpose of my going.'

'They are trying to get in touch,' he said again. 'They may ask you to cocktail parties and to dinners.'

'How hospitable,' I said, 'I like parties.'

'Did they', he said, 'talk about anything but publishing and books?'

'No,' I said. 'Just publishing and books.'

'Thank you,' he said. 'If they ever talk to you about other things, perhaps you will let me know.'

'Can I whistle up a taxi for you?' I inquired.

'No thanks,' he said, very solemnly. 'I came in a fast car.'

Despite the extraordinary experiences compressed within so short and in a sense so bewildering a week, we were not sorry to emplane again for Heathrow and England. There was a last-minute hitch on the runway. We were, the pilot announced, being held while other planes took precedence. He did not know why and one was aware of a quickening of the pulse. We had encountered no problems; the climate seemed freer than ever we imagined it would be; there was more laughter, more conviviality, few signs of restraint. And yet a certain brooding, an inescapable neurosis. During our stay some minor governmental changes were announced. I was to have breakfasted with a British journalist, but as I was dressing he telephoned to say that he could not make the date for this reason. He was not certain of the portents. A little anxious I descended in the lift to the foyer where I was meeting Tom. There were Americans in the lift with me and I asked of one solemn-looking Southerner what he made of the news. 'I don't understand you,' he said, a trifle scared, 'you speak with an English accent. I only speak New York English,' and he darted away. It was an encounter I was able to relate to the Russians without hesitation and they roared their heads off. Few Americans would find it funny. We somehow seemed to have an affinity of humour with the Russians which permitted more uninhibited talk than ever with the Americans, however well one might know them.

At all our meetings one common denominator had been in attendance. He played no great part, but was immensely helpful if any difficulty of understanding arose. He watched intently, and no doubt worked to a brief. But he was wholly delightful. The time came to say goodbye. 'If ever you come to England,' we said, 'you must let us know.'

A year or so later the Russian Trade Mission staged its mammoth show at Earl's Court. MezhKniga's representative in London telephoned me to say that Donev (which was not his name) would be coming. I was mildly surprised, but delighted. We must all meet, I suggested. I asked him to get in touch when a date could be set and I would arrange something with Tom Girtin. 'I do not think there will be time,' he said.

But to our astonishment there proved to be time, for he telephoned a week or so later to say so. An evening was contrived and we collected the two of them from a seedy hotel in the Earl's Court area. First we took them to the Garrick Club for dinner. 'Here', I explained, 'you can see real communism in action. The members share it all. You have nothing at all like it.' They neither could nor would believe it. It was utterly beyond their comprehension. Old Joan, the greatest character of her day among the waitresses, took them to her capacious heart. She enchanted them and after dinner they gravely sought her out and thanked her for her care, shaking her warmly by the hand. It was most charmingly done, and a brave gesture in a strange land.

From dinner we took them to the Tower of London, floodlit on a summer's night. The stars shone clear and the moon was rising and we thought they should experience the Prospect of Whitby lower down the river. The place was crowded and there was singing and laughter. The Russians drank their beer in wonder. Donev had never been to London before, nor even left Russia. Suddenly he put down his beer and put his arms around me. 'Mr Loosty, you have given me the evening of my life. I have never imagined London like this. It is something I can never forget.' He picked up his beer again and I was oddly moved.

On our way back to the drabness of Earl's Court we dropped

in for a last drink at Tom's home in Montpelier Square and they looked at his Girtin watercolours in the elegance of their setting. They had experienced quite an evening. The man from Highgate departed thence and I drove Donev to his hotel. He hugged me again and there were tears in his eyes. 'I will never forget this evening,' he said again. I doubt if he has and I often wonder what became of him. I can still see the dancing excitement in his eyes and hear his gay laughter and I am glad to have experienced a Russian embrace. When, years later, I was to meet Svetlana Alliluyeva and publish her *Twenty Letters to a Friend*, the recollections of that week in Moscow and its outcome were instantly helpful.

19
Diversion Ahead

T HE Thursday morning of June 15th, 1967, was one of
singular enchantment. The sky was blue, the sun lay upon
the garden and the birds were in full song. Babs and I
were breakfasting in the garden, enjoying the scene, when the
telephone rang. The voice at the other end sounded ominously
strained. It was Lady Normanbrook, wife of the then chairman
of the BBC. 'Is that you, Bob?' she said. 'Norman is dead. I would
be grateful if you would cope with everything.'

It was the saddest news, but not totally unexpected. For many
months Lord Normanbrook's colleagues at the BBC had watched
with increasing concern the onset of frailty. After periods of
treatment he had rallied, but for shorter whiles. On the afternoon of only Wednesday he had been at Broadcasting House
preparing for the fortnightly board meeting due at eleven o'clock
this very morning. The national governors (those representing
Scotland, Wales and Northern Ireland) would have come overnight to London while others would be on their way.

I managed to catch Hugh Greene, the BBC's director-general,
at his home and we quickly decided that the meeting should go
ahead. It was the obvious thing and Norman would certainly
have wished it. I suggested to Hugh that we should make our
separate ways immediately to Broadcasting House, for there was
much to be done. 'I am afraid I cannot do that,' said Hugh in
that slow, cool, calculated voice which is so authoritative an
ingredient of his manner. 'I have an appointment with Roy
Thomson at Thomson House. I think I must keep that.' To
hell with Lord Thomson, I thought not for the first time. 'Well,
it's up to you,' I replied, 'but we have our meeting at eleven

o'clock. At any rate, Hugh, let us get our flags to half-mast,' I added as though accustomed to such imperialism at breakfast-time. 'Good God, I wouldn't have thought of that,' said Hugh.

A few moments later the telephone rang again. It was Hugh. 'I think you are right,' he said, 'I have changed my date with Thomson and am leaving now for Broadcasting House.'

When I arrived there the usual serenity prevailed. The ordained procedures were under way. Lady Normanbrook had been telephoned; the agreed announcement was to be made almost at once. The Postmaster-General had been notified and would I be so good as to prepare an appropriate comment to be broadcast along with that to be written by the director-general? I suggested that Harold Macmillan, a close friend of Lord Normanbrook, was the right man to record a full appreciation; and fortunately the necessary apparatus was in the vicinity of his Sussex home.

I had another word with Goss Normanbrook. She was wonderfully composed and glad to hear that we were to go ahead with our meeting. I returned briefly to my own office in adjacent Great Portland Street and during the few minutes I was there, the secretary of the then Postmaster-General, Mr Edward Short, came on the line. He conveyed Mr Short's sympathies and asked that I should pass them on to the BBC. He would like to be informed of any funeral arrangements and meanwhile was happy to think that as vice-chairman I would be taking over Lord Normanbrook's responsibilities. It was, I thought, an intimidating prospect for a quiet man of the printed word; and I returned in what might be described as a sombre mood to Broadcasting House.

The Corporation was in good heart. It had a brilliantly contentious director-general and he headed an outstanding board of management. Lord Normanbrook had taken quiet command and had long since won the respect of the director-general, which was a very necessary thing to do, and he presided over a singularly united and informed board of governors. The 1960s had seen, in the view of very many, public-service broadcasting in its finest hour of liberation and only a few were aware that distant signals were faintly ominous.

In a memorable address given shortly before his death, Lord

Normanbrook had declared, as he understood it, the precise and proper relationship which should exist between the BBC's board of governors and its board of executive management. It was an admirable statement and much of its importance lay in its recognition that the BBC had become unique in the world not despite but because of the delicate balance of its control, which worked. A strength of the system was its ability to accept change, but ill-conceived change thoughtlessly imposed could threaten disaster. Normanbrook's paper was read at a time when the board of governors numbered nine and the board of management, a team of BBC executives equal in rank to each other, apart from the director-general, numbered seven. It was this numerical precision and modesty which ensured a compact, rigid axis of sufficient strength to control the whole of the BBC's activities. The threat to this pivotal axis could develop from an increase to the numerical strength of either, from an inequality of status on the board of management or from change in the relationship between the chairman of the board of governors and the director-general. No one at that time could foresee or even, I think, imagine that within a few months the introduction of new policies would achieve precisely all these things.

I had wondered, when first joining the board of governors in 1960, why its number should stand at nine. It required very little experience to learn of its exact rightness. Eight would have been one too few, ten would have been one too many. There is little in logic to justify this precision. It required a constancy in attendance, but during the eight years of my experience it was only on very rare occasions that any governor was absent from the fortnightly meeting. There existed an intensely felt involvement hard to explain and later to be dismissed by Lord Hill as, until his arrival, the sentiment of ciphers dancing attendance on the director-general. But apart from Lord Hill, busy at that time with the Independent Television Authority, I remain convinced that the diminished status of the BBC in this country, if not in the world, derives considerably from the increase to twelve in the membership of the board of governors imposed by the Labour Government, despite protests from both the director-general and Lord Normanbrook when it was first mooted, and the acting chairman when it was announced. The incoming Lord

Hill had been told nothing about it nor at any time was he consulted.

Another and more delicate situation needs a place in the background of events which followed Lord Normanbrook's death. Sir Hugh Greene had been appointed director-general early in 1960 by the board of governors over which Sir Arthur fforde presided. It was an unexpected and courageous appointment which began, or so I remain convinced, one of the most beneficial, progressive and liberating eras in public-service broadcasting that any society has experienced. Many windows were opened and many minds expanded. Above all there was compassionate understanding and a probing into human problems not previously thought appropriate for public consideration. Its assumptions were that democracy was adult and that those who lived under it were percipient, questioning and responsible. I would rank Hugh Greene equal in status with John Reith, although neither could have accomplished the achievements of the other. I owe much to Hugh Greene and I can find no period in BBC history when I would more have valued a seat on its board of governors.

But there is an engaging element of mischief in Hugh Greene which can also be detected in his brothers Graham and Raymond without much difficulty. It is attractive to those who understand it but can disturb others. Not every pronouncement made by Hugh Greene is to be taken at its face value, nor is his every remark a considered one. Hugh, I think, may have been inclined to make occasional pronouncements about the BBC and its policies which with greater wisdom would have emanated from the chairman in terms of greater tact. Nothing, however, had gone wrong between Hugh Greene and Lord Normanbrook (or, at any time, between Greene and fforde), although there certainly existed in Normanbrook's mind some anxieties that the forces aligning against the director-general were becoming more formidable, and that they derived from sources of much greater consequence than Mrs Mary Whitehouse. These anxieties he expressed to me when we lunched together shortly before he died. Who, he wondered, would or could replace Hugh Greene if, for any reason, he should go? There seemed to him no outstanding claimant among the younger men. 'How about Charles Curran?' I asked. He looked mildly shocked. 'Curran? Certainly not. Curran wouldn't do at all. We should never have a Roman Catholic at the head of the BBC.' I mention this as an indication of how swiftly in our time long-standing prejudices and certainties can be swept away. This was in 1967 and Lord Normanbrook was a man of exceptional enlightenment and liberality. At that moment he was probably right; but within a very few years the editors of *The Times* and the *New Statesman* and the director-general of the BBC were all to be staunch Catholics. Nevertheless, the important fact to recall is that the slightest outline of a question mark had already put in its appearance over the head of Hugh Greene who, by all other portents, should have enjoyed a further five years at least in furthering his policies of progressive and liberal broadcasting.

This then, so it seemed to me, was the general and prevailing picture when the Postmaster-General's secretary again telephoned the day following Lord Normanbrook's death to ask if I would carry on as acting-chairman until, in all probability, the late autumn. They did not wish to make any quick decision on so important an appointment. I replied that I would carry on to the best of my ability, but could not go beyond the autumn as I had my job to do as a hired hand at Hutchinson's as well.

Hugh Greene has stated on more than one occasion that Sir Arthur fforde was probably the best chairman the BBC has ever had. It was during his reign that I took up my appointment, and to have worked under his wise guidance and secured his friendship I regard as one of the highest privileges I could hope to enjoy. When ill-health obliged him to retire before the expiration of his term of office it was a moment of intense personal sorrow to every member of his board and a most serious deprivation to the BBC. The usual speculation arose as to his successor but it was not prolonged, as the admirable, wise and endearing Sir James Duff succeeded him briefly and much against his will. He made it clear that he would not remain as chairman for a moment longer than it took to find another.

The choice of a BBC chairman is entirely a matter for the government of the day. It is not a matter for consultation with the BBC at any level. Various names are bandied about in the press and from a variety of quarters come suggestions that a Strong Chairman is what the government has in mind. Mrs Mary

Whitehouse usually has something to say, and rumours naturally proliferate within and without broadcasting circles. On this occasion there was not long to wait. His name, so far as I can recall, had never been mentioned. The announcement was made that Lord Normanbrook, until recently Secretary to the Cabinet and head of the Civil Service, was to preside over our destiny. He was at once invited by Sir James Duff to attend a board meeting as an 'observer' so that he might meet his new colleagues and gain some impression of the climate of affairs. Both the national and the ordinary governors invited him to private dinners before his arrival and he was to say in due course how valuable and pleasing he found these early courtesies to be. It became quickly clear that the BBC was in exceptionally capable and dedicated hands.

My five-year term of office as a governor came to its end in November 1965. Sir David Milne, national governor for Scotland, had been appointed on the same day and thus together we were given a farewell dinner at Television Centre. It had all been a great experience of absorbing interest and I had been singularly fortunate to encounter it. Nothing seemed less likely than that within a few months I should return to the board as its vice-chairman. Lord Fulton had succeeded Sir James Duff in that capacity, but in the late spring of 1966 was appointed head of a commission to consider all the problems of the Civil Service. This necessitated his resignation as vice-chairman, although he continued as a governor. There was a need for continuity, and Lord Normanbrook, whose health by this time had entered into decline, would find delegation to a vice-chairman who knew the ropes easier than to a newcomer. This was a view acceptable to Harold Wilson, then Prime Minister, and so it was that I returned to the fold to find myself at the centre of events during one of the most traumatic periods yet encountered by the Corporation.

Within a month of Lord Normanbrook's death arrived, innocently enough, Wednesday, July 26th. There was nothing in the air to suggest that it would pass into the history of the BBC as probably the most shattering day it had endured and that after its close nothing would be quite as it had been before. During the morning of that Wednesday there came to my office in Great

Portland Street a telephone call from the Postmaster-General's secretary. Edward Short had never met me; he had nothing in particular to discuss but he thought it would be useful to have a brief talk before the summer break. Could I make it convenient to call upon him at the Post Office on Thursday afternoon? There seemed nothing portentous in this, and I of course assented, pointing out that I could not be precise as to time as I did not know when a governors' meeting, due for the next day, would reach its end. This was perfectly well understood. I could turn up at my own convenience.

Less than an hour later the same voice was on the line, but this time with a note of urgency. Mr Short was extremely sorry but an emergency had arisen. It was imperative that he should see me that Wednesday afternoon. Would I kindly be at the Post Office at half past four? It was highly inconvenient but I agreed and telephoned Hugh Greene to inquire what was happening. He had no idea and was as mystified as I was. All seemed quiet and no new rumour of any significance appeared to be in circulation. I arranged to borrow Hugh's official car and his driver, who could be expected to know where the Post Office and its general were housed. I would return to Broadcasting House with his car, his driver and any news I might acquire.

Without any particular foreboding but with curiosity I presented myself at St Martin's Le Grand at 4.30 p.m. precisely. I was conducted to an uninspiring institutional kind of room and was alone for a moment or two. Then the door opened and it seemed to me that a regiment marched in, headed by Mr Short. He greeted me kindly, rather as a headmaster would a pupil, thanked me for what I was doing at the BBC, and took his seat at the head of the table. I could see no one I had ever met before and I felt singularly alone. Mr Short seemed curiously ill at ease. He kept his eyes fixed on a rather high point on the wall ahead. 'I must apologize for sending for you in this way,' he said, 'but it has become urgently necessary. Our future plans for the BBC have unfortunately leaked. They were not to be made known until the late autumn. But it has been necessary for the Queen to hold a meeting of the Privy Council in her box at Goodwood this afternoon.'

I had the impression that I was about to be sent to the Tower for summary execution. 'Following this,' continued Mr Short, still examining the far wall, 'the name of the new chairman of the BBC will be announced at ten minutes past eight this evening and he will take over from you on September 1st. I promised that I would notify you of our plans well in advance so that you might inform your board before any public announcement. I much regret not now being able to do this and I shall be glad if you will convey my apologies to your fellow governors.' For a second he paused, and there was a certain tension in the air. How many around that table knew what was coming I shall never know. I was conscious of being watched. The Postmaster-General cleared his throat. 'The new chairman of the BBC', he said 'is to be Charles Smith.'

How very odd, I thought, and was determined to remain poker-faced. The final truth did not dawn. Mr Short's secretary, seated opposite me, seemed in a state of some agitation while his master remained in the immobile image of a rather acid schoolmaster about to leave his class. The secretary raised a hand to conceal a whisper. 'Hill,' he said with some urgency, 'Charles Hill, sir, not Charles Smith.' Mr Short accepted the correction with a nod. He clearly was not pleased. There was a deep silence. Every eye in that room was searching me for some reaction, which I was determined not to reveal. The full horror of the situation numbed my mind. All I could wonder was how to break the news to Hugh Greene and the others.

It was the end of the BBC as I knew it, and the end of Hugh Greene too.

In his book *Behind the Screen*, Lord Hill relates that Edward Short reported to him that I received his announcement in 'dumb astonishment'. This is not quite fair. After seven years at the BBC I knew what was thought of Charles Hill by the BBC. 'I hope', I said, 'he will recognize that we are a horse of a very different colour.' It did not seem to me a very bright thing to say and I felt Mr Short shared this view. But at least it was a shade less than dumb and I would certainly not question my astonishment. Time inclines me to think that this was shared by Mr Short. However, he maintained his fixed glance on the wall ahead. 'Lord Hill', he said rather icily, 'is a very wise man. He will be getting in touch with you.' I'm bloody well buggered if he is,

I thought to myself as combative life returned, I shall be getting in touch with him. Mr Short rose to his feet. The class was clearly at an end. He thanked me for coming and his secretary conducted me to the BBC's waiting car. It was not an agreeable journey back to Broadcasting House for it was not an agreeable prospect which lay ahead. Had any chairman, I wondered, let alone an acting one, found himself with such dire news to convey to Broadcasting House?

The director-general's office is on the third floor of Broadcasting House and at that time connected through a secretarial room with the chairman's office. This arrangement was deliberate and sacrosanct and considered vital to the proper relationship between the director-general and his chairman for their informal to-ing and fro-ing. I had no foreboding that the bomb I was about to detonate would blow even this hallowed arrangement to pieces, and probably for good. In point of fact, my wife was subsequently the first person to be told by Lord Hill at some dinner of his intention to remove himself and a separate secretarial staff to a higher floor. 'The room into which I was put', he complained, 'was panelled and I cannot bear the smell of wood.' It was as though an incoming Pope were casually to announce the abolition of altars in St Peter's.

I went straight to Hugh Greene's room. He was alone, seated at his desk. 'Hugh,' I said, 'I am sorry but I bring you the worst possible news. Charles Hill is being switched over to us. He is to be our next chairman.' I might just as well have shot the director-general. He is a large man and he bounced — almost out of his chair. His hand went at once to the telephone. 'Get me the Postmaster-General,' he commanded. 'No, Hugh,' I said, 'don't do that. If you will, then I will. Let us send for Oliver.' The call came through, but Mr Short was, fortunately, not at home. 'Tell Mr Short', said Hugh,' that I shall be in touch with him in the morning.' Oliver Whitley, when he came in, was adamant. 'There should be no talk of resignations tonight,' he said. 'It may well be what they are hoping for.' Whitley, at that time chief assistant to the director-general, had been a tower of strength within the BBC for many years. He made no concessions to firmly held principles, and his integrity of purpose was absolute. His father had been one of the BBC's outstandingly successful and respected chairmen and he himself was to follow Charles Curran as director of External Services at Bush House. Some rumour, it soon appeared, had already reached him during the course of the afternoon. A BBC man had reported meeting Harold Wilson at a party on the previous evening. Wilson had seemed to be in good form and rather pleased with himself. He had said jovially to the BBC man that he had just done something that the BBC wouldn't at all like. He was right. 'But how', Hugh kept asking, 'can I work with such a man?'

We talked for a while around the problem. There was no escape from it. We were somehow aware that the curtain had fallen on the past. The future was certain to be very different. Of the three of us there — and indeed of all those personally affected — it was for Hugh Greene the most bitter blow.

Hugh thought that I should join a party which the board of management was giving that night at the Dorchester Hotel for Anthony Barber. I told Hugh that I had a pressing family engagement — and that in any event I doubted the wisdom of doing so; I would write to Hill in the morning, inviting him to lunch with me privately at Broadcasting House as soon as possible. It appeared that he would continue as chairman of the ITA until the final moment. On the night of August 31st he would go to bed as chairman of the opposition. In the morning he would awake chairman of the BBC. This was hard to stomach. Hugh Greene considered protocol. 'It would be quite wrong', he declared, 'for me or for any other director of the BBC to be in any communication with Lord Hill until he has seen the acting-chairman.' He made arrangements for a meeting with all the directors prior to the Dorchester dinner party. 'I think, Hugh,' I said on parting, 'that all we can do tonight is to drink.'

I drove home to Hampstead and immediately from there we set out for a remote public-house in Essex where we were to meet for the first time the mother of the girl my elder stepson was to marry on the next Saturday. It was after zero hour when we reached our rendezvous for dinner and I wondered what might be happening in newspaper offices and how the BBC was coping with the form of its own announcements. It was difficult to explain to my stepson's future mother-in-law quite why the nearest her daughter would get to a father-in-law was in so disturbed a state of mind. During the meal and after a few drinks had done their work I telephoned Hugh Greene at the Dorchester. He came with caution, expecting the press. I inquired after his health and that of his party. He reported favourably and doubted if it was an evening Anthony Barber would forget. 'Hugh,' I said, 'for the second time in my life I suggest that all our flags should be at half-mast tomorrow morning.'

I have the greatest admiration for David Attenborough, then controller of BBC2, but contrary to legend it was I, and not he, who next morning likened the appointment to Churchill inviting Rommel to command the Eighth Army before Alamein. Perhaps we said it together. It was true enough. The papers on Thursday enjoyed a field day. It was a natural enough sensation and it was generally interpreted as a brutal rebuff to the BBC. Some thought it made sense, but most were alarmed and dismayed. Later Edward Short was to write to me that 'the press generally welcomed the appointment'. Lord Hill, in his book, blandly states that Greene and Lusty prolonged the controversy in the press. We had other things to do and I cannot recall that I had a single contact with the press at all.

At eleven o'clock on that Thursday morning the board was due to meet at Television Centre. A shocked and numbed assembly met me there. There was no contrary mood. Something akin to despair prevailed and there was deep sympathy for Hugh Greene. None, that I can recall, knew Lord Hill personally and there was little animosity towards him. But it was thought odd that he should have felt able to accept the transition — and odder still that he could accomplish it overnight. The resentment and mystification was towards an apparent act of political malice. We had not expected to be consulted, but, following tradition as we knew it, we had hoped for a chairman more of the calibre of Lord Normanbrook and Sir Arthur fforde. As a board we had not been impressed by Lord Hill's chairmanship of the ITA.

I thought it better to have no discussion at our meeting when it started. This, subsequently, was to disappoint Lord Hill, who records that one of his first acts was to search the minutes for just such a discussion and frankly acknowledges his chagrin on finding none. All I did was formally to convey the apologies of the Postmaster-General and report that I had written to Lord Hill inviting him to lunch at the earliest possible date. After that encounter I would relay my impressions to members of the board on holiday. During the course of that day the date of Hill's lunch with me was agreed: the earliest possible date was August 8th — some ten days distant. Lord Hill in his memoirs complains bitterly that no message of any kind reached him from the BBC. In his account he chooses to imply that my invitation to lunch — which was in fact delivered by hand — reached him some ten days later. The dated copies of my invitation and Lord Hill's reply now repose in the BBC's archives. Hill's distortion is a curious one, the only point of which must be to sustain his oft-repeated assertion that he was badly received by the BBC.

But the events of my day were far from over. Hugh Greene asked me to stay behind and we went to his room at Television Centre. He said that every sort of problem had fallen into my lap whilst I was at the BBC and he was afraid he had yet another to add. He had to tell me with sadness that his marriage was breaking up and that there was to be a divorce. He knew it would distress me since both he and Elaine were my close personal friends. I went home sad and anxious. Were the news to break within the next week or two, the situation could be a tricky one. However liberal the climate it seemed to me then, as it seems to me still, that the director-general of the BBC stands in a position of exceptional vulnerability. The problem was not one I had any wish to confront; and I was additionally anxious that Hugh Greene's domestic anxieties might well disturb even his equanimity in the days ahead — indeed, I think they played a certain part in the outcome. Fortunately, there were delays of one kind and another and Lord Hill was in charge of events when the divorce finally came about.

A merciful if tedious element of farce erupted almost at once. It was played out in Brighton hotel bedrooms with hideously complicated telephone calls in the early and chaotic days of S.T.D. My wife and I had gone to Brighton for a weekend of relaxation. Hugh Greene was on holiday in Suffolk and Lord Hill was reputed to have gone fishing. It seems that he had brooded over the lack of enthusiasm he had detected in the BBC. He had at some time met the BBC's newly knighted director of engineering, Sir

Francis McLean, and on the telephone to him had poured out his woes. McLean then telephoned Hugh Greene to suggest that a call from Hugh to Hill might not come amiss. Hugh had been adamant in his insistence that everything should await the meeting between Hill and myself. McLean thought he should consult me in Brighton. I felt a little sorry for McLean since an engineer's obvious response to any problem must be to pour oil around the source. I managed to get a call through to Hugh Greene in Sussex. He thought the whole thing was a nonsense and so did I. If McLean had got himself involved then he should somehow get himself uninvolved. 'I am on holiday,' declared Hugh, 'and Charles Hill is not part of it.' I thus telephoned McLean somewhere in Surrey and a little later reflected that it would do no harm were I to telephone Hill. He was not available and I spoke to Lady Hill.

I have been, and will continue to be, critical in my assessment of Lord Hill's contribution to broadcasting. But Lady Hill is an altogether different matter. She is delightful, wise, friendly and amused. Their mutual devotion is touching and rather movingly evident whenever they are seen together. I explained the situation to her, assured her that no affront was intended to her husband, that I was looking forward to meeting him at lunch and hoped he would in the meanwhile enjoy his fishing.

Luckily after that there was quiet until the Tuesday date with Lord Hill arrived. But I was glad and amused to hear from Hugh that he had arranged to break his holiday and to meet Lord Hill at the Reform Club for tea after Hill's lunch with me. Again, in his account Hill gets it wrong and places his meeting with Greene before and not after our lunch together. Trivial although this may be, it contains a relevance worthy of note.

For his lunch Lord Hill arrived promptly at Broadcasting House and was conducted to the third floor where I awaited him. Our discussion went off in the most friendly fashion until the time arrived for Hill to betake himself to the Reform Club for his tea with Hugh Greene. As Hugh had already done, he promised to telephone me afterwards. Over lunch I stressed the difficulties of the situation, which were obvious enough, and assured him that there was no personal animosity towards himself. It was the chairman of the ITA who introduced the element of discord. This, in Lord Hill's account, becomes a 'lecture on public service broadcasting to the detriment of commercial television'.

I went on to suggest that he might find it useful if I were to arrange an informal lunch or dinner with the board of management. No — he would prefer to cope with them in his own way. Remembering the arrangements which had seemed helpful to Lord Normanbrook, I said I would most gladly contrive a similarly informal meeting with the board of governors so that he might know them personally before his first board meeting in September. Again a polite refusal. He would not be in favour of that. Lord Hill's account makes no mention of these proposals. Instead, he reports that I offered to 'mediate' between him and the director-general. I cannot think that I did. Hugh Greene was to meet him at a later hour and no thought of mediation had occurred to me. I knew Hugh quite well enough to appreciate that he was not a man to require an intermediary in any situation. Lastly, and again recalling Lord Normanbrook's installation, I said that although he, Lord Hill, would be chairman when next the governors met, he might find it useful were I to take the meeting on that occasion. It would also give me the opportunity of expressing a welcome to him on behalf of the board. It was an unwise move. Not only did Lord Hill reject that well-intentioned proposal out of hand, but it enabled him ever afterwards to proclaim far and wide that I had invited him to come along as an 'observer'. 'This suggestion was more than I could take,' complains Lord Hill.

He told me that he was hoping to bring with him a secretary of many years' standing and to make use of a car already provided for him by the Laporte organization of which he was chairman. These I suggested were matters he should take up with the BBC, but I expressed no view.

At one point we reached, I thought, the nub of the problem. 'I cannot understand', observed Lord Hill, 'what all the fuss is about. It is just another job.' 'You must forgive me,' I replied, 'but I think that is exactly what all the fuss is about.'

'Yes,' said Lord Hill when confronted by David Frost with this remark in a television interview, 'I did say that.'

We parted on friendly terms but each, I suspect, realized that any close partnership would be unlikely in the few months we would be together. Later that same afternoon both he and Hugh Greene reported that their meeting had gone well. They seemed to share a certain optimism. It had not been an unsatisfactory day, and after it Lord Hill sent me, with a friendly note, a copy of his first volume of autobiography, *Both Sides of the Hill*.

In fulfilment of my assurance I wrote to every member of the board of governors in terms rather more hopeful than I think any of us had anticipated after our last meeting:

> I think you will like to know that Lord Hill lunched with me privately at Broadcasting House yesterday, and we talked very fully and frankly for some three hours. Following this Lord Hill met Hugh at the Reform Club and had what both subsequently described to me as a pleasant and useful talk. Hugh returned to his holiday much cheered by the understanding which they had managed quickly to establish.
>
> I think Lord Hill felt with me that our own long conversation was useful. Certainly many of the anxieties which we have been feeling became less substantial and my own fears for the future are to an encouraging extent diminished.
>
> Lord Hill looks forward to meeting the board in September.

I had thought in my foolish political naivety, that the Postmaster-General, Edward Short, would have been somehow aware, or made aware, that the appointment to the BBC of the chairman of the ITA, was unlikely to be accepted with unquestioning equanimity by those most directly concerned. I had indeed, at Hugh Greene's request, written a short formal letter to the Postmaster-General acquainting him with the BBC's anxieties in the matter. Hugh Greene thought, and I agreed, that some such letter should find its place in the archives. I concluded therefore that it would be civil, although in no sense obligatory, to send Mr Short a copy of my letter to the governors with its more optimistic forecast. I received a reply which continues to astonish me to this day and which seemed at the time so contentiously ridiculous that I refrained from reporting it to the governors. I am now able to quote it by kind permission of Mr Short.

Thank you for letting me see your letter to the Governors.

Of course I am not concerned with communications between the chairman and the governors, but as you have been kind enough to let me see this letter, I cannot but comment that I am very sorry indeed that it should have been felt necessary to write it. There is a clear implication that something was not quite right about Lord Hill's appointment. Apart from the fact that the appointment of the chairman of the governors is entirely a matter for the Government, it will I hope be borne in mind that Lord Hill, has a long and distinguished record of public service. His appointment has been generally welcomed in the press and I do regret that his coming to the BBC should have been clouded in this way.

As I pointed out in the final section of the recent White Paper on Broadcasting, I am very anxious that there should be a much closer liaison between the two Authorities. Lord Hill's appointment is in furtherance of this policy. I hope everyone will make him welcome.

This, so it seemed to me, was rather too much for even an acting-chairman to accept without retort. I refrained from pointing out that our appointments derived from the Crown with the express purpose of dissociating us from government, and I wrote:

Thank you for your letter of 21st August. You can rest assured that I am doing my utmost to make as easy as possible Lord Hill's transition from the ITA to the BBC. It is, of course, appreciated that Lord Hill has had a long and distinguished record of public service, and the doubts encountered are not personal in any way to Lord Hill, but simply arise from his position as chairman of what the BBC rightly regards as its chief competitor in the field of television — competitive and quite properly so by government decree.

If I may say so, it is hardly realistic to expect that the appointment of the chairman of the ITA to the chair of the BBC should be at once welcomed by the Corporation. It was only natural for the staff, the higher executives and the Board of Governors to feel disconcerted, and although the appointment was welcomed by some sections of the press, there was equally general comment to the effect that it was a severe rebuff to the BBC.

I am not concerned with the rights or wrongs of this, and I of course agree that the appointment is entirely one for the Government to make. However, it happened to fall to me to confront the very real doubts which immediately arose within and throughout the Corporation, and these I am doing my utmost to resolve. There was a very natural anxiety expressed by every member of the board at its last meeting before its recess and immediately following the announcement, of which I had no time to prepare the board. The purpose of my subsequent letter, following a long conversation with Lord Hill — who himself recognizes the natural difficulties — was to allay, so far as I could, the initial anxieties of the board. I am convinced that to gloss over these points would be far more detrimental to the success of Lord Hill's term of office than to face them squarely at the outset, and I am sure that this would be the view of Lord Hill, with whom I enjoyed the fullest and frankest talk.

The BBC as you will know is dedicated to what it regards as public-service broadcasting with a deep conviction, and I can assure you that it is the most sincere wish of the Corporation from the Board of Governors downwards to welcome Lord Hill's wisdom and guidance.

There was no acknowledgment, but in due course I was to receive a brief letter of thanks from Mr Short when my term as Lord Hill's vice-chairman came to its welcome end. He was afraid, he wrote, that I had experienced a difficult time.

The question has long been debated as to why Harold Wilson took a step which from any viewpoint was both contentious and extraordinary. There were some who thought it wise and shrewd, but none, I think, other than Mr Short, who found nothing unusual about it. There was the early story of the 'leak' and of Mr Wilson's alleged remark to a BBC commentator. Our relationship with the Labour Government had not been easy and had proved worrying to Lord Normanbrook: there seemed to be an even greater sensitivity than we had experienced with the previous Conservative Government and this surprised us. There was a certain superficial frigidity about Lord Normanbrook and it had to be doubted if a warmth of understanding could ever have existed between himself and Harold Wilson.

The appointment was certainly no act of charity or good-will on Wilson's part. But many continue to think that it was an act of premeditated malice. This I accepted for a while but came to doubt. A short time after I left the board, at the end of January 1968, I was in Dublin on publishing matters and met at a party some members of the Irish broadcasting authority with whom I had once lunched. They had a strange story to relate which they thought I might verify. A few days previously they had entertained Lord Aylestone as chairman of the ITA. Throughout the world of broadcasting the BBC is news and any part of its experience is eagerly discussed. The appointment of Lord Hill had been regarded as sensational by the whole world of broadcasting. The Irish had questioned Lord Aylestone and he had astonished them by declaring that he, in fact, had been offered the BBC by Harold Wilson, but had declined it in doubt of his abilities to 'deal with that fellow Greene'. The Prime Minister then returned with the proposal that if Hill were to go to the BBC he, Aylestone, could take on the ITA. At that time this version of events had not reached the BBC, for I made inquiries on my return to London. For various reasons I now believe it to be true and it demolishes the theory that Harold Wilson acted in pursuit of any long deep-laid plan. There is an added pith to the episode, for when I first broke the news to Greene of Lord Hill's coming almost his first remark was 'if only it had been Aylestone'. A quite remarkable shot in the dark.

Lord Hill entered into his new kingdom on September 1st, 1967. I was his vice-chairman and would continue to be so until the expiration of my time at the end of January 1968. At the ITA Lord Hill had had a deputy chairman and apparently there is some significant difference between the two, but I think Lord Hill had small regard for either. I understood this to be so from the ITA, and I knew very well that it was so at the BBC. He at no time consulted with me on any point. I do not altogether blame him, for it was unlikely that any advice I proffered would be acceptable.

On that September 1st I was on holiday in the Scilly Isles and Hugh Greene was on holiday in Suffolk. I dispatched a colourful and expensive greetings telegram to the new chairman. It was never referred to. Reports reached me that Lord Hill, dismissing his taxi some way up Portland Place, had arrived on foot and was much photographed being greeted by the commissionaire to whom clean white gloves had been issued. Inside, homage was done by Oliver Whitley, deputizing for the director-general. Later Hugh Greene returned from his holiday and at the end of the month the board assembled for its first meeting under Lord Hill.

I have no desire to emulate Lord Hill in the disclosure of what most would regard as confidential material, for which he was severely taken to task by many who reviewed *Behind the Screen*. It is not an easy tightrope on which to maintain balance but I think it wrong to involve and identify others who may be unaware of one's intentions. But I was still vice-chairman with responsibilities towards the board and towards the BBC which overrode any obligation I might feel towards Lord Hill, who quite clearly regarded me with suspicion and says as much in his book. I had learned in various ways of procedures and approaches which, within the tradition of Arthur fforde and Lord Normanbrook, I found alien and disturbing and which were beginning to spread uneasy apprehension within the BBC. In these circumstances I thought it prudent and right to warn by letter members of the board that life was going to be different and often difficult and that the board was likely, in my opinion, to find itself in situations new to the experience of any of us. I neither consulted nor acquainted Hugh Greene about this letter. It would have involved him in a decision which was mine alone. I later gave him a copy so that it might find its place in the archives of the Corporation. One recipient revealed its contents to Lord Hill.

The first meeting with the board must have been a difficult one for Lord Hill. He had rejected all proposals which might have made it less so. He declined my suggestion that I should utter a few words of welcome, and in his book complains that no word of welcome greeted him. My conviction seems confirmed that the shrewdness of the long-sighted politician could at this stage evaluate the advantages of a reception he might later criticize; but there was nothing I could do about it. He came into the room on the third floor where we habitually foregathered prior to our meeting and shook each of us by the hand, introduced by Sir Ralph Murray who was attending his first meeting as a governor in succession to Sir Ashley Clarke. It appeared that he and Hill were known to one another. We settled ourselves in our accustomed places around the oval table. There was no introductory word; no reference to Lord Normanbrook; no courtesies. The voice, which seems to come from the stomach, and is familiar to all who remember the war-time broadcasts, suggested we should get down to the minutes of the previous meeting. It was neither an auspicious nor a happy beginning.

In all the eight years I had been on the board there had been a vote on only two occasions. The first was in Sir Arthur fforde's day, when we debated over three meetings a request from the board of management that the BBC might broadcast the odds before the race. The ITA. permitted this and we were losing an audience. A Reithian principle was involved and two governors were opposed to the change. Two against is too many, said fforde. In due course one became converted. One against is too few, said fforde. The second was during my period as acting-chairman: we had to decide if in any circumstances at all the BBC should be allowed to contrive secret recordings. It was an unpleasant and difficult point, but finally, although unanimity was not quite possible, the justification, under most rigid control, was maintained and this view was subsequently endorsed by the general advisory council.

Lord Hill at once took an opposite view. Almost every point required a 'counting of hands'. It was, and quickly proved to be, a mistaken conception. Governors could not be equal in experience of the BBC and its problems. In his early days a new governor would need to feel his way; he was not equipped to judge difficult matters until to some extent enlightened by experience and persuasion. Previous chairmen had found it wiser and better to move to decision by consensus: a method much derided by Lord Hill.

There was never, of course, the slightest chance that Charles Hill and Hugh Greene could work for long in any sort of deep accord. Both were, and remain, astute realists. They would each be ready to appear in concord when the circumstances made it convenient for each of them to do so. But in the depths of Lord Hill lay, I suspect, a profound suspicion of Hugh Greene and an almost total inability to understand him. Hugh Greene, on the other hand, while occasionally ready to 'rather like the old buffer', was intellectually contemptuous of Hill and found him devious in his ways. What he underestimated was Hill's ability to find — and then exploit — a dangerous chink in his mass of protective armour. For Hugh has never concealed that a major ambition of his BBC life was to be one, if not two, up on Reith. It was a weakness of which Lord Hill would not remain long in ignorance and it was precisely to suit his purpose. In the mid-summer of 1968 my wife and I were to join a dinner party of Hugh Greene's at Television Centre. During the evening Hugh took me on one side. 'I have some very good news for you,' he said. 'I am to resign as director-general and then be appointed a governor. Charles Hill has got the appointment agreed by Harold Wilson.' I was appalled and said so: 'And you regard this as good news?' 'Yes,' replied Hugh. 'It solves many problems. It's one up on Reith, isn't it?' and the glint of Greene mischief was in his eye. It certainly was 'one up on Reith'. Reithian students will know how deeply distressed he was when, upon his impetuous resignation as director-general in 1938 (which he was ever afterwards to regret), he was not at once made chairman let alone a governor. It greatly embittered him.

It is of course monstrously wrong that the director-general of so sensitive an organization as the BBC should at once (or indeed ever) join the board of which he has been chief executive. It is wrong for him; it is wrong for the board; and it is an impossible imposition on his successor however protective he may think his role to be. I suspect that today Hugh Greene (who left the board within a short time) would concede as much. What was expected of Lord Hill by Harold Wilson and his Government cannot be known. Lord Hill declares that no directions were given him. Certainly Hugh Greene was brought down and a remarkable era of adventurous public-service broadcasting reached its close.

The BBC possesses and exercises an extraordinary authority over its adherents. Of those who become at all deeply involved in its affairs few remain unchanged; and until the publication of his memoirs I doubted if Lord Hill were among them. It must be said that during his time he stood four square against political and commercial pressures. These are the essentials and they were kept inviolate by other chairmen than Lord Hill. It has to be said that there disappeared in the time of Lord Hill elements of extreme importance in the relationship between the chairman and the director-general, and between the governors and the management, which may never again be found — and without which the BBC could never have attained its stature in the world.

The worst affront to truth accomplished by Lord Hill in his reflections is the extraordinary assumption that he was the BBC's first effective chairman and his governors the first effective board. As Hugh Greene has pointed out, 'should such a falsification of the true facts pass unchallenged, doubts would be cast on the whole constitution of the BBC if, after nearly half a century, a Lord Hill was needed to make it work'.

Consider these random quotations from *Behind the Screen*:

It soon became clear that governors' meetings were friendly Christian name affairs. It also became obvious that they decided very little and that a common form of so-called discussion was what the governors agreed with the director-general.

My first impression of the General Advisory Council was of a decorative and distinguished body which was allowed little influence.

I chided him [Lord Reith] that it was his strong director-generalship which had laid the pattern for the future, based on a powerful director-general and a weak board of governors.

There was a negative spirit and little control over the producers by anyone.

I ought to have realized that a document stemming from the board of management, however imperfect, stood a much better chance of acceptance ... than one which came from the boardroom table.

The board discussions, however exciting, however valuable, seemed to lead nowhere.

'That', said Greene, 'is an editorial matter.' I intervened to point out that governors could raise any point they liked.

No such 'intervention' by either Arthur fforde or Lord Normanbrook would ever have been required.

We could talk but that was all. Policy was made by management.

I am sure that no one would suggest today that we should return to the old system — or lack of it. They want to be active governors, not ciphers.

The governors on the whole are becoming clearer as to their role and firmer in their decisions.

If these quotations mean anything, it is that until Lord Hill's arrival, members of the board were ciphers, the chairman an inactive nonentity and the lot subservient to the whim and dictation of the director-general. It was to such a system apparently that Sir Arthur fforde, Sir James Duff, Lord Normanbrook and very many others of distinction over many years devoted their time and their energies.

Towards the end of his life Lord Reith became rather hard of hearing and, as so many deaf people do, he was apt to speak louder than he knew. A high executive of the BBC was lunching with him in the dining-room of the House of Lords. Lord Hill became a topic of conversation. In language of unparalleled strength the verdict of Lord Reith echoed and rolled around the room.

20

Warmer Waters

B Y the middle 1960s I began to feel that we were indeed
attracting a few more favourable reviews from the *Sunday
Times* and that perhaps it could be claimed we were nearer
to the rounding of that corner. It had taken some ten years and I
retain no doubt myself that but for pressures beyond the scope
of any survey I intend to make it could have been achieved in
less.

Editorially, the Hutchinson list was gathering strength with
some momentum, and the imprints associated with it had settled
down within the rough degree of specialization each had been
allotted. The various group services, which the publishing operation had retained, were developing well, and a much younger team
than previously was in charge of them. On the sales side, a first-
rate bunch of youngish travellers had learned the message and
there had been a considerable reappraisal of our overseas markets.
It was no longer regarded as a playful indulgence when someone
from Great Portland Street ventured across the Channel. American publishers and those from other countries added Great
Portland Street to their essential itineraries. I felt able to reflect,
in moments of optimism, that Sir Hugh Greene down the road
at the BBC was not the only one intent on opening windows.

I found I missed very much the continuing involvement with
authors, and what they were up to, which had played so major a
part in my life in Bloomsbury Street. It was a little depressing to
be called into action only when things appeared to be going
wrong. Consultation upwards is not a popular pastime. Editorially Hutchinson still lacked identity and I had failed altogether
either to cultivate or persuade others to cultivate a team of

readers or literary advisers aware of, and excited by, what we were about. It was a large requirement, but too many of the group's readers still derived from a past age and depended, alas, on the wretched pittance paid then and now within publishing for this literary drudgery. It was a deprivation understood by Iain Hamilton, but less so by Harold Harris. No publisher of any size exists who can give the necessary attention to all the manuscripts which flood in upon his office, and the success of many publishers rests as much on the quality of the literary advisers they recruit, as upon any innate hunch they might themselves possess. It is disconcerting to find that a *Born Free* or a *Day of the Jackal* has been thrown out with the bath-water, for lack of percipience in a reader jaded by a surfeit of drudgery.

None the less, I like to believe that by slow inculcation and the kind of animation given first by Iain Hamilton, and after him by Harold Harris with other younger editors, there had imperceptibly come about a climate of 'involved enterprise' capable of accommodating the widest diversity of creative eccentrics. It is doubtful if Dr Bronowski had expected to share a list with Ursula Bloom, or John Bratby with Barbara Cartland, or Lord Reith with Brendan Behan, but each did so and added their contribution to a climate each appeared to find congenial.

Perhaps even more important, we were, or at least appeared to me to be, a tolerant bunch of people; and a certain spirit of lively independence and civilized congeniality dissipated at once any threat of inter-office strife or pettiness from whatever source it might come. It may well be that this derived from my own propensities to arouse apoplectic fury on suitable occasions, and if so I no longer regret them.

I had an occasional divergence of views with those in authority over me, but apart from the disagreeable episode of *Mein Kampf*, with its exceptional implications, no editorial decision of mine was ever questioned either by the board or by Mr Holt, who was not only its chairman but also of the multitude of companies emanating from it. It was my responsibility to sign every publishing agreement and my privilege to go to prison should any publication of ours require it. I found it not a bad cautionary reflection to retain at the back of my mind. In such matters I would be perfectly willing to accept the apparent ignominy of gaol should the principle seem large enough, but I would have needed much persuasion that it was.

Printers in the main are timorous and I was myself glad that ours would continue to query passages or phrases or words unlikely, in fact, to affront a refined lady Sunday-school teacher in the Outer Hebrides. Instructions were that such queries should be referred to me and only on the occasions that I found one I thought justified did I get editorially disgruntled. I did not relish our editorial work being undertaken by our printers.

There are always those around ready to turn an incident into a sensation, especially in the wide world of communication where editorial judgment and discretion too often become interpreted as sinister and reactionary censorship. A widely publicized incident centred upon Brian Aldiss's novel *The Hand-Reared Boy*. Aldiss's considerable reputation was based largely on the brilliance of his science fiction; and *The Hand-Reared Boy* was an attempt, and finally a successful one, to widen his range. Messrs Faber were his normal publishers, but they had rejected *The Hand-Reared Boy*, or perhaps declined might be a more appropriate word since quality was not in doubt. Michael Dempsey was at that time a young whizz-kid editor of great talent who had been sent to me by Iain Hamilton and whose principal concern was New Authors Ltd. The author of *The Hand-Reared Boy* was by no means qualified for that imprint, but Dempsey, with commendable initiative, secured his script. He was enthusiastic about it and so were his readers. There was a unanimity of enthusiasm and no report suggested that its basic theme was one for contemplation. Nor at that time did the title sound a warning and I gave my necessary blessing to the enterprise. In due course proofs of *The Hand-Reared Boy* appeared in their customary profusion, and a message reached me from an editorial source far removed from the office suggesting that I should read them. I took a very great dislike to what I read. It dealt exhaustively, and in my view exhaustingly, with masturbation; and it was clearly going to affront a great many decent people. Well and good: it is occasionally necessary to affront a great many decent people if some frontier of understanding and compassion is to be extended. On such occasions I simply want to be convinced, in an editorial sense, that there is this compensating factor and that the author is well aware of the affront he has deliberately contrived.

I was unable either to be persuaded or to persuade myself that *The Hand-Reared Boy* was a title I wanted in the lists for which I happened to be responsible, or one that, if called upon, I would feel able with conviction to defend. There was, in my mind, no question of censorship or suppression. A publisher was admitting a wrong decision for himself but not for the two hundred or so competing colleagues at once alerted to the situation. In point of fact, my friend Tony Godwin, then the magician with Messrs Weidenfeld, promptly seized upon it and sold a great many more copies than might have been achieved without the acres of fortuitous publicity. The author was understanding and reasonable throughout. He was quite unable to agree with me, but at the same time was unhappy to have a reluctant publisher. In the outcome the prospects seemed so much enhanced that he contemplated dedicating the novel to me in tribute for the publicity my action had secured. A year or so later I took another look at the book and found myself wondering what all the fuss had been about.

Within the foreseeable future it will be difficult to contemplate this sort of problem without bringing to mind the esteemed name and image of Lord Longford whom I am happy to regard as my friend.

It was not pornography which first brought us together, but our publication of his autobiography, *Five Lives*. It had its moments of revelationary hilarity as almost every contact with him has, though this never detracts from respect and affection. At a late stage of the book's production, Lord Longford telephoned in some agitation. He had just lunched with a gentleman of notoriety who featured briefly in that part of his book which dealt with the less commendable members of the human family. Over lunch he had become so impressed by the virtues of his guest's Christian humility and his work of restoration that would we please remove the passage from its present place and insert it more appropriately in the chapter dealing with Christianity? *Five Lives* in due course featured prominently in one of our advertisements in *The Times Literary Supplement* and I was personally sorry that an agitated last-minute correction prevented the announcement of *Five Wives*.

On the spur of a later moment I was to accept Lord Long-ford's suggestion that I should join his now famous commission of investigation into the problems of pornography. I did not scoff at it then and I do not scoff at it now. If it accomplished little else, it properly concentrated attention on a question both complex and important. I very soon decided, however, that I had made a mistake and that Lord Longford's committee was no place for an active publisher whose more proper role was to grope his own way to salvation as best he could on an *ad hoc* basis.

From the beginning it seemed to me that Lord Longford and the majority of his colleagues were far too obsessed with the iniquities of sex, which I happened to think of less importance than violence, sadism, racialism and the rest; I also thought that if these evils could be somehow reduced, sex would more or less take care of itself. I was, too, taken aback by the vehemence of those who seemed to find that an imposed censorship would solve all problems and I came to the conclusion that the sins of oppression could in the long run prove more dangerous than any sins of expression. Thus, after a little while and with what tact I could muster, I beat a retreat which I am afraid sadly disappointed Lord Longford. That the report, when it finally appeared, achieved a degree of tolerant liberality reflected the greatest credit on those who remained with Lord Longford to overcome the persistent tumult of the repressionist extremists I had listened to with such foreboding.

The combination of the Sitwells and Hutchinson seemed improbable, and I was thus particularly elated when David Higham, their literary agent, suggested we might publish a new book by Sir Osbert. All went well despite the difficulties of my one and only meeting with Sir Osbert. The distressing illness from which he suffered was taking him inexorably to the end of his life. He asked me to lunch quietly with him in his London flat. At the time my hearing was exceptionally bad. He was distressingly frail and his voice weak. While conviviality was hardly the order of the day, a more lively exchange of views should have been possible. At the end I felt that he was as perplexed as I was distressed. However, all seemed well and *Pound Wise* duly and successfully appeared.

That all went well was a useful factor in our acquisition of Edith Sitwell's autobiography *Taken Care Of*. We had a young editor in our office whose function — before the days of Michael Dempsey — was New Authors Ltd, but who rightly took a lively interest in everything else. He was Graham Nicol, and was not only a devotee of Edith Sitwell, but a close friend of her secretary Elizabeth Salter. It was Graham Nicol's persistent and dogged determination over quite a few years which, with Elizabeth Salter's help, produced the completion of Edith Sitwell's script. I found her more remarkably a human being than ever I had been led to imagine. Formidable she certainly was, but intensely kind, extremely amusing and totally lacking in that arrogance suggested by the Sitwellian image over many years.

As the book approached publication its author was reaching the end of her life and was more or less bedridden in her Hampstead flat. I had talked with her a number of times and she had been quite extraordinarily kind. I can hardly think that she regarded me as a likely Sitwellian publisher, but at no time did she express misgivings. My hearing was better than when I had to cope with her brother, but her own voice was by no means strong and I was obliged to do a good deal of guesswork, at which most who are deaf become adroit. It was around the publication of *Taken Care Of* that she gave a party; not a large one in numbers but sufficiently so to crowd her flat. She knew I had recently married again after Joan's death, and she included my wife Babs in her invitation. We arrived at her front door with two portly, rather hot, gentlemen in bowler-hats who seemed somehow unlikely to be fellow guests, and yet were late if they were supposed to do the catering. The small drawing-room was crowded and Dame Edith, it was explained, was not too well but hoped to be with us soon. Would we please be ready to entertain her when required. A colony of Siamese cats were delicately cavorting around the room, and taking rather too much interest in various plates of tidbits. A rival publisher, who was clearly of the opinion that Dame Edith should be on his list, was suffering an acute onslaught of hay fever. 'Those bloody cats,' he kept repeating, 'those bloody cats. They always do this to me. I must go.' Gathering up his wife, he left.

In due course the whisper was circulated that Dame Edith

was about to appear. The chatter ceased and every voice was lowered. And then through a door came the two hot gentlemen we had seen before, but without their bowler-hats. Between them they carried what can only be described as a throne, with Edith Sitwell in carefully arranged majesty upon it. She wore an enormous headgear, and her robes had been draped with meticulous precision. Queen Elizabeth I could not have made a greater impact on her Peers assembled, as Dame Edith upon her guests. To the dictation of some mystic command every head was bowed as the furniture removers, for such they were, deposited their burden on the floor. One by one we were bidden to the presence, mumbled a few words of homage and were replaced by another. Even the cats caught the spirit of restraint. Dame Edith soon tired, and left as she had come. It was the last occasion I was to see her. She was a great lady.

Taken Care Of was one of three autobiographies which by chance came more or less together by very different routes to our list and which in succession were serialized in the *Sunday Times*. It had never happened before to the books of one publisher, and Denis Hamilton, who was then the editor, knew very well what it would mean for Hutchinson and for myself, and seemed almost as gratified as I was. *Taken Care Of* was, in fact, a book agented by David Higham, but the other two had come to me direct in curious ways. One was Sir George Mallaby's *From My Level* and the other Nubar Gulbenkian's *Pantaraxia*.

Having published *Mission for My Country* by the Shah of Persia I found myself summoned, and still do, to the celebrations for His Imperial Majesty's birthday, held each year in London by his reigning ambassador. It is a crowded affair and on this first occasion I found myself in close proximity to the unmistakable presence of Nubar Gulbenkian. With an orchid in his buttonhole, his monocle, his massive beard and his sparkling eyes, he exuded an aura of dignified and appropriate flamboyance. I dislike and rather disapprove of accosting celebrities at cocktail parties, but Mr Gulbenkian seemed disengaged and so was I. 'Aren't you', I ventured rather unnecessarily, 'Mr Gulbenkian?' 'Indeed I am,' he said pleasantly, 'and who are you?' I explained that I was His Imperial Majesty's humble publisher and added, 'I have been thinking it's time you wrote an autobiography.' 'I have been thinking the same thing,' he said; and so it was that in due course *Pantaraxia* came to our list.

'Call me Nubar,' he was soon to say and it somehow gave me singular pleasure. It was impossible not to enjoy every moment in his rumbustious yet sensitive company, and there were to be many of them over the next years and indeed until his death not so very long ago. Larger than life at its largest and always in Technicolor, he was an extraordinarily attractive character, uniquely able to add charm to the ostentation he could hardly be expected to avoid. His 'life-style', very naturally, was flamboyant, but disarmingly so. 'What would you expect from an Armenian Jew?' he was frequently to say. It may not be easy for a rich man to enter the kingdom of heaven, but it must be very much more difficult for him to journey through life untainted by cynicism and doubt. Nubar Gulbenkian moved very warily and was instantly suspicious that any proposal put to him was somehow designed to exploit his worldly innocence or his wealth. It was necessary to regard this innate caution as something of a joke. His book gave him a great deal of pleasure, but its production required patience and diplomacy, since he welcomed it as a God-given opportunity to give vent to his hates and air his detestation of those who ran, in his view misguidedly, the Gulbenkian Foundation. In the preparation of his book he was guided with great skill by George Scott, now editor of the *Listener* and a distinguished journalist. When the time came to settle with lawyers and their endless consultations, he thought it perfectly reasonable that George Scott should share his costs.

He very much enjoyed the serialization in the *Sunday Times* and the various junketings which attended publication. During the progress of the book and when it still lacked a title, he and his extremely charming and devoted wife joined a dinner party at Television Centre at which I was host. In a building for most hours of the day a-swarm with celebrities Nubar made a great impression as we toured the studios; and outside the famous car, dolled up as a London taxi, was very much on view.

Babs, very sensibly, had swotted him up in *Who's Who* and noted that his hobby, or one of them, was 'Pantaraxia'. 'What does it mean?' she asked him. 'It means', he said, 'keeping people on their toes.' It seemed to me a splendid title, but he had some

273

doubts. 'It sounds like a disease of the feet,' he said. He may have been right, but nothing better came along and *Pantaraxia* the book became.

At one time he was rather taken with the idea that it might be translated into a musical comedy. It possessed splendid ingredients — wealth, sex, colour and character — and many of the chapter titles simply await their music: The Three Requirements of Monsieur Nubar; Oilmen are like Cats: A Corner in Caviar; More Comfortable than Happy; Leave it to Radcliffe; An Orchid a Day.

He invited us to the celebrations of his seventieth birthday — an event not easily forgotten. Originally to be at Claridge's it was switched at the last moment to the Hilton after some tiff with the management. It may be that Claridge's felt unable to offer hospitality to the hounds of the Whaddon Chase who with attendant huntsmen bayed and trumpeted in with the birthday cake. The party began at 9 p.m. and continued until breakfast was served next morning. A solid phalanx of orchids ran the length of the enormous room. Champagne cascaded like Niagara in flood and caviar seemed available by the ton. Dramatic belly-dancers were flown from Turkey for the occasion, accompanied by appropriate bands. We shared a small table with Lord Radcliff and George Scott, and discussed our host who dominated the proceedings with ease and charm. He had explained on some previous occasion that his impressive cummerbunds were made from his wife's discarded evening dresses.

He observed with scrupulous care the Lenten requirements of his faith, and on the appointed day his beard and his eyebrows would be brushed down in humility and not restored to upward growth until the fast had ended.

I last saw 'my friend Nubar' not long before he died. He had become more or less an invalid in his house up in the hills near Grasse. We were staying at Antibes and he sent a message that he would like to see me. A young English chauffeur appeared to collect me in the largest Mercedes ever seen, to which a special perspex roof had been contrived to enable Nubar to view the skies. He had, I gathered, the full-time services of four nurses; his doctor paid daily visits and he had his valet and two secretaries. A barber would call daily to trim his beard and a chiropodist was in regular attendance. He appeared in better form than I had expected to find him, but had aged and seemed reduced in size. We had tea and talked, and then a specially constructed beach-car arrived to drive me round the estate with its olive orchards. On my return we quietly consumed a bottle of champagne together and I was driven back to Antibes. The young English driver, clearly devoted to his master, related a perfect Nubarian anecdote. It seems that he had long since decided that, when the day came, he would be buried in a small graveyard above Grasse. With care he had chosen and purchased a site with a fine panoramic view. Not so long ago he had decided to have a rehearsal of his funeral and was driven to the cemetery. To his intense indignation he discovered that the view from his grave had become much obscured by a newly erected Shell petrol-station. In wrath he wrote to the management protesting at this vulgar violation of decency in general and of his view in particular; and would Messrs Shell have the goodness to remove their petrol station to another site. The reply regretted Mr Gulbenkian's distress; there had been no intentional affront and perhaps Mr Gulbenkian would reflect that he of all men had little cause to complain should a product of oil diminish the view from his final resting-place. Mr Gulbenkian did reflect and replied that he thought the point a valid one and would be happy to withdraw his request.

I sadly attended his memorial service in St Margaret's, Westminster, which was notable for the splendid singing of the 'Harrow School Song'. Nubar would have loved it. It kept the congregation on its toes.

Sir George Mallaby's *From My Level* illustrates again the chancy way by which manuscripts come to a publisher. We had staying with us for the weekend some old friends of my wife's from Suffolk. They were friendly with the Mallabys, who lived near by, and had understood from Sir George that his own publisher had just turned down his memoirs and he was uncertain what to do next.

I wrote to Sir George and received in response the script of *From My Level*. This I read with increasing interest and expectancy. It seemed to me to illuminate a quite exceptionally important aspect of state affairs, seldom divulged and of the greatest value. Sir George Mallaby had been a distinguished civil servant and an Assistant Secretary to the Cabinet during much of the war. Writing from a level rather below the top Sir George did much to humanize the whole operation of affairs without exposing anything at all to which exception could be taken. It seemed to me just the sort of book which Denis Hamilton would like for his *Sunday Times* and he took no time at all to agree.

Vague suggestions were made that the book contravened the Official Secrets Act and that the author had, in any event, overstepped the bounds normally respected by senior civil servants. Lord Normanbrook, at this time chairman of the BBC, and George Mallaby's old boss, was much disturbed. He had no criticism to make of a publisher wishing to publish what was offered him, but he shared the bureaucratic view and urged Mallaby to change his plans. It was possible to see his point, but neither Denis Hamilton nor I could agree with it. If the author was ready to confront the possible dangers of the Official Secrets Act and the brickbats of old colleagues, we certainly were; and the whole plan went ahead to considerable success.

The man with a story to tell would, of course, have been Lord Normanbrook himself. As Secretary to the Cabinet through momentous years, he knew it all. A geologist could more easily extract revelations from a rock than a publisher from Lord Normanbrook. The only confession I heard from him, and it a little shook me, was that he had destroyed every note and every paper in his personal possession concerning the Suez war.

These three books were a useful shot in the arm and enabled me to present a more confident presence at the monthly meetings of the parent board, particularly as two of them had come without the intercession of agents and thus enabled us to handle all rights and add the useful commissions which normally elude the publisher. An important book which gave us much satisfaction was Helen Joseph's *Tomorrow's Sun*, which was somehow smuggled from South Africa to land on Harold Harris's desk. It told the dramatic and horrendous story of its author's unceasing battle against apartheid operations in her country, for which she had long been under house arrest with all the loneliness and stress that this involved. She was a deeply religious woman whom nothing daunted and when Babs and I were in Johannes-

burg in 1971, I was determined somehow to see her. By this time
she was permitted a certain amount of freedom and was able to
come to our hotel one morning for breakfast. My wife and I
awaited her in the vestibule. When she came she was easily
recognizable and we stepped forward to greet her. She was at once
concerned and apologetic. My wife would have to go. To be seen
with more than one person was a breach of the regulations which
surrounded her. She was allowed to have breakfast with me, but
my wife would have to have it elsewhere. She was, she said,
under continual surveillance on such occasions and she indicated
a man in the hall, who was her sleuth and had followed her from
her home. She appeared to be in the highest spirits, sustained by
her faith and quite undaunted. A few weeks previously Dr
Ramsey, then Archbishop of Canterbury, with his wife, had been
in Johannesburg and, knowing of her, had invited her to breakfast. He too had assumed that his wife could be present, but she
too was banished from the scene. The Archbishop had given her
Communion and this had touched and inspired her.

I had the impression that we, at certain times, were also kept
track of. Certainly two letters from my 88-year-old mother had
been opened somewhere along their line from Cirencester. Unfortunately, before leaving for home from Cape Town, I made
some critical remarks which I thought to be off the record
but which were reported, rather to the embarrassment of a
number of people who had been most kind and hospitable to us.

James Plunkett's novel *Strumpet City* was for me, and I hope
also for its author, a remarkably satisfactory operation which
restored me to some of the more personal pleasures of publishing.
The novel derived from the days of Iain Hamilton's successful
plunder of the Irish literary scene, but its author, an executive in
the Irish television service, was a perfectionist whose progress
was so slow that we had almost abandoned hope that his manuscript would ever be finished to his satisfaction. It had some
affinity with James Farrell's *Thy Tears Might Cease*, which some
still claim to be the better novel.

Just making impressive headway on the Hutchinson water-
front was Brian Perman who had come to take charge of our
publicity and advertising. It is nowadays a major assignment,
often bringing directorial status. It is an activity which tends to

277

proliferation and requires on occasions a drastic confrontation with reality. In publishing it hardly existed before the last war. Brian Perman was new to the book world but this was no handicap and indeed the introduction to its occasionally reactionary thinking of fresh, uncluttered minds unlikely to be inhibited by reverence or timidity was an indulgence I enjoyed.

I had always at the back of my mind the urge to get back into publishing on my own account, making use of the administrative and publishing services reputedly in my charge, which were able to accomplish very well what might be asked of them. It was perhaps an approach of some arrogance, but as I was often accused of possessing such, it seemed reasonable enough to make positive use of so undesirable a trait. If, I thought, I could find the right book I would, as an exercise, cut a swathe through the procedures of my own devising, and concoct a ploy with young Brian Perman. Just as I was setting off for a short and lazy holiday in Devon, the manuscript of Plunkett's long-awaited novel reached me. It had the right 'smell' and I took it away with me. It was a long novel, but once started upon I found I wanted neither to stop reading it nor — a more rare experience — to reach its end. I felt once again that sense of overwhelming excitement which a publisher can hardly hope to encounter on more than a few occasions in his working life. Here I thought is the sort of injection required to give a boost to my personal publishing morale.

Much more depended on Brian Perman than he knew. One man's enthusiasm in an organization of any size, is not enough. An ally is essential from the start. I posted the manuscript off to Perman and asked him to read it. I may have encouraged him to like it, but no more; and he had, in any event, enough independence of mind to disagree. A merciful providence coincided his view with mine and we set forth in a joint activity to smash through every obstacle which might stand between *Strumpet City* and stardom.

For the first edition (after which the reviews took over) I wrote the blurb, and for the first time in my life signed it as THE PUBLISHER. I doubt if it was an act of wisdom, but there is no evidence that it did any harm, and *Strumpet City* in due course burst through the barriers and enjoyed a success which continues to this day. It has always astonished me that it has not as yet become a film. It had a quality of greatness; and Father Giffley, for me the dominant figure, would be a splendid part for Alec Guinness. But today, alas, Ireland is out of favour and aspirations to greatness in its literature have for a while become contaminated by the facts of its life.

An involvement of a different dimension added much to the environment of 1967 with the sudden appearance of Svetlana Alliluyeva on the centre of the world stage. There is not much in principle to be said for 'cheque book' publishing or for participation in the frantic auction which follows sensation and feeds upon it. This can erupt at any time and set the bells ringing in publishing offices all over the world. Transatlantic calls are made 'in the strictest confidence' between the originator (most likely to be in America) and half a dozen English publishers. Each of these, again in strict confidence, makes contact with the leading paperback publishers to ascertain their views. It is a lunatic operation conducted by lunatics and often enough by the end of the afternoon the truth emerges: it is not, after all, a book by the Messiah himself but a new portrait by a Jewish philosopher written after twenty-five years in a kibbutz and already under option to Weidenfeld. None the less, such is the climate; and it is sometimes necessary to engage in it, especially if one is battling for a position in the top league.

Svetlana Alliluyeva provided the opportunity we had awaited. It was known that, in 1963, she had smuggled the script of a book to India which she collected on her arrival early in 1967, and took with her to America. An authorized translation was to be done by Priscilla Johnson. The Russian authorities were angry and were peddling an alleged version of their own. To prevent this, it became necessary to publish Svetlana's book in the original Russian, and this was done both in America and in England. In America the book publishing rights had been acquired by Messrs Harper; and the project was being handled in New York by Messrs Curtis Brown (by this time divorced from the London firm) and in London by Messrs A. P. Watt. By great good fortune Harold Harris was in New York and was thus able to keep me informed of the picture as it developed. Hutchinson's chairman, Mr Holt, seemed ready with the money, when I told him that I thought we would have to go to £50,000. This did not deter him, and I pressed our claim on Messrs A. P. Watt and sent a cable to Harris economically worded 'Have offered fifty Bob'. The post office dropped the capitalization of the signature and occasioned Harold great alarm — he was obliged to have the truth explained to him by the Curtis Brown office before he recovered.

Other offers were, of course, being made and other considerations than money were being taken into account by those making the final decision. I could only hope for the best. It was certainly the 'biggest' and most sensational book to take the stage for many years and its acquisition at that moment would be of great benefit to us. I had made no forays with it into the world of paperbacks and I had one advantage over those who had. I happened to know both the whereabouts on that afternoon of Sir Allen Lane and the various reflections agitating his mind. The obvious paperback publisher for *Twenty Letters to a Friend* was Penguin, and although they were in less need of a sensational acquisition than we were, it would suit Allen very well to secure it himself. He was at that time anxious to reassert his editorial authority following doubts as to where the policies of his current editorial eminence, Tony Godwin, were leading him. A typical Lane disenchantment was under way.

In a very short time the answer had come. For a number of reasons our offer was acceptable. There was obvious elation; and negotiations with Allen Lane were of the simplest. 'Allen,' I said over the telephone, 'we have got Svetlana's book. How much is it worth to you?' There was the briefest pause. 'I think £25,000,' he replied. 'That is exactly the sum in my mind,' I said. 'Can you let me have the money?' 'Yes,' he said, 'I can. Thank you very much, Bob.' I knew what it meant to him and he knew what it meant to me.

The next issue of *The Bookseller* contained a full-page advertisement. It showed a large press photograph of Svetlana descending the steps from an aircraft on her arrival in America. She is smiling and clasping what might very well be a manuscript. Beneath were the two words 'It's Ours', and in one corner at the foot of the page was the Hutchinson colophon of taurus and in the other Allen Lane's penguin. I gazed upon it with satisfaction and remembered that first visit with Krishna Menon to Vigo Street just over forty years before.

Few books, I would in fact think none, have been so widely, persistently and sensationally proclaimed before publication. Serial rights were acquired by the *Observer* and for them, of course, it was a scoop to be made the most of. By the time the book itself appeared, there was a certain anti-climax. It had been very thoroughly serialized; every nuance of meaning and implication had been discussed; many who had eagerly awaited the book felt already familiar with it. In normal terms its sales were very large, but they were not what had been hoped for. Thanks to the sale to Penguin, financially there was no disaster; and with one thing and another we about broke even. It had certainly achieved its major purpose. So it did for Allen Lane, though the sales of the ultimate Penguin edition were not good. None the less Allen declared that he had no regrets whatever.

Twenty Letters to a Friend was a splendid book. 'A unique masterpiece,' wrote Edward Crankshaw; ' ... all past histories of Russia will have to be re-written in the light of this book.' It must surely be certain that the passage of time will add *Twenty Letters to a Friend* by Stalin's daughter as one essential to the understanding of its period.

In the spring of the following year my wife and I were in America and spending a weekend at Hopewell with Alan Collins's widow, Catherine. Svetlana was installed in a house in nearby Princeton and she was to come to Hopewell for dinner. We had had a certain amount of correspondence, but had not met.

I went with Alan's son to collect her. She lived alone, with a daily woman and a man on occasions to tend the garden. The house seemed sparsely furnished with few signs of comfort. Svetlana Alliluyeva possessed great charm; she was simply dressed for the evening and greeted me with warmth and friendship. Yet there was clearly a distance to be kept and observed. She seemed to contain the reserve of royalty. She was not to be caught off guard. One had to be careful. She expected a certain deference and when she joined the small dinner party, it was clear that she received it.

After dinner she signed a copy of the book for me and gave me a list of corrections to be made in any reprint. She had not altogether approved of every word of the translation. The wrapper blurb she had marked severely, and she deleted Edward Crankshaw's comment which had been printed at the top. 'It is not true,' she said. Reviews elsewhere had already placed her with Turgenev, Tolstoy, Chekhov and Pasternak. 'Nonsense,' she said, smiling, and deleted the lot. The blurb referred to her unwavering love for her father. 'This is not so,' she said, and crossed it out.

I suggested she might visit England and assured her of its welcome. She would like to come, but for the time there would be difficulties. She had great vivacity, a strong sense of humour and enjoyed living in Princeton. I asked her what protection she was given. A bell, she said, had been installed in her house. She had only to ring it and the policemen of Princeton would swarm around. On New Year's Eve, her first away from Russia, she had felt a little lonely. On the spur of the moment she rang the bell and as the police arrived she welcomed them. 'I am in no danger,' she said to them, 'but it is New Year's Eve and I am lonely on my own. I want you all to drink with me.' Quite a moment for a policeman in Princeton, should he care to think about it.

I have always tended to think that Svetlana Alliluyeva's second book, *Only One Year*, was in many ways of greater value and interest, although it attracted nothing like the attention of her first. In it she was able to take a more distant view of the life and of the country she had left behind. Her assessment of her father is quite different to that given in *Twenty Letters*: in that book, the portrayal of the father was by a devoted daughter, and the account of his death has a most impressive and moving poignancy which should merit a place in many anthologies for centuries to come. *Only One Year* is much more critical; she is looking at Russia and its masters from the democratic freedom of America and the climate of a university town. When I had talked with her there was the assumption that she would have more to write, and, having watched her with children and listened to her talking of her own, I suggested that one day she should write a book for them. She appeared to like the idea and she may indeed still have it in mind, but the news, when it came, was of *Only One Year*.

Our contract with Svetlana contained no option clause. Messrs

Harper in New York acquired all rights in *Only One Year*, which was a natural enough arrangement and simplified the contractual position. Svetlana herself and Messrs Harper assumed, and rightly, that we would want to be its publisher in London and the Commonwealth. There was no problem and terms, very much more lenient than those covering *Twenty Letters*, were quickly agreed.

Out of the blue of an afternoon came a transatlantic call from an obviously distressed Cass Canfield, the head of Messrs Harper and an old friend of mine. He told me that, to his consternation and regret, I could not have *Only One Year* for the Hutchinson list. He was finding himself obliged to complete a contract with Messrs Collins. I inquired the reason and became very angry indeed when I heard it. I knew that some difference of opinion had arisen between Svetlana and Priscilla Johnson, who had, admirably I thought, translated *Twenty Letters* from the Russian. Svetlana had somehow become determined that the translator of *Only One Year* should be Manya Harari. Mrs Harari, who, alas, died within a comparatively short time, was a brilliant woman and in association with Messrs Collins ran the Harvill Press. Svetlana, very properly, was deeply impressed by translations she had done. I had known, admired and liked Billy Collins (now Sir William) for nearly all my publishing life. He had always, and still marvellously retains, a fire of enthusiasm which many lesser spirits envy, but which at times obliges some fellow publisher to dial 999 and call for the fire brigade either to contain the flames or to drench surrounding property. Billy Collins is single-minded. The only place for an author of any quality is within the Collins list. He had not enjoyed the spectacle of *Twenty Letters to a Friend* in another's list any more than we would have done had it eluded us. Hearing now that Svetlana was insisting that Mrs Harari be pressed into service, Billy Collins announced that if she were to translate the book then Collins must publish it. For us to lose Svetlana's successor to *Twenty Letters* would be a fearful blow. It would suggest some default or lack of confidence and effectively dissipate any advantages accruing to us from our publication of *Twenty Letters*. Cass Canfield was sympathetic, but there was little he could do and Svetlana herself could not be expected to understand the internecine conflicts of the capitalist world. The only one who appeared to view the scene with the utmost serenity of righteous conviction was Billy Collins himself.

I was determined to upset this serenity and I asked Mr Canfield to be so kind as to hold his hand before signing up with Messrs Collins. I sought in my mind for the one word which might express my view and disturb Billy's equilibrium. The word I chose was 'squalid' and it appeared in the public print of *The Times* Diary.

Only One Year under its proper imprint was translated by Paul Chavchavadze, and the outcome of the affair was one that never fails to delight me and that makes any continuing breach with Billy Collins quite impossible. I heard no more from him until a few days before our publication of *Only One Year*. My telephone rang. 'Is that you, Bob? Billy Collins here. I do want to congratulate you on that splendid book you are publishing, *Only One Year*. I think it comes out next Monday and I know you have a big success on your hands.'

'That is extraordinarily nice of you, Billy. Have you read it?'

'Yes, Bob. I managed to get hold of a proof copy. I have asked Tommy Joy at Hatchards [owned by Messrs Collins] to give you all the help he can. It will get a big display there.'

'Well, Billy, that is very kind. I appreciate it enormously and will send you a proper copy to replace your proof.'

In this I wrote an affectionate and sincere inscription, and thus came to its end the only serious altercation I have ever had with any publisher I have held in high regard. There have been others, but this is no place for them.

I have always enjoyed the story of Sir William Collins receiving one afternoon the news that one of his many successful authors had dropped dead at lunch. 'What,' said Billy in horror, 'after all we've done for him?'

In the spring of 1969 and on the spur of a moment which derived from some newspaper item, I wrote to Mrs Harold Wilson suggesting that she might consider the possibility of getting together a selection of her poems for publication. I had never seen her, nor was I able to contrive any more personal approach than this letter out of the blue. The outcome, after a brief delay, was a telephone call from Mary Wilson inviting me to 10 Downing Street and coffee.

My only previous visit to No. 10 had taken me no further than the doorstep with Sheila MacDonald, when her father was its incumbent. This time I was ushered into the lift which ascended to the modest flat provided for Prime Ministers on the upper floors. There to greet me was unmistakably Mary Wilson. I noticed a tray of coffee and three cups and wondered, idly, if the Prime Minister was expected. I could not at the time have been in his best books, since on leaving the BBC I had at once denounced his appointment of Lord Hill to its chair. I had been given to understand that I had 'rocked the boat' which, indeed, had been my purpose.

I quickly found that Mary Wilson possessed all the virtues of charm, modesty, frankness and humour, guided by compassion and an acute awareness of life's realities. She was at once immensely kind and friendly and a human being to whom one instantly warmed. In fact she was so instantly and extraordinarily nice that I almost at once began to doubt the purity of my motives for being there. These, I had to admit, centred around a conviction that we could sell a lot of copies of a book of poems by Mrs Harold Wilson. I now realized, within a very few minutes, that I had to take other and much more important matters into account; of which paramount was Mary Wilson herself. I rather wished I had not come.

At that point the telephone rang and Mrs Wilson, answering it, had a friendly conversation with one John. 'A mutual friend, I think', she said when it was over. 'That was John Guest.' He was indeed a mutual friend but he was also a publisher. Had he, I wondered, any enterprise at the back of his mind? In point of fact, I do not think that he had, but the impetus of competition arrived at the right moment.

Mrs Wilson showed me one or two of her poems, and read the verses she had written on the Aberfan disaster, which I thought most moving. There was a depth of sincerity and feeling which would assure them a wide reading, but which added to their vulnerability to the gibes of the merciless. The idea of publication I thought attracted Mrs Wilson, but she had her doubts. Did her writing warrant it? Had they been written by some unknown hand, would I still feel the same? I had to confess that I would not, since all attention would elude them. Being who she was she could introduce to the reading and appreciation of poetry a great many people who normally found it inexplicable and tortuous.

Once or twice Mary Wilson referred to her friend John Betjeman and I made a mental note to enlist his services. I had obviously to find support for my view, for the destruction of Mary Wilson the poet, either by failure or virulence, was not to be countenanced in any circumstances. The outcome was that Mrs Wilson would think it all over and would be in touch again.

I had known John Betjeman since his days in Bloomsbury Street with *Time and Tide*, and I now sought him out. He was in complete agreement with me and he would encourage Mary Wilson to go ahead.

Every now and again I made inquiries as to progress, but it was not until March 1970 that I was again bidden to No. 10. After much thought she had completed her selection and here was the manuscript. I was delighted and asked if she would write a short preface about her approach to writing and so forth. I read the script the same afternoon and was greatly elated by it. Again it seemed to me that the appeal of such a book would be very wide; and I could not envisage from anyone who mattered the sort of savagery wounding to any writer, but very much more so to Mary Wilson in the context of all the attendant issues.

There was by this time the prospect of a fairly early general election, and much debate as to whether Mr Wilson would go to the country in the early summer or the autumn. At all costs Mary Wilson's book had to be kept away from the political arena. It was an entirely personal matter. At this stage, and for the first time, I proposed terms and drafted an agreement which was signed instantly. We agreed that, if possible, we would publish in the autumn but our plans might change should politics intrude.

I thought that the *Sunday Times* might like to contemplate some form of serialization and I had a word with its editor, Harold Evans, and sent him a duplicate of the script. He promptly accepted the proposal and I was again fortified in my view that we had not only a potential seller on our hands but a deserving one at that.

The Prime Minister was accommodating and solved all prob-

lems by plumping for a June election. All would be over before
the autumn and it was a foregone conclusion that it would bring
the publication of a book of poems by the Prime Minister's wife.
There might, apparently, be some promotional problems since as
such she could hardly appear on television to talk about her
poems, because Mr Heath had no wife to offer as a balancing
attraction on the next night. 'Is it as silly as that?' I inquired.
'Yes,' was the answer, 'it is.'

Two days before the election Mary Wilson kindly asked us to
watch Beating the Retreat on Horse Guards Parade. She was
having a brief respite from electioneering. On leaving I took her
corrected proofs and on the morning of the election my wife and I
left for a holiday in France.

'You have in England a new Prime Minister,' said the hotel's
hall porter in Marseilles the next morning. 'Nonsense,' I said.
'It is Mr Heath,' he insisted. 'Good God,' I said to my wife, 'our
poor author,' and sent an immediate telegram assuring her that
this would make no difference whatever. The only address I had
was 10 Downing Street, and the message never reached her. Her
instant thought was that our interest in her book would evaporate:
it would be a disaster. There was no such danger and in a curious
way the total unexpectedness of the political defeat added to the
speculation and interest as publication neared.

I have told already of the Garrick dinner party which brought
together the unlikely combination of Mary Wilson, Joan the
poetic waitress, Ogden Nash and John Betjeman. Ogden Nash
fell for both Mary Wilson and her poems and inscribed the
following to her:

> Diogenes would not admire
> The Morals of this versifier
> Who became a man of letters
> By simply stealing from his betters.
> His method is to snatch and scoot;
> Here's a sample of his loot.
> But since your book is not yet due,
> There's nothing here that's filched from you.

This was later reproduced in the *New Statesman* where, unfortunately, 'versifier' became 'thirsty fire'.

Mary Wilson's *Selected Poems* was a triumph on publication day and ever since. In the morning she had agreed to sign copies at Messrs Claude Gill in Oxford Street. Longer queues than had ever been seen outside a shop trailed down Oxford Street. There were men and women of all ages and all conditions. Patiently, in the centre, with two copies clasped to him stood a recent and distinguished ambassador to Washington. There were similar scenes at other shops. Reprints followed a large first printing and it was said that no book of poems had sold in such quantities since the days of Byron. Honest and sincere verse had won through to an extraordinary acclamation. Overnight the wife of Mr Harold Wilson had become Mary Wilson the poet. And this she remains.

> This is an unfortunate mixture of fact and fiction ... the writing is never better than competent, and the author's use of metaphor and simile are usually unpictorial ... The book is vastly over-written, studded with James Bond type characters and reality-boosting data; not all of which is accurate. *Verdict:* Poor.

A judgment from an experienced reader not calculated to raise hope in any publishing office. The particular novel had already, to some extent, disenchanted its author. It was his first and derived from a film scenario which had already been sold. He had entertained fruitless hopes that some percipient publisher would commission the novel he planned to make of it. None had and we were of the number. The author had thus completed the novel without encouragement and two or three leading publishers had rejected it before it found its way to Great Portland Street. With the report quoted above was another of some enthusiasm by Michael Dempsey. The verdict, however, went against it and a letter of rejection was composed by Harold Harris. It was of a routine nature, but mercifully added, 'I am sorry about this, and will probably be even sorrier when someone has a tremendous success with it.' Why there should be only probability of sorrow is an editorial nuance which escapes me. However, the author was to remember this expression of probable sorrow, and when an enthusiastic French publisher accepted the book he telephoned

Harold Harris to acquaint him with the news.

'Where is the manuscript now?' inquired Harold.

'It is with Michael Joseph in Bedford Square and has been for the past three weeks.'

Harold came to consult me. 'What should we do?' he asked.

'Tell that Frederick Forsyth of yours', I answered, 'to get along to the Joseph office as quickly as he can, somehow to retrieve his manuscript and bring it back here.'

Having invented and devised the intricacies and ingenuities of *The Day of the Jackal*, the hi-jacking of his own manuscript presented no problem to our first novelist, and within hours the script was with us.

It was exceptionally bad luck for my old firm. They cannot be said to have turned it down, for it was not even read. The sort of mishap which occurs every now and again in every publishing office had simply left *The Day of the Jackal* high and dry. It was extraordinarily good luck for me personally that so uniquely profitable an unagented 'property' should have coincided its arrival at Hutchinson with my terminal days of dotage. It enabled me to feel that in financial terms I had at last accomplished what had been expected of me in 1956.

As always happens on such occasions in publishing offices the world over, incredulity was expressed that any literate nincompoop could have failed to discern the potential of *The Day of the Jackal*. It was a natural, and yet I was still a little hesitant to accept Harold Harris's proposal that we should at once complete a three-novel agreement with the author. 'Wholly wrong', I scribbled with some irritation, 'to commit ourselves to *whatever* might emerge next.'

The Forsyth saga has become now almost a part of legend. It was an intensely exciting operation to conduct. Since no literary agent was involved, it was possible to plan and integrate with publishers all over the world. It was a promotional exercise on a scale very rarely possible in publishing, and I know of no literary agency anywhere which would even have attempted the integrated plan which a unified control made possible. It is no part of my purpose to quote a turmoil of facts and figures and finances, but the editions involved, and the immensity of the finance covering Frederick Forsyth's *The Day of the Jackal* and the two subsequent novels *The Odessa File* and *The Dogs of War*, would have astonished Mr Walter in his days at Paternoster Row and surprised even his heirs and successors at Great Portland Street and now of Fitzroy Square. I was proud to feel that I had got together a team of enthusiasts able to plan and work on such a scale, but I still felt sorry for the Michael Joseph people in Bedford Square.

A climate of success is no less welcome in a publishing office than elsewhere, but what gave particular encouragement was the fact that, despite the thrust of development with current books, a lengthening back list was for the first time overtaking the current list in the volume of sales it was achieving. This was something that had never before happened within the Hutchinson group and I had no cause to hang my head in dejection.

Many years previously, at Michael Joseph, I had a first contact with Earl Mountbatten of Burma, then First Sea Lord at the Admiralty. King George VI was to review his fleet. C. S. Forester would be in England and I wrote to Earl Mountbatten to suggest that the creator of Hornblower had possibly earned a right to witness it. The next morning I arrived at my office to be greeted with the news that Lord Mountbatten had telephoned in person the previous evening. He entirely agreed with my view but he deeply regretted that I was too late. Not a spare berth could be found for Mr Forester and he was very sorry about it.

I was not to know it at the time, but it was the typical gesture of a man utterly lacking in pomposity, extremely considerate and generous in praise. This I found to be so when we arranged to publish the book version of the memorable television biography made by John Terraine and Peter Morley. Lord Mountbatten took the greatest and most meticulous interest in every aspect of publication. I travelled with him to Leeds where he was to talk at a *Yorkshire Post* lunch in honour of the book, and men from H.M.S. *Kelly* were on the train. He had been in command when she was torpedoed. There was a procession of his old shipmates to the carriage and it was a moving experience to watch the sincerity and friendship of every greeting. He talked to me of his father and mother and of his wish for a biography about his father. Thus came about in the end Richard Hough's memorable study *Louis and Victoria*, which told not only of Lord Louis' parents but the long chronicle of a family which provided the whole of Europe with its royalty, and at the same time were fathers and mothers and brothers and sisters to an extent which the normal records of history tend to forget. Not, by nature, a dedicated publisher of Royal Books in Large Handsome Volumes Profusely Illustrated, these deriving from Lord Louis were ones I gladly reflect upon.

I had one more hazardous duty to fulfil. The attractions of a life in publishing, or for that matter in any of the creative areas of 'communication', lie in its complete involvement. Willy-nilly it is one's life, and a complete separation becomes unthinkable and intolerable. Thus the question of a successor is an intensely personal matter, apart from a responsibility to one's colleagues. I did not care to contemplate handing over the reins, however much I might have bungled the rest of the harness, to some alien invader imposed from above.

My researches in due course led to Charles Clark who was in charge of the remarkable developments at Penguin Books in the fields of education. I knew of the high regard in which he had been held by Sir Allen Lane, who had talked to me of him shortly before his death. I invited him to lunch, ascertained his interest and passed him on to those who would have to make the decision. Two more disparate people able to stand on the same principles of publishing than Charles Clark and myself could hardly be found. All to the good. Those responsible took one look and grabbed — quite rightly. My days with Hutchinson were very nearly over. Whether Mr Walter would think I had 'helped a lot', I really do not know. His portrait remains uncommunicative.

21
Prospects from a Harbour

THERE would appear to be some affinity between old publishers and old soldiers in their tendency to fade away. It is, or at any rate it has been until the proliferation of departments and the introduction of unions, a life commitment from which controversies about 'unsocial hours' have been mercifully absent. I am glad and fortunate to have been involved in publishing during a period which might be thought traditional, but which, at least, has been questioning as well. The last forty years have witnessed, it could be claimed, the elimination of the more tiresome aspects of tradition but without so far fully accepting all the apparent requirements of this impersonal, computerized, accountant-ridden present.

In very many aspects the book has been almost wholly changed in one twentieth-century lifetime, and it confronts conditions and a society almost wholly changed as well. What is remarkable, and one would think contrary to all expectation, is the international recognition that books are important. Who, even thirty years ago, would have expected the governments of the world to proclaim an International Book Year? Not even the late Stanley Unwin. Who would have expected a government to present to every newly married couple throughout that year the nucleus of a personal library? This, in fact, is what the French did.

Our own government, of course, did virtually nothing. The National Book League organized a Book Bang of staggering futility and extravagance in Bedford Square. It rained for most of the time and an elephant somehow interfered with Lord Longford. It was all said to be great fun for children, but whether in first or second childhood was never explained.

The publishers of this country — the home of the English language — face problems of great complexity deriving from our colonial past. No other country has done more than our own to create a desire for knowledge throughout the world and then to seek to satisfy it. In the late '20s and early '30s I do not remember the word 'export' being used in publishing. We had 'overseas' sales, on which discounts were so considerable that minimal royalties were paid on them. A percentage of every binding order would require 'colonial' cloth. This was not because such possessed any quality which could stand up to climatic variations, but because it was cheap. The British Empire and colonial market covered most of the English-speaking areas of the world. As our colonies tended to diminish, the phraseology was amended to 'the British Commonwealth market', but the territory still includes a number of strange little areas few Britishers have heard of. These 'exclusive' areas are now, not unnaturally, increasingly questioned and indigenous publishing is widely encouraged in all of any substance where, traditionally, the publishers of England have been relied upon to supply the bulk of reading matter.

Even when I returned to Hutchinson in 1956, 'export' was not regarded with any great seriousness. It is true that the firm had its own representatives in both Australia and South Africa, but there was little pressure and virtually no travelling by executives or representatives. One of the London travellers had once visited Holland and one editor had visited New York. Unfortunately he contracted chicken-pox on the way, and spent his time in quarantine.

One of the great misfortunes of British publishing is the persistence of the Americans in regarding their language as English. They can amass more finance, assume more sales and develop with greater intensity than their British colleagues. They are more aggressive in the so-called 'open' markets and now see no reason why books originating in the American tongue should await publication in London before being welcomed into Sydney or Melbourne or Johannesburg. At the same time the 'developing' countries of Africa, with all their nationalistic fervours, are less eager to have their educational books prepared by the educationists of their old colonial masters.

It is difficult to know quite what the technological panjandrums and the financial whizz-kids of the present are going to do about this increasingly difficult problem. For some five hundred years the predominant means of what today we have to call 'communication' was the printed word, and books have been far and away the predominant vehicle for them: and so they have remained until virtually the day before yesterday. But who can now doubt that the monopoly of the printed word will be neatly encompassed within the five hundred years from Caxton to cassette? It is hard to contemplate the revolution in what is alleged to be 'communication' that is now erupting around us and, as lava overwhelms all in its path, surfeiting and throttling us with so monstrous an excess of information that the balance of our minds becomes gravely disturbed.

A huge new industry has sprung into existence, virtually overnight, proliferating and popularizing a range of electronic gadgetry so extraordinary and alarming that its impact can hardly be imagined, let alone assessed. I find it incredible to reflect that little more than fifty years ago in a Somerset farmhouse on a Sunday afternoon, I heard miraculously the dim playing of a military band from the end of the pier of Weston-super-Mare. The adroit manipulation of a cat's whisker was the first intimation that John Reith was getting down to work.

Predictions of disaster for books and for reading followed the advent of radio, but were not fulfilled. That this was so has always seemed a consequence less of any particular activity by publishers than of an enlightened policy of public-service broadcasting by the BBC. Lord Reith and his successors were quick to discover that adventurous and progressive broadcasting could not make much progress unless supported by an enlightened and literate audience. Thus the BBC from its beginning, and notably in its programmes for children, has encouraged the reading of books as an extension to many of its programmes. Many publishers seem incapable none the less of understanding that the main preoccupation of broadcasting is not the welfare of publishers, but intelligent communication by means other than the printed word.

In general terms, and while broadcasting in this country remained dedicated to public service, I would suggest that those who previously read a great deal tended to read less, but that many more who never read at all were encouraged to do so by broadcast programmes which aroused their interest. I wish I could believe that this will continue to be so in the future. But with the coming of electronic wonders designed for home entertainment and not wholly inspired by notions of public service, doubts arise.

The dilemmas of commercial broadcasting derive not so much from its programmes but from what is lightly called its 'natural breaks'. It is no criticism of advertisers or advertising to think that both in the main are concerned with the standards of life. Most of what is advertised demands little but the money to acquire it. The dangers of the natural breaks are that they confuse, especially for the young, standards of living with the quality of life. They require the receptive and not the questioning mind. It is a requirement that the programmes cannot completely ignore.

The challenge thus for public-service broadcasting is to ensure that the dominance of the questioning mind is absolute. This must be why contentions about broadcasting and its programmes centre almost entirely around the BBC and will always do so. The commercialization of the BBC would be deadly not only to that institution but to the intellect of our democracy. An Orwellian nightmare could become reality. This is why the governors of the BBC must have always before them the requirements of public-service broadcasting rather than the convenience of the BBC.

The publisher who has lived for long in the ivory tower of typographical monopoly has now to understand that a child of our age can somehow become adult and pass fairly successfully through life quite well informed, but with no recourse to serious reading at all. The standard of such a life may be high; its quality abysmal. Against the facile assimilation of broadcasting programmes, the reading of books is concerned more with the enrichment of life; and thus it requires a positive discipline and a determination which are not needed if only standards are to be advanced. Enrichment is up against inertia. This, of course, is not wholly true, but true enough to be significant to those who publish books and have the intention of continuing the process against a competition which is very unlikely to diminish, but which, indeed, is likely to proliferate and intensify.

There is, almost inevitably, a conservatism about books which renders them difficult to promote as 'marketable' end-products. Their packaging is traditional and there cannot be a succession of new models as such, rendering obsolete what has appeared before. Arranged on shelves and with no regard for what is in them, they convey a certain status but not one of sufficient potency to excite the other Joneses in the street. Sometimes, impressively arranged, they prove not to be books at all but a decoration concealing an array of bottles. But for most, the continuing excitement of books must derive from what is inside them and thus the approach to their marketing can be only a limited exercise.

I am inclined to think that the only dramatic response made by books to the challenge of broadcasting was that of the late Sir Allen Lane with his concept of Penguin paperbacks. It may indeed be wondered if Penguin Books could ever have been successfully launched had not Reith led the way for quite a few years with enlightened policies for broadcasting. Both Reith and Lane refused to underestimate, as so many do, the intelligence and perspicacity and concerns of the average citizen. In any foreseeable future it is difficult to imagine that the printed word can take any greater stride forward than that taken in 1935 by the publication of the first of Lane's Penguins. If there is no plaque in the crypt of the Marylebone church from which they first emanated, there certainly should be.

The book trade is fortunate that so much of its promotional work is done, and even financed, by others. Those responsible for education still appear to regard, as a primary requirement, the ability to read. The National Book League, which exists to keep books in touch with life and life in touch with books, receives wide support from outside the book trade and a notable lack of warmth from within it. What needs to be ensured, for it rarely follows as a natural consequence, is that the ability to read becomes a desire to do so and a recognition that reading can be a useful if not essential extension to every part of living. To accomplish this against the inertia induced by continuous and mostly visual electronics, the book trade will certainly need to become very much more assertive in the market-places, and must rid itself of assumptions of divinity inculcated by five hundred years of monopoly. There still persists a certain damaging remoteness. That a book 'is the precious life-blood of a master spirit' may still sound impressive, but it cuts little ice in the later years of the twentieth century and will mean nothing at the end of it. The life-blood of contemporary master-spirits even now flows often more rewardingly from sources other than the printed word.

During most of my time, the British book trade, and indeed the world book trade for that matter, has been in a condition of crisis. It appears to be an endemic state and I dare say arises partly from the smallness of the parish in which it operates and partly from the articulate propensities of its inhabitants. Of these, in my view, the authors should always come first; the publishers, second; and the booksellers, third. There has somewhere to be found a place for the increasingly powerful literary agents, but my view as to where it can be found is a constantly shifting one. The onlooker might well expect a melodic harmony to be natural when so many common purposes prevail. But, alas, the same song is seldom sung at the same time to the' same tune, and disputations on one topic or another seem always in evidence.

There have been changes in the ambience of publishing which I regret and which I think have become perceptible in the harsher quality of contemporary creative writing. A certain domestic charm has all but vanished from the publishing scene; a certain gaiety of spirit and a humanistic disdain for pure accountancy have given way to tougher qualities of management and realism. These, while sensible enough and necessary to a greater degree than I probably care to admit, are not wholly conducive to the many freedoms which should pervade all the corridors of com- municative power. It always will be, and indeed one can say that it always should be, a difficult balance to attain and maintain between the perfectly understandable requirements of solvency and profit and the reasonable freedom of editorial eccentrics. The impersonal image of the conglomerate has, in my lifetime, taken over the personal relationship between imprint and author. A certain humanity has been supplanted by apparently inexorable trends which are as indefinably evident in the completed book as in the loaf of bread from some multiple bakery.

Book publishing in this country never was the cottage industry it is believed to be by some of the more thrustful of our American colleagues. Before the last war, publishing was certainly a much smaller industry than it is today, and was in the main controlled by family firms in more or less friendly competition. Most of these have been either absorbed within groups or have 'gone public'. Today the real control is financial and lies dangerously within too few hands. We have the Thomson group; the Tillings group; the Granada group; the Longmans group; and so forth. Proliferating departments abound, and the publisher begets an editor who begets copy-editors and managing editors; and with the production department go visualizers, lay-out people, designers, planners and hosts of others, enormously increasing overheads and the price of books. These multitudes achieve in twelve months of mounting hysteria what used to be quietly accomplished in three by a publisher who did not feel capable of operating without knowledge, if not mastery, of the whole procedure. The editorial selection, the production, the advertising and promotion, the selling and, if need arose, the invoicing and parcelling were all to be envisaged as one read a proffered script. Publishing was indivisible.

Already it has to be recognized that books have lost out in the immediacy of events. They cannot compete with the instant documentary on every problem under the sun. Books have become dangerously long-term, if they are to have a voice in any but long-term affairs. It is inconceivable that the Victor Gollancz of today could achieve the impact of his Left Book Club of the '30s. Almost every subject covered by those vivid, yellow-jacketed productions would now be covered exhaustively by immediate debate on television. Protracted delay cannot be other than frustrating to any who write. It is frustrating to others as well, but in all these matters the first and major purpose must be the attainment of a climate best conducive to the liveliness of creative editorial minds. The efficient administration of instant and sustained communication, while important, is a secondary matter.

The role of the book in current affairs should be somehow retrieved and a new urgency restored to the mechanics of its production. It may well be that standards of production, and typographical niceties, will diminish at least for a time, but this would be a price worth paying if books are to have other than a reflective role to play in the urgency of world events.

There are other facts of publishing life which require reflection and explanation. Those of us with responsibilities in the matter have created great misunderstanding by the thoughtless trade vernacular we have adopted of hardbacks, softbacks and paperbacks. We have made no attempt to explain how books are priced and why it is that two books, apparently comparable in every physical particular, may be widely disparate in price. Those involved may know well enough that paperbacks and softbacks are not relatively cheaper than hardbacks by any process of binding, but the public remains completely uninformed and with completely wrong and dangerous impressions. Anyone who reads a paperback should know that its cost has very little to do with the manner of its binding, but everything to do with the size of the edition which has been printed. It should be widely known that only a very small proportion of the new books appearing every year can ever become viable propositions as paperbacks and that no publishing industry could survive on an output of nothing but paperbacks. Every publisher at all in touch with readers must be familiar with the refrain 'why can't every book be a paperback?'. Were it so, creative writing in the English language would be throttled at its source in no time at all. Should publishing ever be confined to what can be done only in paperback, it would be pap-publishing of the most deadening kind.

One of the major glories of book publishing, which must never be surrendered or for a moment forgotten, is that, almost alone, it operates the medium through which new creative talent nearly always finds its first expression. No other communicative medium can achieve its ratings or its viability with so small an audience. This is why it is vital to publishing and to creative expression that the attainment of at least financial balance should be reached by editions much smaller than have become necessary today. It used to be possible to 'come home' on a sale of 750 copies of a first novel published at 7s. 6d. The equivalent today in 1975 would be nearer 4,000 and the price around £3.50. Here, then, is another area requiring explanation and public understanding, for it is readers who bestow recognition on what is new and fresh and vigorous and they should somehow be brought within the excitements of discovery.

In yet another category — and a very wide one, for it involves educational areas — new ingenuities and new methods of textual presentation have to be found if books are to play a continuing role. It is hard to accept that the present instructional and informational book, with its static pictures and diagrams, can stand against the competition of the video disc or tape or the miracles of computerized retrieval systems. Within a very short time the mechanics will be a part of every television set. The voice and the coloured movie will demonstrate dramatically and easily what now requires the concentrated study of printed pages. None the less, as with the University of the Air, a book will be required to give permanence, portability and extension to what has been seen and heard. It will be for publishers to ensure that their productions are designed to meet these new requirements.

But what of the retail and institutional outlets through which books become available to those who want them? Nothing that the author or publisher can accomplish will be of much avail unless attractively, efficiently and rapidly their joint product is brought to the market-place. The task of the bookseller has never been an easy one. Within the activity of retailing, as within the world of publishing, it is permissible to point out once again that books are 'different'. It is not a claim or a plea but a fairly minor fact to be taken into account. Bookselling requires a dedication and a constancy and a knowledge of one's customers not demanded of many. The output with which a bookseller has to contend is gargantuan, but he has the remedy of selection and he should be ruthless in applying it.

One of the most alarming experiences of my life was to address an annual conference of booksellers on how I would profitably run a bookshop. Cadness Page, at that time manager of Harrods' book department, was the Booksellers Association's president, and it was clear from the terms of his invitation that only flattery would induce a publisher to risk his neck — and in Bournemouth of all places. One of the proposals I made was that an enterprising bookseller might do well to dispense coffee as well as books. A good many years later I visited, at mid-morning, a delightful bookseller in the main street of Bulawayo. 'Come,' she said, 'and have coffee at your own stall.' It was an agreeable moment. But, I declared in Bournemouth and since, it is, to my mind, imperative that books should be seen and should be available in all the market-places to which they have application, and not only in the shop of a bookseller where customers somehow feel that they have to behave with a greater hesitancy and decorum than elsewhere. The barrier between books and life is still a very real one. For the local foodstore to display cookery books and the local hardware shop to display how-to-do-it books and so forth should not be beyond the wit of man. It can be arranged by local licence or some other mechanism to protect the autonomy of the bookseller. The air of reverence and veneration for books and bookshops has no place in today's world. Books have to be thought about as machine-tools of the mind. None of the traditions of bookselling need disappear, but the bookseller has now to understand that his role has expanded and he is the retailer of 'communication' in all its forms. His bookshop should regard itself as the local 'communication' centre, and if he can put across this message to younger generations he may retrieve some of the ground he has surrendered far too easily to the public library and the public librarian.

I have never understood the reluctance of booksellers to provide a variety of services to their customers. I would willingly pay an adequate fee to a bookseller able to reduce the continuing chaos of my own modest shelves to something like order. A bookseller should be equipped to advise upon, if not provide the installation of, bookshelves in unlikely nooks and crannies of the modern home. Personal libraries, however small, should be a necessity of life; and if they are to remain alive, should be treated as a garden and weeded and pruned to discard the ephemeral, the out-of-date and the never-to-be-read-again. It is a profound pity that such eruptions as Hitler should have brought the occasional destruction of books into disrepute. The private bookshelves of the world must contain thousands upon thousands of miles of unloved and unread books occupying space required by a living literature. Once, when crossing the Atlantic, I watched an old lady sitting by the rails of the *Queen Elizabeth*'s promenade deck, engrossed in a Penguin. As she completed each page her hand, with a great economy of gesture, ripped it away, screwed it up and threw it into the waters of the ocean. She had the right idea.

The almost total collapse of the circulating subscription libraries has been a social phenomenon so far as I know neglected by everyone. It has certainly proved a deprivation to authors, publishers and, I think, to themselves, had they shown some awareness of what was going on. The commercial libraries were the mainstay of the general publishing trade during the 1920s and 1930s. There was Messrs Boots, with a range of 'classes' to which their customers might subscribe. The Boots Library, as a general rule, was accommodated at the back of Boots stores on the assumption that subscribers would be obliged to take note of their other wares. If I remember rightly, Boots' 'On Demand' service cost three guineas a year. It undertook (in fact I think it guaranteed) to provide any book within three days. Its presiding authority was Freddie Richardson and by the pattern of his ordering it was possible to gauge with some accuracy (and with rather more than the present-day analyst is able to from his computer) the success or otherwise of a new book. A good review in the *Sunday Times* by Ralph Straus and another in the *Observer* by Gerald Gould would be reflected in Mr Richardson's order on the following Friday. The arrival of Boots' weekly order in any publishing office was a highlight or lowlight of the week. In his retirement before the war, Richardson engaged in an operation of singular ingenuity based on the principle which every purveyor of books knows to be sound. It is that the best and surest tactic to get a book selling is by the personal recommendation of one reader to another. It is the one certainty of success. From his own experience Richardson knew this perfectly well and he sought, shrewdly, to exploit it. He devised his chosen panels with care, and for an agreed sum would circulate to one hundred or two hundred or so members free copies of the book. These would be provided by the publisher, who would also pay Freddie Richardson his fee. Each recipient of the book would be expected to talk about it at least within the circle. It was not a particularly expensive advertising allocation, but war put an effective stop to the experiment and it has never been revived.

There were of course other circulating libraries too: Mudie's, The Times Book Club, W. H. Smith, Harrods, and others. They were a very significant part of the book trade and almost overnight they disappeared. Only one now remains at Messrs Harrods and the service it provides is a sorry shadow of its heyday. These organizations between them satisfied a great section of the reading public which regarded the free public libraries as dubious institutions for the 'lower' classes, tinged somehow with charity and certainly a dangerous source of unpleasant infection.

The war and the consequent demise of the commercial libraries changed all that. Deprived of their Mudie's and their Boots, the great middle classes went 'public' and discovered that they possessed, on their doorstep almost, a free library system unequalled in the world and now providing a service almost as good and sometimes better than the defunct commercial libraries at their best. The commercial libraries should, I believe, at the right moment, have increased their charges and provided additional facilities of one kind and another beyond any possibility that could be considered by the public library system. The position has long since been lost and the public library is pretty well in control, offering a range of additional services never contemplated by Mr Carnegie.

Shortly after the war on my first visit to the United States I was being kindly entertained for the weekend in a log cabin on the shore of Lake Netcong. The schoolgirl daughter was delegated to take me for an afternoon row. It seemed a hazardous outing since Lake Netcong was once, apparently, a forest, the tops of whose trees were for ever threatening to penetrate the fragile hull. The necessities of war had deprived the delightful child of much contact with travellers from distant lands. She looked at me with curiosity. 'Do you', she inquired, 'have such things as public libraries in England?' 'Yes,' I replied 'as a matter of fact we have. But there is another big tree coming up through the boat. I think we should avoid it.' It is, of course, this concentration of power within the public library system that so justifies and makes necessary the imposition upon it of the Public Lending Right. It is in no sense a tax, but is at least a token financial gesture which recognizes that authors do have something to do with books, and become thus entitled to some part of their proceeds.

From the confusion of interests and purposes which has

developed in publishing over the past twenty-five years would seem now to be emerging a certain pattern of compromise of considerable significance. Communication, basically, must be an editorial process — an association between writers and publishers. All the rest is administration of one kind and another. What matters when all is said and done is the climate in which creative men and women can work freely and in reasonable confidence that they will be heard. But this should not be a certainty — a fight may be necessary. If the climate is right, any challenge to its condition of health brings alerted forces into play, as does the threat of disease in the human body.

The concentration within a few huge financial organizations of the communication media has alerted such forces in those un-suited by temperament to observe the regimentations of size. But size, it is recognized now, has considerable advantages in administration. It can run the machine with infinitely greater resources and an expertise in management; it can streamline and unify the procedures; it can provide finance for new projects; it can do very many things with an efficiency financially impossible for the small unit. Wisely managed, it can also, on occasions, accommodate editorial eccentricities and requirements. But to some will still remain feelings of frustration and the suspicion of exploitation. An accelerating tendency in recent years is for young, creative men and women, feeling such doubts, to break away from organizational life and fragment themselves into numbers of personalized, independent editorial imprints. In publishing they operate to the point at which the book becomes a marketable commodity; and then, by a variety of arrangements and contrivances, it is handed over to the elabo-rate distributive machinery of the conglomerate.

It is, I believe, a movement of quite exceptional importance. It can be discerned also in broadcasting (and indeed in other areas of creative activity far removed from the media). In broad-casting many brilliant producers find it possible to work freely and with satisfaction within the climate of the broadcasting authorities — and especially in the BBC. Should public-service broadcasting at any time fail to achieve the necessary climate for tis creative programme people, then it will have failed in a major purpose. None the less, there will always be those conscious of frustration and they too now tend to break away, form small production units, and offer their programmes back to one or another of the broadcasting organizations.

It has been an extraordinary era in which to publish books, and not an easy one. Publishing has developed from a comparatively small industry dominated by publishing families into one at least ten times the size, and then only part of a huge international and interlocking industry of communication almost beyond comprehension. In the matter of books, when I started with Hutchinson in 1928 their printers would query the use of the word 'damn'. Strong language, they would suggest in red ink. I recall an afternoon of editorial crisis in Paternoster Row. The Large, Handsome Volume Profusely Illustrated of a distinguished diplomat was in production. Anxious and strained, Mr Coffin, Hutchinson's overworked miracle-man of production who once asked an author if he had Francis Bacon's permission to quote, rushed into Erle Lunn's cubicle with the diplomat's galley proofs shaking in his hand. It seemed that the ambassador had referred to receiving a letter in the French language, but he had described it with commendable precision. Faces paled; there were confidential mutterings to which I, only lately released from a Quaker education, was not made privy. Something had to be done and quickly, since the machines had been stopped. The offending sentence was rephrased.

And now, in recent years, books one would have been expelled for reading in the schools of fifty years ago are required reading for juniors. A phrase thought to be taboo in the spring fails to raise an eyebrow in the autumn. I continue to believe that the responsible publisher should retain the ability to be shocked, while ever ready to extend the frontiers of compassion.

It is a strange experience, at the end of it all, to browse through the catalogues for which one has been to some extent responsible over nearly fifty years. There are titles and authors — too many — which sadly strike no chord of recollection at all. There are others of a certain sadness which inspired a moment of enthusiasm and the hope that they might somehow have taken off. Colleagues, friends, acquaintances, experiences of all sorts and in many countries crowd one's memory through the catalogue pages which embody so much of the hopes and frustrations and achievements of their span.

The story told in the pages of this book, which I hope is no catalogue, has been that of a most fortunate man, lucky beyond anything that he had a right to expect. There are aspects of it he would have changed. He has never been other than a 'hired hand' and thus not always in control of the story when sometimes it seemed important to be so. But there it is. He would like Miss World to think kindly of the old man who paid a call.

Index